ONCE A COP

ONCE A COP

The Street, the Law,
Two Worlds, One Man

COREY PEGUES

ATRIA PAPERBACK

New York   London   Toronto   Sydney   New Delhi

ATRIA
PAPERBACK

An Imprint of Simon & Schuster, Inc.
1230 Avenue of the Americas
New York, NY 10020

First Atria Paperback edition April 2017

ATRIA PAPERBACK and colophon are trademarks of Simon & Schuster, Inc.

For information about special discounts for bulk purchases, please contact
Simon & Schuster Special Sales at 1-866-506-1949
or business@simonandschuster.com.

The Simon & Schuster Speakers Bureau can bring authors to your live event.
For more information or to book an event, contact the Simon & Schuster Speakers
Bureau at 1-866-248-3049 or visit our website at www.simonspeakers.com.

Interior design by Paul Dippolito

10 9 8 7 6 5 4 3 2

Library of Congress Cataloging-in-Publication Data is available.

ISBN 978-1-5011-1049-8
ISBN 978-1-5011-1050-4 (pbk)
ISBN 978-1-5011-1051-1 (ebook)

For Brendale

For Corey Jr., Natasha, Kenyetta, Diquan, Cordale, and Cori

For all the young people out there who've made bad choices but are looking to change their lives. I hope my story will inspire you.

CONTENTS

The names of most individuals involved in criminal acivities, and all NYPD employees below the rank of Chief with whom the author worked, have been changed.

ONCE A COP

ONCE A COP

It was late in the afternoon. I was hanging out in Baisley Park, chilling on one of the benches next to the handball court, about to start my shift. Prince and Malik rolled up in Prince's black BMW. Malik got out and he came over to me and he said, "Yo, come on. Get in the car. We gotta go somewhere."

I jumped in the back. Malik got in the front passenger side, closed the door, and Prince pulled off. As we drove, Malik reached back and handed me a shiny black 9-millimeter pistol. He said, "Here, hold this."

I took the gun. "Wassup?"

He said, "We're going to take you someplace. When we get there we're gonna point somebody out to you, and when we do you're gonna shoot him in the head."

PART ONE

Hustler

1

Suburban Sugar Hill

No kid grows up dreaming of being a crack dealer. I certainly didn't. My mother did everything she could to put me on the right path, to teach me the difference between right and wrong.

She made us go to church every Sunday. She'd wake us up early—so early that we'd all have to shower the night before. The next morning we'd be running around getting dressed while she'd yell from downstairs, "Hurry up! The Lord don't have no time to wait for you!" There would be fights over the bathroom, because there was only one in the house for me, my parents, and my five sisters.

Ma would have breakfast ready when we came downstairs. We'd eat real fast and rush out the door. Poppa rarely came with us. Every Sunday she tried to get him to go, and every Sunday he'd say, "Eva, I ain't goin' to no damn church." We went to Prince of Peace Baptist in St. Albans, Queens, where we lived. It was a big church, a lot of members, including almost my entire extended family, my aunts and uncles and cousins. Church was all day. Me and my little sister, Latonia—we called her Tawn—we would start out at Sunday school in the basement, then go up to join my mother and my older sisters for the regular service. We had to be there for all three services, the six o'clock, the eight o'clock, and the eleven o'clock. Tawn and I would get restless and start acting up, hitting each other, making noises. Ma would turn her head, grit her teeth, and say, "Sit y'asses down 'fore I beat you." We knew what that meant. We would settle down quietly for a while, until, inevitably, we would start back up again.

Getting through three services was hard but worth it, because after church we'd get Ma's home cooking. Every Sunday was like Thanksgiving at our house. My mother cooked during the week, but Sunday was the day we'd *eat*. To make a big meal like that with six kids wasn't easy. Ma had a system and she ran a tight ship. She had one of us sweeping the floors, another setting the table, someone cutting the potatoes. Tawn and I would stir the cake mix, because we liked to lick the bowl. After dinner we'd play games or do homework. The time we spent together on Sundays was always special.

I was born on Christmas Eve, December 24, 1968, at Mary Immaculate Hospital in Jamaica, Queens. Nobody called me Corey. My nickname was Boobie, or Boo. I don't know where it came from. My mother was Eva Jewel Caple, we called her Ma, and my father, Poppa, Richard Russell Sloan. My four older sisters, Linda, Vicky, Debra, and Angie, were from Ma's earlier marriage in North Carolina, to a man named James Caple. My older sisters are much older. Angie is the youngest of those four, and she's six years older than me, so most of my memories from growing up are just me and Tawn, who's three years younger. We shared a bedroom and have the same father. We didn't get his last name, though; the two of us were given my mother's maiden name, Pegues. (Nobody pronounces it right. It's Pa-*geez*.)

St. Albans was a working- and middle-class black neighborhood in southeastern Queens. It was mostly African-American, sprinkled with some Caribbean, and by Caribbean I mean Jamaican. Some of the better off families from Sugar Hill in Harlem had started moving out after World War II. They called St. Albans the suburban Sugar Hill. A lot of famous names: Count Basie, Jackie Robinson, Ella Fitzgerald, James Brown. They all lived here back in the day. Just next to us were neighborhoods like Hollis and Laurelton and Springfield Gardens, places where blacks who had made it out of the ghetto were able to buy their own homes. To the south, down Guy R. Brewer and

Sutphin Boulevard, was South Jamaica, home to the Baisley Park Projects and the South Jamaica Projects, which people called the 40 Houses. That was still the ghetto, pretty much. That's where things got rough.

When I was growing up, middle-class black families were going even farther out, to towns like Hempstead and Roosevelt on Long Island, and St. Albans saw a lot of less-well-off families like ours moving in. It was definitely becoming a low-income neighborhood, but it was a stable, working-class neighborhood: kids playing in the park, people sitting in the front yards, barbecues in the summer. St. Albans had been all white before blacks started moving in, but by the time we lived there the only white person left on our block was Mr. George, this grumpy old fat guy. He was nice, but he was a loner. We only saw him when he'd take his garbage out.

We lived on 198th Street, south of Murdock Avenue, in a small row house. Up at the corner, at the intersection with Murdock, was the bus stop and a commercial strip with a beauty shop, a Jamaican restaurant, and a bodega. Only we didn't call them bodegas. We called them candy stores. A couple blocks down Murdock was O'Connell Park, with the basketball courts where everybody would hang out. Other than that, the surrounding blocks were all residential. Row houses and detached, single-family homes. People had little front yards and driveways for cars. Kids were always in the street, playing skelly, Frisbee, tag, baseball, football. It was a nice place to grow up.

The best thing about living in St. Albans was family. I had twelve aunts and uncles and twenty cousins within a few square miles. My aunt Mary and her husband Gene lived across from us with my cousins Val and Jeff. My grandmother, my mom's mom, lived there, too; she had a room in the basement. Aunt Mary's house was the unofficial gathering place; you'd find seven or eight cousins running around over there at any given time. We did birthdays together, played after school together, went to church together.

Christmas was a big deal for us. My birthday was on Christmas

Eve and my mother's was on Christmas Day. Every Christmas Eve, my aunts, uncles, and cousins would celebrate and exchange presents. There was a lot of laughing and singing and dancing. My aunts would take turns singing Christmas carols and hymns in the living room. With all those cousins, presents would be piled up under the tree. Every Christmas Eve, I'd get nice gifts from my aunts and uncles—train sets, toy soldiers, toy trucks—and I went home happy. But one year I realized that my parents never got any presents for the other kids. I asked, "Ma, why don't we get presents for them?"

She said, "Son, we can't afford it."

I'd never thought of us as being poor, but as I got older I learned that we were on welfare. I learned what that was, what it meant. Ma was from a town called Laurinburg in North Carolina, where she'd had my four older sisters with her first husband. He was no good. He wasn't just cheating on her; he had a whole second family going at the same time. Ma couldn't take it. One day she took the girls and left. My aunt Mary had already moved up here. My mother followed, hoping to give her daughters a chance at a better life. Ma was a beautiful woman, smooth cocoa-brown skin with a big Afro. She was strong and hardworking, but she'd never graduated from high school. She didn't have the skills or the education to get a decent job. With four young girls and no husband to help out, she wound up on public assistance and never left.

In New York she met my father, who'd come up from Tallahassee, Florida, where he had two older sons running around, my half brothers. I've never met them. My father was tall and slim, about six-one, handsome, a bit of a player and a charmer. He hadn't graduated from high school, either. He drove a bus for Creedmoor Hospital, an institution for mentally challenged adults. Throughout the day he'd drop the patients off at appointments and pick them back up. Whenever we weren't in school, he'd take us to work to ride the bus with him. That was my favorite memory of him, riding around on that bus and watching him work. Some of the other memories aren't so good.

My father drank. Smirnoff. He'd drink it straight, no chaser. I actually don't have any memories of him without a glass or a bottle in his hand. As far back as I can remember, every day my father smelled like liquor. I don't think I ever saw him sober other than when he got up in the morning. I'm sure he drank while he was at work, too, driving the bus for the hospital. But the man could hold his liquor. He was a functional alcoholic. He was never sloppy drunk to where he couldn't hold a conversation. He'd kill a fifth of vodka and carry on like it was nothing.

I didn't like that my father drank, but other than that I was a happy kid. My parents had a genuine love, but they weren't always good at being together. They'd fight a lot, mostly about the drinking. For a while, thanks to my father's job, we lived better than most families on welfare. Rent wasn't too high in a neighborhood like ours, and we had clothes to wear and presents on our birthdays. But my parents never got married. They couldn't.

Technically my father wasn't supposed to be living with us. Single women on welfare couldn't have a man living in the house. If Social Services found out, she'd lose her benefits. Once in a while caseworkers would do these pop-up visits to check the house. Ma would say, "They're coming today for a face-to-face," and we'd have to run and hide my father's things. We'd empty his dresser and his closets, stuff his clothes in the trash can or under the bed. That's also the reason my sister and I went by my mother's maiden name. We had to pretend my father wasn't a part of our lives.

Then, at a certain point, we didn't have to pretend anymore.

2

Loosies

I was in the third grade when everything fell apart. That year we moved down Murdock to a new house on Dormans Road. When we moved, everything felt good. On 198 we'd been in a row house. On Dormans the house was unattached with a big backyard and lots of bedrooms. Tawn and I shared a room, and so did Debra and Angie. Vicky had the attic, and Linda, the oldest, had moved out on her own.

It was an area with good families. Right in front of our house, Dormans Road intersected with Murdock at an angle that made the intersection shaped like a baseball diamond, with a manhole cover for home plate. Almost every day, the boys from the block were out there playing baseball. Most of them were older than me, but I caught on fast and soon I was signed up to play shortstop in the St. Albans Little League.

Tawn and I went to elementary school at PS 136. When we moved to Dormans, even though it was only a few blocks away, we were in a new school zone. Technically we should have transferred to PS 36, the designated school for that street. But Ma wanted to keep us at 136 and didn't tell the school we'd moved. That lasted a few months. Then I screwed it all up.

The prettiest girl in third grade was Michelle. She had long, wavy hair, light brown eyes, a cute smile. I had the biggest crush on her. Most eight-year-old boys don't want anything to do with girls. Not me. I was obsessed with them. One day we were heading back to the classroom after lunch, the class lined up on the stairs, the boys lined up on one side and the girls on the other. Michelle and I were at the front of each line at the top of the stairs. She was messing around and having fun and she pushed me. I told her to stop and she did it again, so I pushed her back. She fell over backward and the whole girls' line went down, falling down the stairs like dominos, screaming and yelling. Nobody broke an arm, but there were definitely some bumps and bruises. All the girls were crying, and all the boys were laughing.

The teacher grabbed me and asked what happened. I told her, "Michelle pushed me first." She didn't buy it. I got sent to the principal's office. She suspended me for the rest of the day and drove me home in her car, but she took me to 198 and Murdock, because that was still the address that the school had. I told her, "We don't live here anymore." She asked where we lived, and I had her take me to Dormans Road.

When we pulled up to the house, I could see Ma in the window, waiting for us. She and the principal talked briefly. Once she was gone, Ma tore into me. "How dare you!" and "See what you've done!" and all that. She whipped me with a belt until she got tired. We didn't have much money, but my mother was a proud person. Having the principal bring me home like that was embarrassing, and now the school knew that we weren't living in the right school zone. Tawn and I had to transfer schools immediately. We enrolled in PS 36 the next day.

Walking us to our new school, Ma was furious, cussing me out under her breath. I'd never seen her so mad in my life. I kept saying, "I'm sorry, Ma. I'm sorry." I knew how much she was dealing with, having six kids on welfare, and I was mad at myself for putting her through it. When I got home that first day, I went to her and said, "Ma, I'll never disappoint you again."

She said, "Okay, son."

And I meant what I said, but even though I resolved to do better, I couldn't stop everything in the family from going downhill.

My mother and father had always fought, but now it was constant. Ma had reached the end of her rope. Poppa was staying out all night, some weeks drinking his whole paycheck. Some nights he was so drunk he'd piss the bed. He'd pass out, urinate all over the sheets. Middle of the night my mother would wake up furious, cursing him 'cause she was covered in piss, again. There was a lot of screaming, a lot of cursing. Fuck you. Fuck this. Fuck that. He'd yell, "Fuck you, bitch!" And she'd come right back, "If you see a bitch, slap a bitch!" Then things would get violent.

Ma always threw the first punch. She was the aggressor. Poppa was the passive one. He wasn't abusive. He didn't fight back. He was probably too drunk to fight back. She would go off. *"Drunk son of a bitch! Tired of this!"* He would take it until one of my older sisters went in to break it up. Tawn and I would be crying in our room, waiting for it to be over. I prayed every day that it would stop. But no matter how bad it got, my father never put the bottle down. He never even tried.

The biggest fight came at the end. My father came home drunk from hanging out with friends. Ma started in on him. This particular night, he decided he was tired of getting hit. He said, "That's enough of this shit!" and he went off, punching and hitting her back. All of a sudden Ma picked up this big, porcelain cereal bowl, and cracked him in the face. Poppa screamed out in pain and grabbed his nose. Blood was pouring out of his face. Poppa said, "I'm going to the emergency room," and he left. A few days later I came home from school and he'd moved out. Once he was gone, he was gone. He lived close by in Queens, at a place on Linden Boulevard, but we never saw him. He drove for the hospital for a few more years. Then he was in an accident and wound up on disability. Out of a job. Still drinking.

After that Ma was on her own. Now I was old enough to know what it meant to be poor. I'd need a new pair of sneakers because I had holes in the bottom of mine. Sneakers only cost $25 back then, but my mom couldn't even manage that. I still have one of my class photos from PS 36. The teacher made me sit in the front row, Indian-style, and I'm sitting there holding my feet, trying to cover them with my palms because I had cardboard in the holes on the bottom of my shoes and I was embarrassed. All kids get hand-me-down clothes, but I only had sisters, so I'd get girls' jeans and have to wear those. Going to school with cardboard in my shoes and wearing hand-me-down Jordache jeans. It was humiliating.

We were on food stamps, and I hated when Ma sent me to the store. Hated it. The stamps were in this booklet. The $10 bill was green, the $5 bill was purple, the $1 bill was brown. I called it funny money. I was embarrassed to be up there paying with it. Ma would send me to the Little Giant Supermarket, and I would do the shopping and get up to the counter and one of my friends would walk in. I'd wave the cashier off, like, "Nah, Forget it. I don't want it." I'd walk out, leave the groceries on the counter. I didn't want to be seen paying with food stamps.

At home, things started happening: the lights getting cut off, the gas, sometimes the water. We kept candles in the house, and some nights that's all we had. We couldn't use the bathroom because we couldn't flush. We had to go to a neighbor's house, Mr. Brown's, and ask him for buckets of water so we could flush the toilet. After a week or so, Ma would get things right and the utilities would be back on for a while. Then they'd go out again. Eventually we fell so far behind on the rent that we had to leave.

In seventh grade we moved to a two-bedroom apartment above a store at the corner of Murdock and Farmers Boulevard, halfway between Dormans Road and our old place on 198. You went in downstairs, down this narrow hallway to this staircase that took you up to our apartment. My older sisters had moved out. Tawn and I shared a bedroom, like before, and my mom took the other one, which was separated from the living room by a set of glass doors. It was cramped. The bathroom was small, and the kitchen wasn't in great shape. It had old, cracked linoleum floors. There was a dinette in there we'd eat at. Ma did everything she could to make it a home for us, cleaned the whole place every weekend, but it was an old apartment that never got clean no matter how much she washed and scrubbed.

We were only a few blocks from our house on Dormans, but this was a completely different world. No families out in their yards, no baseball games with the neighbors' kids. We weren't on a residential street. It was a commercial strip, and the store we lived over wasn't actually a store. It was a numbers joint. Back in the seventies there were numbers joints everywhere. They were fronts for the mob. They're easy to spot—they don't sell anything. All the guy had in there was some potato chips, a few boxes of candy. We had these characters from the neighborhood coming and going, playing numbers.

Those years on Farmers were bad. I was hungry all the time. End of the month and no food in the apartment. My aunts and uncles helped us out when they could. I can remember walking to their house, getting baloney and rice. Some mornings we ate cereal with water. Try that shit. Mayonnaise sandwiches. Mustard sandwiches. If I was lucky, a grilled cheese sandwich. We had mice. I'd go in, turn on the kitchen light, and see them running along the counters, on top of the stove. I'd come home and Ma would have a sandwich waiting for me in the fridge. I'd open it up and there'd be roaches in there crawling and running around on everything. But I needed that sandwich. I'd brush it off and eat it. What else you gonna do?

Sometimes at night I'd hear Ma crying in her room. She would have her moments where it got to be too much. She wanted to do better for us and she didn't have the means. Even if she'd gotten a job, it probably wouldn't have paid better than the welfare, which at least came with food stamps and other benefits. She was doing the best she could. As I got older I started to understand why things were so hard for us. I started to see what racism was, how it worked.

Starting in seventh grade, me and a bunch of the other black kids from St. Albans were bused to JHS 158 in Bayside, on the north side of Queens. Bayside was white. Irish and Italian. Middle- and working-class families. We'd catch the yellow bus on Linden Boulevard and ride up there. The first day, the older kids who'd been bused the year before said, "Look, when the bell rings at three, you *run* to the school bus."

I said, "Run to the bus? For what?"

"Yo, man. These white kids? They bring their big brothers from the neighborhood and they'll chase you to the bus. You get caught and they'll beat you."

I didn't believe them. Then, sure enough, that afternoon I came out of class and these white kids were coming for us. They were chasing us with sticks, baseball bats, throwing rocks at the bus. The kids who couldn't run fast got beat to shit. I don't remember a single teacher or principal stepping in to do anything about it, either. I didn't get messed with too much. But I didn't make any friends over there, either. The white kids didn't talk to us, and we didn't talk to them. If I didn't have basketball practice, I'd catch the bus and go straight home to hang in O'Connell Park.

O'Connell Park was my spot. It was just this little playground at 196th Street and Murdock, but that place was legendary. A lot of basketball legends came out of that park: Boo Harvey, Anthony Mason, Mark Jackson. It had a concrete area we used as a baseball diamond, cages for basketball and handball. O'Connell was where my friends would be. All the girls were out there, too, watching the basketball players.

I'd go and play pickup games after school. I was good, a naturally gifted athlete, and the older guys would pick me to be on their teams. O'Connell Park was where I met Smooth. Smooth was a pretty boy with a flashy game. He was two years older than me, but one afternoon we wound up playing together and hit it off immediately. After the game, he was like, "Yo, let's hang out. Come to my crib." From that day on, we were inseparable.

Smooth's life was completely different from mine. His real name was Mike Russell. Smooth was his street name. The Russells were living the American Dream. They were the perfect middle-class family, like the Huxtables. Smooth's mother and father were married. She worked for the phone company, and he was a supervisor at the post office. Smooth went to Catholic school, Bishop Ford in Brooklyn. He was Mike over there, and he was Smooth on the block. He had an older sister who was in college and an older brother in the military. They had a nice house on 113th Road, just up from O'Connell Park. It was a detached Colonial, three full bedrooms and a big family room in the basement where a lot of neighborhood kids would hang out.

While I was going around with holes in my shoes, Smooth was one of the best-dressed guys in the hood. He had the freshest sneakers, the nicest clothes. He could drive his sister's car when he wanted. He was incredibly generous and never judged me for being poor. He knew I didn't have much, so he started giving me things. I remember one day he was wearing this leather jacket. I told him I liked it and he took it off and said, "Here, that's you." He'd do things like that all the time. His parents always invited me for dinner so I could get a good meal.

One afternoon in the fall of '82, the start of my eighth-grade year, Smooth and I were hanging in the park. I was thirteen, and he was fifteen. I didn't know much about selling drugs. I'd see these guys hanging around the park, standing around on the corner, and I knew they were hustlers or they were in a gang, but I was young enough that I wasn't any part of that. Smooth was older. He'd gotten to know a lot of these guys. We were in the park that afternoon, hanging by the basketball cages, and he said to me, "Yo, my man Mack want us to sell these loosies for him."

Loosies were marijuana joints rolled up in cigarette paper. Smooth said Mack had offered to give us a hundred joints; we'd sell them for $1 each, give him back $80, and keep $20 for ourselves. If we were interested, he'd meet us that evening over on the corner at 198 and Murdock and give us the package. I thought about it. I knew weed wasn't a big deal. Everybody smoked weed. My older sister Angie smoked weed. Mostly I thought of what I could do with my half of the money. I could buy some clothes, a new pair of sneakers. Maybe I could buy myself something to eat.

I didn't have to think about it long. "Yo," I said, "let's do it."

3

The Golden Age

Back when I was nine years old and we were still living on Dormans Road, an old guy named Stevie lived a few doors down. He died, and the family and friends and neighbors gathered over there one afternoon for the funeral. This young guy showed up; he must have been a nephew or a cousin or something. The second he walked in everybody started talking and whispering. This guy was still young, maybe eighteen years old, but people were in awe of him. Guys were going, "Yo, that's *him*. That's Supreme."

I was like, "Who's Supreme?"

"He's the man. He's a big deal on the South Side, over in Baisley Park. He runs things over there. He runs with Fat Cat."

That's when I started hearing these names: Supreme, Fat Cat, Ronnie Bumps, Pop Freeman, Tommy Montana, the Corley Brothers. Street legends. They were hustlers and gangsters who controlled the drug trade and the numbers rackets and the crime in southeast Queens. Over on Dormans, there wasn't much criminal element. Once we moved to the apartment above the numbers joint, we were closer to the epicenter of everything criminal that was going on in the neighborhood.

You can stand on any street corner in St. Albans and look at the single-family houses, the people playing ball in the park, and it looks like any other neighborhood. But chaos was going on underneath the surface. Black families moved out to places like Hollis and St. Albans to get out of the ghetto, but when you're black and trying to get ahead in this world, the ghetto has a way of following you. You've got no-good relatives from the old neighborhood. You've got folks poorer than you running away from the same troubles and bringing their problems along with them. Gangsters and mobsters also know that poor black neighborhoods are easy places to operate—the community doesn't have the leverage to get them out.

Poor people don't gamble or do drugs any more than rich people. Rich folks go to Vegas to play blackjack, get Valium prescriptions from their doctors. Poor folks play the numbers and buy loose joints on the corner. Same thing, only rich people make sure their vices stay legal. Poor people don't have that option, so the black market comes along to provide the vices they want. Crime inevitably follows.

After black families moved out to Queens in the forties and fifties, the mafia followed in the sixties and seventies. Pop Freeman was the man back then. He ran numbers and the heroin trade out here for the mob, for the Genovese crime family they say. He had the whole neighborhood locked down. After Pop Freeman it was Ronnie "Bumps" Bassett who took over. Ronnie was an old-school hustler, with the superfly suits and the big Cadillac. He ran southeast Queens like Nicky Barnes and Frank Lucas ran Harlem. He was one of the first black dealers to cut out the mob; he went straight to Miami and bought uncut cocaine and heroin and brought it back to New York to sell.

Coming up behind Ronnie Bumps was a new generation of young street gangs: the Seven Crowns, the Savage Skulls, the Savage Nomads, the Peace Gods. These were young black cats amped up with talk of Black Power, but nowhere to go with it. They wanted to be like the Black Panthers or the Muslims, but they mostly ended up being neighborhood gangs that got into fights, stole car radios, and sold drugs to make a little money. By the 1980s, a lot of guys from those gangs had stepped up to take a big piece of the drug trade under Ronnie Bumps. The Corley Brothers controlled the Forty Projects.

Tommy Montana had neighborhoods like Hollis and Laurelton. Supreme took over the Baisley projects and Baisley Park. Lorenzo "Fat Cat" Nichols, who was with the Seven Crowns, he was the biggest of all of them, the biggest gangster in southeast Queens.

Other than that one time seeing Supreme on Dormans Road, my earliest exposure to gangs was through my sister Debra's boyfriend, Spank. He started coming around when I was twelve years old. He and my sister lived together off Murdock near O'Connell Park. I grew up with sisters, my father gone, no male influence around the house. Spank was the big brother I never had. He would bring me gifts, give me a couple dollars here and there. I loved hanging out with him, loved having a big brother to play with me. But Spank was a straight gangster. He was with the Seven Crowns. He'd sold heroin and everything else back in the day. He'd just got out of maximum security prison for shooting someone. It wasn't the first maximum security prison he'd been in, either.

Spank was fucking nuts. He was one of those guys nobody wanted to mess with. He opened up a bar on Farmers Boulevard. He had a couple of used pool tables, a few arcade games like Pac-Man and Galaga, an office in the back. I'd hang out there with him from time to time. I was there with him one night—twelve years old and hanging out in a pool hall with a convicted felon. Spank was playing a game with one of his friends and they started having this beef. Spank told the guy to come in the back office. They went back there. I heard screaming and yelling and then—*boom! boom! boom!*—three shots. Next thing I knew two guys were carrying this dude out wrapped in blankets. I don't know if he was dead or what. Spank walked back out, came back to the table like nothing had happened, and went back to shooting pool.

As I got older and started hanging around in O'Connell Park, I started to see who the hustlers were, how they worked. Smooth had been around them a lot more. He had two years on me, and his older brother Patrick used to hang with a lot of these guys before going into the army. Guys like Cash and Diquan and Mack. They were the hustlers who worked around O'Connell Park. They looked out for Smooth because they knew Patrick. They brought him along, made sure he was good. They'd tell him, "Yo, this is how you wear your hat. This is how you wear your sneakers."

Smooth was hanging with those guys up in Cash's attic one day, and they were rolling joints to sell. Smooth was like, "What's that?"

Cash said, "Yo, didn't you know? That's how we get a couple dollars. But you ain't ready for this here."

Smooth convinced them to give him a shot. They gave him a few loosies to sell, and he was good at it. He was popular. He had the clientele. He moved the product fast. Smooth started out selling for Cash, but Cash was only a part-time hustler. He had a job at Queens General Hospital and was dealing on the side. He wasn't putting his foot forward like he could have. So Smooth started selling for Mack. Mack was a gangster for real. He was in the streets, the baddest dude from Hollis Ave. He had the connect to get the good weed, and soon Smooth had more loosies to sell than he could handle on his own.

Me and Smooth, right away we were like brothers. That's the code we learned from the older guys. Once you embrace somebody as a brother, that's it. Nothing can come between you—not money, not girls, nothing. So of course he was going to bring me in on what he was doing, and I wasn't going to let him do it without me. That first night, after we'd talked about it in the park after school, me and Smooth met Mack on the block at 198 and Murdock. He gave us the package, a brown manilla envelope with a hundred joints.

We sold that in less than a day. Selling weed was easy. Me and Smooth, we're both personable guys, smooth talkers. But you didn't need a personality to sell weed. Shit sold itself. Everybody smoked it. If you had good shit—and we always had good shit—word got out and people came to you. Soon business was rolling. We were selling and selling and selling, getting that money. We'd meet up with Mack on Sunday night, get five hundred joints for $380 to start fresh on Monday. We'd sell that in two days, get another five hundred for Wednesday, and another on Friday for the weekend. Sometimes more. We were pocketing a buck-twenty on each package, so by the end of the week we were walking around with four, five hundred dollars in our pockets. I was thirteen years old.

I needed the money. Smooth didn't. I had the mom on welfare and the absent father. Smooth had the stable two-parent home, the private school, but he made the choice. It was the culture, the environment we grew up in. It was seductive. The hustlers working the park, they were the baddest guys around. Mack and Cash and Diquan, they were the coolest motherfuckers to be with. If you looked up cool in a dictionary, you'd see their pictures.

Diquan was this skinny dude, wore a Kangol hat, used to custom paint his Pumas all these different colors. Mack was this laid-back, lanky, light-skinned dude, always had the latest outfits before anybody else in the hood had even heard of them. Those were the guys we wanted to be like. They had the women, the fresh outfits. Smooth, his mom would buy him a new pair of Keds, but she wasn't buying him the new Pumas. Pumas were dope, and if you wanted them, you needed that little extra money—sell a few loose joints, you were good.

It was also the Golden Age of Hip-Hop. That was in full effect, and we were right in the middle of it. Street hustling and hip-hop grew out of the same environment. Our older brothers and sisters would bring home the singles, "Rapper's Delight" by the Sugar Hill Gang, "The Breaks" by Kurtis Blow. Everybody had their boom box out in the park, playing those songs. The one I remember most was "Super Sporm" by Captain Sky, because I was young and all I knew was sperm was a bad word and I wasn't supposed to say it.

You had Grandmaster Flash and Melle Mel up in the Bronx. Marley Marl and Roxanne Shante over in Queensbridge. But hip-hop wasn't just blowing up in other parts of New York. It was happening in *my* hood, in *my* park. LL Cool J is the same age as me. We grew up together. He lived right around the corner from my house on Dormans

Road. We'd see him walking around, his headphones on, bopping his head and mouthing along to the lyrics, coming up with rhymes for himself. His DJ, Cut Creator, was one of the guys we'd play baseball games with out on Dormans Road. Russell Simmons and Run-DMC were from Hollis. They were older than us, but they'd gone to high school at Andrew Jackson with our brothers and sisters. LL Cool J shot the cover of his *Bigger and Deffer* album in front of Andrew Jackson. Ed Lover, from *Yo! MTV Raps*, he was a security guard at Andrew Jackson. He had a high-top fade with an orange tail in the back.

We knew all of those guys. LL Cool J and Cut Creator would do jams right in O'Connell Park. They'd come in, take the electricity from the light pole, bring the big speakers out, the turntable and crates of records, and we'd have a party. Run-DMC would do free concerts every summer in Hollis Park. Everybody would go. We had so much pride in what was happening. It wasn't like listening to the Delfonics sing about love. This music was about being poor and growing up on welfare, drug dealers on the corner. It was ghetto poetry. It was like, Wow, this is our reality, and the whole country is hearing about where we come from.

Everybody was caught up in the culture of hip-hop. That's how Smooth had got his name, doing graffiti with Diquan, tagging subway cars and buses. He did a few gigs as a DJ, had his name on a sweatshirt and everything: DJ Smooth. I tried to be an MC myself. For about a week. I tried to write some rhymes and recorded myself doing them. I was terrible. I stuck with selling drugs. It was easier. And to be honest, being a hustler was cooler than being a rapper. Rappers didn't make any money in those days. Hustlers had the money, the girls, the swag. Rappers emulated the hustlers to try to make themselves look cool.

Being in a poor community and having that extra bit of money to buy nice clothes, take your girl out, that was cool. You're young, you're black, you don't see any prospects. Then you see these dealers, and they're living the American Dream. That was how we were raised: mobbed up numbers joints and pool halls and street hustlers. It was impossible to hang around people selling drugs and making money and not get caught up in it. It don't work. People are products of their environments. If you're raised in a pigsty, you learn how to be a pig. You can say you're not going to eat shit, but eventually you're going to eat shit.

4

Life

Smooth's parents thought that by sending him to a nice, private Catholic school they were putting him in a better environment than where we grew up. But the rich, white kids he went to school with? They bought more drugs than anyone. Smooth would take a bunch of joints to school and sell them in between class or on the school bus in the morning. He could take two hundred loosies to school and they would be gone by lunch.

I wasn't selling up at Bayside the way Smooth was at Bishop Ford. I was still in middle school; thirteen-year-old kids aren't buying weed. Plus I tried to keep those two things separate. When I was at school I was at school. I guess I was an unusual drug dealer. I liked school. I never missed a single day. I never forgot the time I let my mother down by getting kicked out of third grade and the promise I made to never disappoint her again.

Ma knew I was selling drugs. She had to know. I was out there every day, down the street from my aunt and uncle's house. I was also giving Ma money. I was a fourteen-year-old kid coming home, helping my mom out with a couple hundred bucks here and there. Where else could I be getting it? So she knew. She wasn't happy about it, but she'd take the money. She needed it.

None of my older sisters graduated from high school. Ma would say , "I just want to see one of my kids graduate from high school." She wanted that for us because she didn't get it for herself, and she knew how it held her back. Since she wasn't educated, she couldn't help us with homework, didn't know which programs we should get involved with. I had to figure that out on my own. Those were the cards I was dealt. I knew I was letting Ma down by selling drugs, so I made a promise to myself to make up for it by staying in school and being the first to graduate.

I did okay at Bayside, as well as anybody could after hugging the block all night and spending an hour on the bus to get to school. I never sat with the clowns in the back, but always in the front row. I was getting Cs and Bs, some Ds here and there, but I was passing. If I'd actually been studying, who knows how well I might have done?

In the spring of '83, I was getting set to finish ninth grade and graduate from Bayside. In New York, students could test and apply to different magnet schools if they wanted to go to a high school outside their zone. I was zoned for Andrew Jackson in St. Albans. It was a terrible school, a dropout factory. Older guys I knew from the park went to Andrew Jackson, and they were all just clowning over there.

I knew if I went there, I'd end up flunking out with everybody else, so at the end of ninth grade I looked at the aptitude test for some of these better schools. I picked engineering. I knew engineers made decent money, and since everything I did was about maximizing my financial potential, I gave it a shot. I passed and got into Newtown High over in Elmhurst in northwest Queens, near Laguardia Airport. I started there in the fall of '83.

Even though I was doing well in school, I never thought about getting out of the streets. I still had to eat, and business was only getting bigger. Me and Smooth were moving up. Most people in St. Albans couldn't afford cocaine, but Smooth started getting a bit from Mack to sell to the kids at Bishop Ford. And we stopped messing around with loosies. We had too many clients. We started buying weed in bulk from some West Indians who were selling out of one of those candy store fronts. We'd bag it and sell tre bags for three dollars, nickel bags for five, and dime bags for ten. That was easier than selling the loose joints.

Then we started getting mescaline. I never smoked weed when I was selling it. I was never into getting high; I never wanted drugs controlling me the way alcohol controlled my father. I smoked it maybe once or twice. The other guys would make me just to see me do it. "C'mon, man! Smoke up! Take a hit!" I didn't care much for it. When Mack first offered us mescaline tabs to sell, Smooth said we should try it so we'd know what we were selling. "We gotta know what the product do," he said. We got together over at his house one night. We had a bottle of golden Champale. We popped those little tabs under our tongues, drank the Champale, and got the buzz of our lives. All we did was laugh. We laughed and laughed and laughed all night long. The next day, we were like, "Okay, this shit ain't too dangerous." So we started selling that, too.

The mescaline came in these glassine bags, one tab in each. We were killing 'em with that. In the summertime, if a big block party was going on or whatever, we'd get two hundred of these tabs from Mack, head out to the park. Sell the tabs for $10 each. We'd be out there hustlin', gettin' that paper, and we'd be finished by late afternoon with two grand in our pockets. Fourteen hundred of that would go back to my man Mack, and me and Smooth would split the rest. It was a joke how easy it was. We never worried about getting shot, getting busted, any of that. The Jamaicans had the big stash houses. They were moving serious weight. They might get their door knocked down, get busted and locked up. But the street sellers? The cops weren't looking for us.

There weren't a whole lot of cops around, period. I never got stopped or questioned over the weed. Not once. We didn't have to deal with gangs, either. There wasn't any one gang that controlled St. Albans the way the Supreme Team and the Corley Brothers controlled the projects over on the South Side, primarily because of geography and real estate. For a gang to take over an area, they need public housing towers to control. They need corners to occupy. South Jamaica has public housing and industrial and commercial properties. St. Albans is mostly a suburban, family type of environment. The only storefronts near us were on that commercial strip at 198 and Murdock. Most of the corners in our neighborhood were people's yards. You can't sell drugs in people's yards.

Without a gang controlling the territory, there was no hierarchy. No higher-ups bringing us along. We had a few older homies, guys like Cash and Mack, giving us the work, but that's all they did. We learned as we went. The guys selling around O'Connell Park and 198 and Murdock were freelance. We had an understanding. Everybody did his own thing. We had our own product and we made our own money. Nobody stepped on toes. There was no violence, no beefs, no "Get the fuck off my corner!" It was loosey-goosey. Nobody had a gun or anything like that.

We weren't a gang. We were more like a crew, a bunch of young guys hanging in the park after school, playing basketball, and the weed and the mescaline was how we made a few extra dollars. It was me and Smooth, my man Dre, my man Mark, my man Smiley. Everybody was cool. We'd go to parties, go to clubs. Dre was funny, tall, a real pretty boy. He was like Smooth, from a good family, both parents working, but he still gravitated to the streets. He was the closest to a real gangster of all of us, real quick-tempered, always first to throw a punch. Anybody disrespected him it was going to be a problem. Mark, he was a skinny, light-skinned dude, laid back but would fight if he had to. He smoked weed. Drank a lot, too. He had a brother in the streets who got killed. Smiley was a great guy. Like his name sounds, he smiled all the time, was always friendly. But Smiley smoked and drank way too much. He's messed up now, still to this day.

Cash was part of the crew as well. He was our older dude, our protection, our political tie. Those older guys from back in the day, like the Seven Crowns and Ronnie Bumps, Cash was down with them. Nobody messed with Cash. Because we were down with Cash, the older crews accepted us as well.

We were a bunch of kids playing at being real gangsters. One day we were hanging out in the basketball cages in O'Connell and we were like, "Yo, we need to come up with a name for our crew." I don't remember who, but somebody said, "Let's call ourselves the Life Mob." I was "Boo Life." Smooth was "Smooth Life." Cash was "Cash Life." That was us trying to be cool. I don't think it even lasted a week. But my name stuck. People started calling me "Life." That became my street name.

Around that time I was becoming three different people. At home and with my Ma I was still Boo. Across town at school I was Corey, varsity basketball player, doing my homework, sitting in the front of the classroom. And out in the streets I was Life. Life was more of a persona than the other two. It wasn't me. I was a happy kid, happy-go-lucky, outgoing, friendly. But in the streets I couldn't be like that. There was a code. Somebody disrespected me, I had to respond. Somebody owed me money and couldn't pay, I had to take care of it.

I started putting this front up, like, "Yo, I'm this tough guy," which I wasn't. I wasn't some gangster killer. In O'Connell Park, people knew we ran with Cash and Mack, so we didn't have to prove ourselves much. But we were all over southeast Queens, playing pickup games in different parks, on other guys' turf. We'd go over there and run into different crews and hear them talking behind our backs. "Yo, that's them niggers Life and Smooth." Those guys were going to try us. We had to stick our chest out a bit.

It was the same thing going out to the clubs. Once our gear was stepped up, once we were wearing the nice clothes and the nice jewelry, we started seeing that eye. We started seeing that envy. Dudes would want to fight us just because we were a couple of handsome guys in their club, putting a little money down, checking out their girls. We'd be hanging out and some dude would come by, bump into us on purpose. I'd say "Yo, what's up?" And he'd be an asshole for no reason, like, "Yo! My man don't like your man!" Or whatever. So now that macho bullshit had to come out. I had to be like, "Yo, I ain't no punk. Let's get it." I had to protect myself, protect my rep, build my street cred.

"I ain't no punk." That's the code of the streets, and once we were in that life, we were in it. I took on that persona, and it became a part of me, even though it wasn't ever how I saw myself. I started getting caught up in all kinds of shit. Somebody'd say, "Hey, let's go up to Bayside and steal bikes," and we'd go up to Bayside and steal bikes. We did robberies, got in fights. We won some, we lost some, but eventually that respect came.

I never liked that part of it. I wanted to look fly, get money, and get girls. That was it for me. Drug dealers get women. Pretty girls, too. Either they wanted that money or they wanted that hookup. Girls were the thing that got me in trouble. That was true going back to third grade, when my crush on Michelle got me acting out and forced me to change schools. Smooth was the same way. He was dating a girl from Bishop Ford at the time we started selling. She got pregnant and he had a baby by her before the end of junior year.

Once I started making money, getting girls was no longer a problem. I was fifteen, messing around with girls five, six years older than me. Take them out, buy them clothes, buy them jewelry. At the end of my sophomore year, I met Theresa. I was playing basketball in O'Connell Park and noticed her hanging out with this girl I knew. I called over from the court, "Yo, I want to meet your friend." On the next shot I ran into the pole, cracked my tooth, and went down on the pavement. I got up, all embarrassed and bleeding, and that's when this girl walked Theresa over and introduced us. We started dating, my first real girlfriend.

Theresa came from a nice family. Her father was an electrician who worked in Manhattan. He died not long after we started dating. Her mom, Mamma Willis, had a job with the Social Security Department. They lived around the corner from me at Theresa's grandmother's house, in the basement. They didn't have much furniture—a small table, two beds, and one couch that turned into a bed.

I didn't know what to do in a serious relationship. My father certainly never taught me how to treat women. Everything I knew came from the streets. Everybody had different girls in their lives. I'd step out on Theresa with girls over at school, from around the neighborhood. Theresa was a good girlfriend, even if I wasn't a good boyfriend. She was beautiful, full lips and a sexy walk, but she was quiet, down to earth. She made me want to be the better person I knew I could be.

At the end of that same summer, I had a chance to get out of the streets, a chance to stop dealing. There was a guy around the neighborhood, a basketball scout. His name was Joe Bostic. He was always looking for up-and-coming players; he'd hooked up guys to go play at different schools. One day he said to me, "Listen, I want to hook you up with St. John's Military Academy. It's outside Milwaukee. I think you'd be good over there." The way he pitched it, I'd finish my junior and senior year at this military school and go on to college. I wanted to go. The only reason I'd started dealing was so I could eat. The other shit—the money, the sneakers, the jewelry, the girls—I was having fun with it but I wasn't stupid. I was happy to give it up for the chance to do something positive with my life.

I made up my mind that I was going. I started making plans, imagining the future I'd have. But even though they were offering me a scholarship, I'd still have expenses, maybe a couple hundred dollars a month. My mother didn't have that kind of money. I went around to my aunts and uncles to see if they could help. They couldn't. I had to turn it down. A window had opened, showing me another world. Then it closed again and there I was, back on the corner.

A couple months later, Mack came down one day to bring us the package. He opened up the envelope and handed it to us, but this time it wasn't weed or mescaline inside. It was these little glass vials. Mack said, "Yo, I want y'all to start selling this now." That was the first time I laid eyes on crack cocaine.

5

The Perfect Drug

We'd been hearing about this new drug for a few weeks. Smooth had only ever dealt with a bit of powder cocaine. We knew you could snort it, shoot it. Some people would freebase it, but to do that you had to cook it down, which was complicated and dangerous. Now people were talking about selling cocaine already cooked, in rock form. You'd put it in a cigarette and smoke it, put it in a pipe and smoke it. We didn't really know what that meant. When Mack gave us the vials, he said, "Yo, you do what you want, you stand where you want, but this is what you need to be sellin'. This is the shit here. Them weed heads y'all got? They about to become y'all crackheads."

Mack was right. We stopped messing with weed the day we got crack. Some guys started out selling what we called woolies, joints laced with crack. But me and Smooth didn't mess with that, either. We just sold the vials. We had two different sizes, ones with small caps and ones with large caps. The small ones we'd sell for $5. The big ones—we called them jumbos or jums—those sold for $10.

Crack was the perfect drug: easy to make, cheap to buy, and insanely addictive. Take $25 worth of coke, water, and some baking soda. You cook that up and you had $100 worth of crack. I knew guys who would cook it up on a stove at home. I never cooked it. I can't boil an egg, so I never tried.

The shit took off. I mean, like a rocket ship. People started coming. They were smoking it, buggin' out, and coming back for more the same day. They wanted that hit. Had to have it. It was crazy. I couldn't believe it at first. I was like, "Where the fuck all these people coming from?" We were the first guys in the neighborhood to get it. They'd been going way down to Sutphin or Farmers Boulevard to get it. Now they didn't have to go that far and were all coming to us. Crackheads. Fiends. They started coming and coming and didn't stop.

We had no idea what crack would do; we didn't know it would be different from weed or mescaline or anything else. We couldn't believe how much money we were making. I probably made $100 a day selling weed, but we were moving so much crack I started clearing $500 a day, easy. Then it was $700 a day. Then $800, $900, sometimes $1,000 a day. It was coming faster than I could spend it. I didn't keep it at my house. I wanted to keep it away from my family. I started keeping it in shoe boxes at Theresa's house. I would roll it up in rubber bands and throw the rolls in the box.

The money was as addictive as the drug. It was easy, quick, and every hit left us hungry for the next one, then one more, then one more after that. Dealing weed or heroin was no different than running a regular business, like a Laundromat or a candy store. You had your clientele, the locals and the regulars. You might have a good week or a bad week, a shortage or a surplus, but month to month it was steady work, hugging the block, grinding it out. Crack exploded and kept going.

Street gangs like the Supreme Team over on the South Side, they scaled up to grab everything they could. Dealing became a monopoly thing. They wanted territory. Me and Smooth, we were never on that. Smooth was getting ready to graduate from Bishop Ford the next spring; he was already applying to colleges. He never lost sight of that. I knew I was going to graduate, too. For us, it wasn't about "Yo, let's be gangstas." We didn't want to be kingpins, didn't want to be Nicky Barnes. For us it was "Hey, we're gonna get this money, we're gonna get women, gonna buy a lot of clothes." On 198 and Murdock, the rules for selling crack were the same as selling weed, at first. Everybody had his own connect, his own package, and he'd be out there selling. We didn't mess with each other. Our thinking was that there was so much money to be made, let everybody make it. It didn't stay like that for long.

We got rid of Mack fast, after only a month maybe. Me and Smooth couldn't meet the demand; we could never get the re-up from Mack fast enough. He was mostly bringing us those small caps. Mark and Dre, they had the big caps, the jumbos, and they were turning that shit over fast. They were dealing direct with some Colombians up in Harlem, buying wholesale, getting better product at a better price than we were getting. Mark and Dre said, "Yo, let us take you uptown." They took us uptown, and that was the end of Mack.

We took a livery cab from a cabstand in St. Albans and drove up to Harlem. It was a mess up there. Whole rows of houses dilapidated, boarded-up, and abandoned. In Harlem, Colombians had the crack business on lock. This particular group controlled a whole block, 131st Street I think, not far from City College. We couldn't even get on the block without being searched by armed guards out in the street in broad daylight. The guards were Colombian, with curly black Afros and gold around their necks. They didn't speak to us except to ask, in broken English, who we were there to see. We told them and they patted us down and took us into the basement of one of those buildings.

Going in there made the hair on the back of my neck stand up. The basement was dark, filthy. It reeked of urine. I was barely sixteen years old, walking into an abandoned building, surrounded by armed Colombians with three, four thousand dollars cash in my pocket. They'd built this maze of tunnels down there we had to get through. We walked for a while, through four or five different brownstones connected underground, until we reached a room in the basement of a different house from the one we'd entered aboveground. We got in there and there was this guy sitting at a table, bricks of pure cocaine stacked all around him, and plastic tubs full of crack vials that had been counted out and put in packages for guys like us.

The main guy, the top Colombian dude, I'll never forget: His name was Kilo. Perfect name. Kilo was this wiry Hispanic guy, didn't speak any English, or at least he acted like he didn't. But he didn't need to. It was simple. We put down the cash, he laid out the package, we took it and left. That was it. After that first trip, we didn't need Mark or Dre to go with us. Me and Smooth went on our own. We started out buying two, three hundred vials at a time, paying $5 each and turning around and selling them for $10 each on the block. Soon we were going up there several times a week, buying a thousand vials at a time. The turnover was that quick.

Back on the block, we hired a few guys to start working for us. We'd pay them $20 for every $100 they sold, the same way we'd started out under Mack. We had three or four different guys, a couple years younger than us. Whenever we couldn't be on the block, we'd have those cats out there working for us. Duce was our number one worker. He was my protégé. He watched every move I made and learned the game. I loved him like a brother, and that's how I referred to him. He had a baby by my sister Tawn. There was also Donte, Mohammed, Barnett. All Barnett wanted to do was sit out there and smoke. Mohammed was a good kid, though. He was murdered a few years later.

That was our crew. From the first vial we sold for Mack to setting up our own connect with the Colombians and bringing those guys in to work for us, all that happened in a couple of months, during that first winter of '85. It happened so fast we were already deep in it before we realized what we were doing.

One night it was cold out and me and my crew were huddled inside the Jamaican restaurant next to the candy store. This fiend came up and knocked on the window. We could hear him through the glass. "Yo, yo, I need some. I need some." My man Smiley stepped out to hit him off. They went around the corner to make the sale. All of a sudden we heard gunshots. *Boom! Boom! Boom! Boom!* It was a setup. The fiend robbed him, took his package, and when Smiley took off running the guy fired at him.

We were like, *Wow*. This is real.

After Smiley got robbed, I hired a bodyguard, a guy I knew from the neighborhood just out of prison for shooting someone. Big motherfucker. Between his size and his reputation, nobody messed with this guy. I paid him $100 a day, plus I bought him food whenever he got hungry. He'd eat liverwurst sandwiches all day long.

Up to that point, me and Smooth had never carried guns. We'd never even thought about it. Now we thought about it constantly, wondering if another dealer or some fiend was going to come after us. Smooth went out and bought a nickel-plated .38.

I was on the block one afternoon, and this 'head came up looking to buy. He was all fucked up, twitchy, the hollow eyes, scratching himself. I said, "What you need?"

He said, "Gimme three jumbos."

I said, "That's thirty."

He was like, "I don't have it."

"Man, get the fuck outta here."

"No, no, wait," he said. "I don't have no money, but I got this."

He pulled out a pistol, a .25. I took him around the back of the store. He gave me the gun. I held it, looked at it. I'd never held a gun in my hand before. I didn't even know what I was looking at. He said, "Gimme three jumbos and you can have it."

I said okay, slid the gun in my pocket, gave him three, and he left. I remember standing there, feeling the weight of it on my leg, thinking, Damn, I can't wait to tell Smooth. We're on our way now.

6

In Full Effect

One afternoon that summer, Smooth and I went up to Harlem to pick up a package from the Colombians. We got searched on the street, went in through the basement and down the maze of tunnels to the stash room. There was one light over the table where Kilo sat with the product and the rest of the room in shadows. You couldn't see much.

We gave Kilo our money, five grand for a thousand caps. He counted the money out. Normally we never counted the package, but that day Smooth wanted a count. So he sat there, sorting through this whole bag of crack vials, counting one by one, three hundred . . . four hundred . . . He finished and looked up at me. He said, "Yo, Life. We short."

"What?"

"We short, man! We fuckin' short!"

The package was something like three vials short, out of a thousand, not a big deal. It'd been short once or twice before, but we'd just thrown in the extra $20 to cover it and who gives a fuck? You're talking pennies. But that day Smooth started acting all pissy. He kept on. "We short. These motherfuckers tryin' to short us."

I couldn't believe it. We were a couple of high school kids in an abandoned building in Harlem buying drugs from fucking Colombians, and Smooth wanted to argue over three vials of crack. I said, "Smooth, man. Chill. Let it go. Take the fuckin' package and let's go."

He wouldn't. He got madder. He started yelling. Kilo was looking at us, like "*Que pasa?*" Smooth started getting in his face, screaming, "I'm tired of you motherfuckers shortin' our fuckin' package. I'm givin' you niggers money. I want my paper. I want what you fuckin' owe me."

Then Kilo started losing it. Smooth was yelling at Kilo, and Kilo was yelling at Smooth. This guy didn't speak a word of English, and Smooth didn't speak a word of Spanish, but they both knew exactly what the other was saying. They kept arguing and cursing and finally Kilo yelled some shit in Spanish and we heard *Clack-clack! Clack-clack! Clack-clack!* Four or five Colombian dudes popped up out of the shadows. Fucking shotguns, 9-millimeters, assault rifles. These dudes stood there and stared us down.

We froze. I said, "Smooth, you need to calm the fuck down. We takin' the package and we gettin' the fuck out of here." I turned to Kilo and was like, "Look, man. I got him. It's cool. I'm gonna take him and we'll go." We took the package and left as quietly and calmly as we could. I never took Smooth back to Harlem with me after that day. I went and got the re-ups by myself. To this day that asshole is still mad about that package being short.

If you act like a criminal long enough, eventually that's what you become. Maybe it starts out as a pose, acting tough to get street cred, make money, or impress girls. But once you adopt that pose, you can't drop it. You have to put up that front, be hard, protect your rep, even when it means doing stupid shit. Smooth was a private-school kid on his way to college, with a kid to take care of, and he wanted to start some beef with a Colombian drug cartel? To show he's the man? Being in the street changes you. That's what had happened to Smooth.

It was happening to me, too. That summer, my sister Angie had been dating this guy. He was nineteen or twenty, nice guy, had a job. Then he started smoking crack. Now the dude was all messed up. I kept my stash hidden in the back of the hallway closet of my mom's apartment. I went to get it one day and I could tell: Somebody had fucked with the package. This guy was the only one who could have done it. He thought he was being clever. He didn't take any vials, but he'd tapped every single one of them and taken a rock or two out of each one. He thought I wouldn't be able to tell, but it was obvious. I confronted him right there in the apartment in front of my sister. I got right up on him and I said, "Yo, you took my shit! You took my crack."

He was all, "Nah, nah, man. What you talkin' about? I didn't take anything."

"You took my shit, you motherfuckin' crackhead. Don't fuckin' lie to me."

He kept denying it, saying he didn't know nothing. But a crackhead is a crackhead. They're terrible liars. I got tired of listening to his bullshit. I left and went up to the corner to find my man Al. Al was this big, jacked-up dude. He was a guy around the neighborhood you could pay money to do shit. I offered him $200 to come back to the apartment with me and beat the shit out of my sister's boyfriend. He said okay.

As we walked back, I explained the situation to him. "Yo, my sister's boyfriend fucked with my package. I need you to go in here and fuck him up. But this is my mom's apartment. You can't be messing it up or my mom's gonna be pissed. So you need to take this outside. Just don't kill him or nothin' like that, 'cause he's like my brother-in-law."

We got to the apartment, went up to the living room. Angie saw me with Al and yelled, "Boobie, no!"

I didn't listen. I told Al, "Get that motherfucker."

Al snatched this guy right off the couch and dragged him out and down the stairs. At the bottom of the landing, he beat the crap out of him, kicked him out the door onto the sidewalk. Angie had run out behind us, screaming and yelling and crying, "Boobie, stop it! I'm gonna tell Ma! I'm gonna tell Ma!"

I gave Al the $200 and he took off, left this dude lying there on the sidewalk, his lip busted and his eye swollen shut.

The thing was, I didn't want to do it. The whole time Al was kicking his ass, I felt terrible. I was like, "*Why*, motherfucker? Why you makin' me do this to you?" But him taking my shit? That couldn't happen. If I let him fuck with my package, I'm short the next time I go up and see the Colombians. Other guys on the block hear about it, and they know that I'm soft. Then I'm the one getting my ass kicked, or worse. He shouldn't have touched the package. He got what he deserved. As a matter of fact, he got off light *because* we were family. Anybody else out there would have paid someone to shoot his ass.

———

That summer, the summer of '85, crack was in full effect. It was spreading fast. It seemed like everyone was starting to be affected by it, their house getting broke into, a relative getting cracked out, something. Dealing quickly turned into a 24/7 thing. If it was a school day, I went to school. Then as soon as I got home, I'd get my package and head right out. I'd be out there till three, four in the morning, crash for a few, then head back to school at eight. On weekends, we'd be out there hugging the block two days straight. Didn't even stop to change clothes. Theresa lived a few blocks away. I'd go over there, catch a catnap. But for the most part I was out all day. And come June or July, once school was out, we lived on that corner.

The crackheads, they were out. Morning, noon, and night, they were out. Middle of summer, dead of winter, they were out. The money didn't stop, and I got used to the lifestyle. I was surrounded by guys walking around with rolls of hundreds in their pockets, and I wanted to keep up. I was keeping mine rolled up in rubber bands in those shoe boxes in Theresa's closet. First it was one shoe box. Then two. Then three. I don't know how much it was. I never counted it. It was too much to count.

We'd blow through it, too. We spent it on nonsense. We started taking town cars everywhere. The cabstand we used to take us up to Harlem, we had two drivers there on call: this Jamaican guy named

Roy, and this other guy whose car was numbered 86, so that's what we called him, Eighty-six. We'd give those guys a hundred dollars for the day, and they'd take us around wherever we wanted to go, down to Brooklyn to see Smooth's girlfriend, out to the clubs. They were great. Funny guys. Cool to ride with. It was like having a personal chauffeur. They obviously knew what we were doing, but they were making so much money it was easy for them to keep their mouths shut.

We bought a lot of jewelry. A lot of it. The gold ropes and the big, custom medallions. Me and Smooth were up at Harry's Barbershop on Farmers every three days to keep our cuts fresh. We'd both get Caesars with waves spinning all over our head. I always tipped double the cost of the cut. Sometimes, if I was in a rush, I'd pay the three guys ahead of me to wait just so I could skip the line.

We spent most of the money on clothes. That was our thing. We were the best-dressed dudes in the hood, walking through O'Connell Park with our hustler shit on, the freshest outfits, the flyest sneakers. I developed a permanent pimp roll in the way I moved, a little ditty-bop in my step. The style that summer was the gray sweats with the bike shorts on top. That was the uniform. That was the bomb. We'd get that outfit with the sneakers to match. If we wore the red bike shorts on top, we wore the red Pumas. Green on top, green Pumas. Blue on top, blue Pumas. However we wanted to hook it up. We'd buy that whole outfit, buy it fresh, brand-new, just to go to the movies with our girls. The next day we'd give it away to a kid in the neighborhood and buy ourselves something else.

We hit the biggest clubs. We'd go to Club 50 on Linden and Farmers, to Club Encore on Merrick. Encore was a hard-core hip-hop and R&B club. All the big dealers from the borough would be in there. The Supreme Team was legendary in that spot. Mark Jackson, who we used to ball with at O'Connell Park and who went on to play for the Knicks, he took me and Smooth out one night to celebrate at Bentley's in Manhattan, this hip-hop dance club where you'd find a lot of celebrities. We'd take our girls out, go to a restaurant, buy them clothes, jewelry, whatever they wanted. We would take them to dinner on City Island in the Bronx, where they had a lot of nice seafood restaurants. We'd take a town car up, have the driver wait for us, buy him dinner to eat while we ate ours.

We did all of it without a care in the world. Crack had been on the streets for months, but the police weren't wise to it yet. Cops would fuck with black kids for doing nothing. We'd be out at a club or going to the movies and they'd walk up to us, throw us against the wall, go through our pockets. They'd do that to us for walking down the street. But when it came to selling crack, in the beginning at least, they didn't have a clue.

Cops in New York in the eighties were lazy, corrupt. They didn't give a shit. I only had a couple of close calls. One time when I went uptown to the Colombians, I'd picked up the package and I had it tucked in my waistband, up under my shirt. I stopped to use a pay phone on the way back to the cab I had waiting. While I was on the phone, someone tapped me on my shoulder. I turned around. It was a uniformed patrol officer. I was like, Oh, *fuck*. I'm going to jail for real. Right now. Cop said, "Hey, how long you gonna be on the phone?"

I stammered, "Just, uh . . . Just one second, Officer."

"Okay."

I couldn't get off that phone fast enough. I hung up, nodded to the officer, and went straight to my cab.

My only other close call came one afternoon on 198. I was out there with Smiley and a few others. We were selling hand-to-hand. I had maybe a hundred vials on me when out of nowhere all these cop cars swarmed the block. Guys were yelling, "Jake! It's Jake!" Jake is what we called the police. Everybody scattered. Me and Smiley turned and ducked straight into the candy store, ran to the back, threw our packages wherever we could, in the potato chips, in the freezer. Two cops came running in right after us and they came charging up the aisle. I stood there thinking, I'm done, I'm fuckin' done. I tensed up, waiting for that hand to grab me, but then *bam!* They grabbed Smiley, cuffed him, and dragged him out. They weren't looking for me. They only wanted Smiley, because he'd sold to an undercover.

Busts like that didn't happen often. Any drug enforcement that was going on was at a much higher level, feds and special task forces trying to build cases against major players like Fat Cat and Supreme. Most of the time, we weren't even worried about undercovers. It's hard to emulate a crackhead if you're a cop. Smiley wasn't smart. A smart dealer, he's not selling to somebody who doesn't look like a crackhead, and it's impossible for any healthy person to look like a crackhead. Only a crackhead looks like a crackhead. A real fiend would be undernourished, underweight, jaundiced with the cloudy eyes, ashy skin, lips all chapped. Just dirty, sick-looking.

I did have an undercover try to buy from me once. He was dressed in this ratty outfit, smelled like he hadn't showered. But under his clothes he was obviously in great shape, some young guy fresh out of the academy. I watched him coming down the block, trying to act all cracked out, going, "Hey, gimme a hit, man. I need a hit."

The guy was a joke. I said, "Man, get the fuck outta here."

"C'mon, I need three."

"I don't know what you're talking about. I ain't got shit."

As much as the way they looked, I could tell fiends by the way they behaved. Anxious, twitchy, scratching themselves. The real giveaway was, if I was in a room with a crackhead, he couldn't keep eye contact with me. He'd always be looking at the ground, scanning the carpet, thinking maybe he'd dropped a rock. If there was a spot of something white on the rug, he'd be down there on his knees, picking with his finger, trying to see if it was crack. If I wasn't sure about someone, I'd offer them a free hit and make them smoke it right in front of me. An undercover wasn't going to do that, but no fiend was going to turn it down.

With the women, especially, it was crazy. There were so many girls: Niki, Shan, Yvette. Niki was a professional dancer. She was gorgeous. Yvette was the girl who broke everyone's heart. Deep chocolate skin and a beautiful smile. I'd never seen a girl walk that sexy in my life. These girls were so fine that a year before I couldn't touch 'em. They wouldn't talk to me, wouldn't give me the time of day. They were that far out of my league. Now they were all strung out, coming up and going, "I'll suck your dick for a jumbo. Please."

We called them 'zoids. "Yo, she's a 'zoid." That was a woman who was down to do whatever. She'd fuck anybody. There was an abandoned van in the alley behind the candy store, this rusted-out piece of shit. We opened it up, took it over, and people started taking girls back there. Give 'em a vial of crack and they'd suck you off. Some women would stay in the van all day. You could go back there and give them a rock and they'd let you do whatever you wanted. Later that night, go back and do it again. She'd still be there.

Some guys started taking it too far. They'd disappear for days at a time with one of these 'zoids, hole up in a motel room, smoking their own product. Me and Smooth, it sounds weird to say it, but we had morals. We had a code. We wouldn't sell to family, to kids, or to pregnant women. We'd kick pregnant women off the block, wouldn't let other guys sell to them, either. We wouldn't sell near a church or near a school. A dude that was just a weed cat, or just a coke cat, we wouldn't sell crack to him. If you were a white-collar Wall Street dude, or a college guy, thinking you were going to come out here and have some ghetto thrill smoking crack, we weren't selling to you. We'd tell you to get lost. "Get outta here. I ain't selling you shit."

When we were selling weed, I never had any qualms about it. Weed wasn't hurting anybody. It never has. But with crack, I saw what it was doing to people. It was right in my face. So we had this code of who could buy. "This person's a junkie. They're going to be a crackhead anyway." That's how I rationalized it. That way I could say, "I'm not the bad guy. I'm just making money off of what these people are already doing to themselves."

Even though we were crack dealers, we didn't want people in the neighborhood to think we were bad kids. We'd grown up in this

neighborhood. We knew everybody, and they knew us. It was no secret what we were doing. On the one hand people didn't want us out
there selling. On the other hand they relied on us. Being on the block
24/7, we became the eyes and ears for the community, the neighborhood watch. We looked after the kids. We made sure they weren't getting in trouble, made sure they got home, made sure no crackheads
or drug addicts were messing with them. If we saw a kid out late by
himself, we'd say, "What you doing out here by yourself? Where's
your mom? Get home. Where you live?" We'd take him home, tell him
to get off the streets.

Our corner was the bus stop for the Q3A, which ran through St.
Albans from the Jamaica Terminal. Older ladies from the neighborhood were working and coming home late on the bus after cleaning
up office buildings, watching other people's kids. We knew those ladies. Ms. Smith, Ms. Walker, Ms. Fredericks, Ms. McGee. If Ms. Smith
was coming home late, you couldn't let her walk those four blocks
home by herself. We'd say "Ms. Smith, c'mon. We're going to walk you
home." She'd say "Thank you," and we'd walk her home, carry her bag,
ask about her nieces and nephews, make sure she was okay.

We weren't thugs to Ms. Smith. She knew us from Sunday school.
She knew our moms from church. Ms. Smith was probably the only
one who could actually get us to leave the block. A rival crew could
roll up with 9-millimeters threatening to shoot us if we didn't get off
the corner, and we wouldn't budge. It'd be a fight. But Ms. Smith?
All she had to do was give us that speech. "What you doin' out here,
son? Does your momma know you out here? I hope you ain't out here
messin' around."

We'd smile and say, "No, ma'am. We ain't doin' nothin'."

But we weren't fooling Ms. Smith. She'd shake her head and say,
"Baby, get off this corner. I know you was raised better than this. Go
home and be with your family." We'd lower our eyes down and say,
"Yes, ma'am." We'd go home and feel bad for a while, but the next day
or later that night we'd be right back on the block. We didn't stop.

Partly it was the money, but mostly we were out there because we wanted to be out there. We were with our crew, with our friends. We'd be there on the sidewalk, around the side of the candy store. We had milk crates, a seat we'd taken out of an old car and put up against the wall. That's where we'd sit, chill out, talk shit. Guys were smoking weed, drinking brews. Forty ounces all over the place, St. Ides and Olde English and Colt 45. Somebody'd have his boom box out there, listening to Whodini and Doug E. Fresh and the latest tracks. Girlfriends were coming by, hanging out.

There was a pay phone right there on the block. I still remember the number. If that phone rang, it was for one of us. If someone got arrested, he didn't call his family. He called that phone. One of us would pick up. Guys would call from out of town, from prison; everybody would get on, take turns saying hi. We'd play games. Drift over to O'Connell Park, shoot some ball, head back to the corner. We'd be out there rolling dice, playing Cee-lo. We'd play for big money, too. It wasn't unusual for the jackpot to be in the thousands.

The Jamaican restaurant next door, we ate there all the time. I had so many beef patties from that place. It one of those to-go joints where they serve you from behind bulletproof Plexiglas, with a couple of cheap Formica tables and chairs if you want to eat right there. The owners didn't like us being in there. But the husband and wife who ran the candy store, this older black couple, we never had any problems with them. They knew what we were doing, and they never said anything, never called the cops. We bought a lot of snacks and sandwiches from them, and a lot of 40s.

It was no different than any other place where young kids hang out anywhere in America, only we were drug dealers. Suburban kids hang out at the mall, eat at the food court, and work at the Gap. We'd hang out on the corner, get snacks from the candy store, and sell drugs. We'd play games, flirt with girls, and every now and then a crackhead would wander in, buy crack, and leave. That was normal to us. And it was *fun*. Being on the block was fun. Gangs beefing over turf, drive-bys with machine guns, SWAT teams breaking down doors, in the summer of '85 there was none of that. That hadn't hit yet. It was just me and my crew, being young and wild and having a blast.

I'll never forget coming home one day with this big rope chain and medallion I'd bought. I'd been showing it off down on the corner. I thought I was the baddest cat in the world wearing this thing. I was the bomb. I got home and my sister Angie was like, "Ooh, look what Boobie got on."

My mother looked at me and she started crying. She broke down. "My son is going to die. They're going to kill you."

I said, "Ma, I'm good. I *got* this."

And I thought I did. I was surrounded by danger every minute, but I was too caught up in it to see. It was a crazy, crazy time. But as much as I regret it now, I still have to say it was one of the most fun times of my life. I was young and innocent, and I didn't know what the hell I was doing.

7

The Block Gets Hot

At the end of that summer, I was getting ready to go back to New-town for my senior year. I was on the varsity basketball team. I didn't think I was going to the NBA or anything like that, but I was hoping for an athletic scholarship somewhere. Smooth was on his way. He'd graduated from Bishop Ford and was headed to Morgan State University in Baltimore. He was home at least two weekends a month to see his kid, but I knew things were going to be different with him leaving. What I didn't realize was how different it would be and how quickly it would change.

One afternoon that August, I was in O'Connell Park playing basketball. Smooth and the other guys, they were in a baseball game across the way, but I was in the cage ballin' with these dudes from the neighborhood when three of them jumped me. I don't even know why. All I was doing was talking trash like we always did. "You know I'm better than you." "You can't stick me." Shit like that. Didn't mean nothing, but something set these guys off and they jumped me. I ran. By the time I got away from them I was seeing red. How *dare* they jump me? In *my* fucking park?

I was furious. I had to retaliate. I knew Smooth and them were across the way, but I was like, "Fuck that." I wanted to fuck these guys up. I said, "I'm goin' to get Spank."

I ran over to Spank and Debra's apartment. I went in and told him what happened. "Yo, these dudes jumped me in the park."

He was like, "*What?* Let's go."

I was a sixteen-year-old kid, playing at all this gangster shit. Spank was a real gangster. Without telling me, on the way out he went in the kitchen and grabbed a chef's knife and tucked it up in his jacket. Walking back to the park he was telling me, "Listen, we gonna go back up there. When we get to the park, you start fightin' with the motherfucker who hit you. You go straight to him and start swingin'."

I said, "A'ight."

I walked out in front of Spank. He was coming up behind me and we walked into the park. I ran right up on the guy who'd jumped me and I clocked him. Spank cruised in right behind me and, like something out of a movie, he ran up on the dude from the side and—*boom*—he stabbed the guy three times in the neck. Three quick jabs. Didn't even hesitate. That guy dropped. Then Spank stabbed the next guy. Then the next guy. Just like that he shanked three dudes, boom, boom, boom. They all went down. Blood everywhere. Everybody in the park was screaming, running.

I didn't know anything like that was going to happen. I freaked out. I started yelling, "Spank! The *fuck*?! C'mon! Let's get out of here!" We turned and ran out the park and down 113th past Smooth's house. The cops came around the corner, lights flashing. Spank saw them turn the corner and he threw the knife under a car. I kept running. The cops caught up fast, grabbed Spank, grabbed the knife—and didn't come after me. Maybe they didn't see that I was involved? I don't know, but my guardian angel was looking out for me that day. I guess Spank was the only one who stabbed anybody, so they took him and that was that.

Spank went to jail. He did like five, six years on that. Meanwhile, I had to get lost. One of the guys Spank stabbed had real street cred, and the block got real hot for me after that. I had to lay low for a minute. I decided to go down and stay with my aunt Bell down on the South Side by Baisley Park—Supreme Team territory.

———

Big Dave was a guy I knew who worked for the Supreme Team. He and Smooth were good friends going way back. Because I was tight with Smooth, Dave and I were cool. We used to go to his house, hang out, play ball. Big Dave worked under Malik, one of Supreme's top lieutenants. The Supreme Team was making insane money. They had the whole South Side on lock. Big Dave knew me and Smooth were good at moving the product, and he was constantly trying to recruit us to go over there and join them. He said Malik would sanction us. We always said no. We liked what we'd built up over on 198 and Murdock. Good crew. Regular customers. No cops. Shit was easy.

The Supreme Team was a totally different thing. At the height of the crack cocaine era, they were the most dangerous, most notorious drug crew in New York City. In the late 1970s and early 1980s, the drug game had changed. Before that there was mostly weed and heroin, some pills and a bit of cocaine. Nearly everything was mob controlled. Most of the black hustlers and gangs were fronting for the Italian mafia. Since nobody messed with the mafia, things stayed relatively peaceful. Then a flood of cocaine started coming in from South America, tons of it, more than ever before. At the same time, the mob was slipping. The feds were cracking down on the big families that ran the city, and they were losing control of their territory. That opened the door for a new generation of younger guys to step up, guys like Fat Cat and Supreme.

Fat Cat was the first guy to put his foot forward. He took over several blocks around 150th and Sutphin Boulevard, had a deli and a game room there that he owned, fronts for his drug operation. He moved tens of thousands of dollars in cocaine and heroin a week.

Supreme wasn't far behind Fat Cat, but he had a better game, built a better organization. Supreme's real name was Kenneth McGriff. He had one of those magnetic, charismatic personalities. He was a natural born leader, the kind of guy people wanted to follow. He got the name

Supreme from being a Five Percenter. The Five Percent Nation was a black nationalist movement dedicated to the salvation of young black men; it's an offshoot of the Nation of Islam. The group's name comes from their belief that 10 percent of the population is the evil elite that controls 85 percent of the people by keeping them poor and uninformed about the truth of existence. The remaining 5 percent are truly enlightened and righteous and dedicated to saving humanity. Five Percenters preached that the black man himself was God, that every black man was a divine being, and that we needed to relearn this because slavery and the white man had tried to steal that knowledge from us.

A lot of guys around the neighborhood were into the Five Percenter thing. They usually got recruited in prison, which is where you find young black men hungry for some kind of direction. They had a book, like their Bible, that they always carried around. There were lessons, and everybody had to know the lessons. I never joined. I already had a strong religious foundation through my mother. I could never come home and tell her I had changed my religion. Would have broken her heart. Plus I didn't want to have to carry that little book around and study it all the time. That seemed like a lot of work.

Supreme was a true believer. Didn't drink, didn't smoke, didn't eat pork. He bought into that mystical shit about blacks as supreme beings. Before he was out of high school he started running with a crew called the Peace Gods, a bunch of Five Percenter ex-cons with grandiose street names like God B, First Born Prince, Lightskin Knowledge. The same way the mafia used blood and family to build loyalty, Supreme used that message of black empowerment and black supremacy to bind everyone together in his crew. Five Percenters got offended if you called them a gang. They liked to believe they were a spiritual movement that sold drugs as a way to finance this crusade they were on. That's how they saw themselves. Others saw them as nothing but a gang who used religion to justify the fact that they were a bunch of criminals.

Supreme started out dealing coke and heroin around the Baisley Park houses, mostly small-time, hand-to-hand. He worked as a guard at stash houses for Ronnie Bumps, helping Fat Cat with this or that. He did whatever he could do to learn how the game worked. The Peace Gods were his muscle, and eventually they started calling themselves the Supreme Team. With weed and heroin and coke, Fat Cat and Supreme and a few other crews carved up southeast Queens and took it for themselves, each of them controlling a different pocket and all of them making good money.

Then along came crack.

The money from crack turned the whole game upside down. Small-time hoods became kingpins overnight. Supreme opened up his crew to Hispanics. There was a guy named Puerto Rican Righteous. Supreme made him a top guy in the organization. Reaching out to Hispanics like that, he was able to get in tight with the Colombians to start buying serious weight. It wasn't long before the Supreme Team was running the South Side. They had the whole neighborhood on lock. Baisley Park, Sutphin Boulevard, Guy R. Brewer, the Baisley projects. In some of those project towers, they occupied whole floors, and with a few of them, the entire building.

Supreme became a street legend, a hood movie star, as Nas would say. Whenever he went out to the clubs, he wore white suits like Tony Montana in *Scarface*. The things we'd hear about him in the neighborhood, it was like folklore. His money. His women. "Yo, I heard one time Supreme did this." Or "Did you hear about the time Supreme did that?" No one would say anything bad about him, wouldn't even whisper it, for fear that word might get back to him.

The Supreme Team took the black empowerment philosophy of the Five Percenters and mixed it with the swagger of hip-hop. In a place where young black dudes felt like they had nothing and were going nowhere, Supreme created a culture that made them feel like they were a part of something important. Working for the Supreme Team compared with a part-time job at McDonald's: it was no question which one they'd choose.

In *New Jack City* Wesley Snipes plays the crack kingpin Nino Brown, head of the Cash Money Brothers. People say that whole movie was based on the Supreme Team. Whether that's true or not, the fact that people believe it tells you something. The rooms of naked women bottling up the crack with their tits out, the crew taking over whole buildings and city blocks? All of that was straight out of the Supreme Team's playbook.

There's one scene in the movie where Nino Brown and his crew give out holiday turkeys to the neighborhood. That was another move from Supreme's playbook, one he took from Nicky Barnes in Harlem. Take care of the people. For the residents in the Baisley houses, Supreme did holiday turkeys, paid utility bills for little old grandmas. He made himself into Robin Hood. Supreme Team had community basketball tournaments. The parties they threw were epic. They'd take over nightclubs, everybody stepping out in fresh new suits with the big gold jewelry, lots of diamonds. Supreme had the hookup with Russell Simmons and all those guys. The big hip-hop artists from Def Jam—the Beastie Boys, LL Cool J, Run-DMC—they would play at these Supreme Team parties that would last all night.

But with that fame came attention. Earlier that summer, in June, Fat Cat had been arrested in a raid on his deli that turned up $180,000 in cash and a ton of cocaine and heroin. That September, Supreme got arrested in a raid. They caught him covered in white powder, trying to pour cocaine down the sink. But while he was locked up awaiting trial, the game didn't skip a beat. Supreme was still calling the shots from prison, and his right-hand man, his nephew Gerald Miller, who went by the street name Prince, was running things.

Prince was the son of one of Supreme's older sisters, but they were only two years apart, so they were more like brothers. 50 Cent rapped about the two of them in his song "Ghetto Qu'ran": "*'Preme was the businessman and Prince was the killer.*" That's exactly how it was. People were in awe of Supreme. They were afraid of Prince. Supreme was the cold, calculating CEO. Prince was the brutal, hotheaded enforcer. With the businessman gone, the killer was running the operation.

Working for the Supreme Team was *intense*. I'd heard about it from Dre. He went for like a week, maybe less than that, and he came right back. He was like, "Yo, I can't fuck with them niggas. Shit's crazy over there." But now I was in this situation where I couldn't go back on the block, couldn't work. My money situation was drying up. I had to do something.

Except for the odd weekend home, Smooth was off at college; I'd lost my partner, the guy I knew would always have my back, and I knew if I was with the Supreme Team, nobody would fuck with me. Plus I'd have the chance to make a whole lot of money. I went to Big Dave and said, "Yo, I'm ready. I moved in with my aunt, so I'm over here now. Let's do it."

8

Welcome to the Supreme Team

My first day on the South Side was like the first day of school. Malik came by my aunt's house and picked me up. He drove a brand-new BMW 325i, black with gold BBS rims. I walked out front and he said, "Yo, Boo, come on. Come with me." I got in, we drove into Manhattan, and he took me to this place called Mason's Tennis Mart to go shopping.

The Supreme Team had a dress code, like a uniform. Everybody wore a full sweat suit, or a nylon tracksuit. They had different colors, but you had to wear Le Tigre shorts over the sweatpants. Nobody would wear that unless they were with the Supreme Team. That was the look. They'd get "'Preme Team" monogrammed on the shirts; it was like they weren't even trying to hide. That day Malik bought me five Fila sweat suits, five pairs of Le Tigre shorts, and a few pairs of new sneakers. He dropped $3,000 on me like it was nothing. I was hyped after that. I was like, Yo, I *like* this. It's all good over here.

After shopping, we drove back out to Jamaica, to the corner of Guy R. Brewer and Foch Boulevard. That was the main intersection at the south end of the Baisley Park projects—the epicenter of the Supreme Team operation. There was a cabstand where the top guys would hang out. If you needed to talk to anyone, see anyone, handle any business, that's where you went. Malik was one of four main lieutenants working under Prince. The other three guys were Born Justice, Everlasting, and Knowledge. I didn't deal with Born Justice or

Everlasting that much. Knowledge was the guy you had to watch out for. He was a dark, African-looking brother. Big dude. He had a lot of flash, wore the latest gear, looked like a real hip-hop hustler. He was a no-nonsense, mean-tempered type guy. You looked at him wrong, he'd punch you in the mouth. He drove an Audi 5000. He put it in the shop and had the entire car painted gold, down to the rims. That was the hottest car in Queens.

Then there was Malik. Malik was a good dude. He was a baller from Farmers Boulevard. Grew up in Hollis. He was a true hustler. He was about getting his money, always had the hottest women. He was a light-skinned, freckle-faced guy, looked like Opie from *Andy Griffith*. He was usually mild-mannered, but he had this tough-guy edge to him; light-skinned guys have to act tougher. Malik was also the crew's big connection to hip-hop. He was friends with Russell Simmons and Run-DMC and LL Cool J from way back. If you watch the video of Run-DMC performing on *Saturday Night Live* in 1986, you'll see Malik in the back. One of the most notorious drug dealers in New York, and there he is dancing on NBC.

After driving back to the Baisley projects, Malik and I hooked up with Big Dave and we went over to 118th and Sutphin, the other side of Baisley Park. Supreme Team had that whole block, dealers on every corner, a couple of stash houses, a couple of crack houses where fiends would go and smoke and fuck and do all kinds of crazy shit.

There was a whole system set up. Every crew had different color caps on their vials, so the bosses could measure the performance of the different crews, see whose packages were selling, who was short with the money. It was that sophisticated. Prince had yellow caps, Knowledge had orange, and so on. Malik's were blue. We pulled up on 118, Malik gave me my package, a couple hundred vials, and I got out there.

That first day I screwed up because I didn't know how the system worked. The street guys out there were working for different lieutenants. I had Malik's work, somebody else had Everlasting's, this other guy, Iron Horse, he had Born Justice's. Crackheads would call out a color to say whose they wanted. You weren't supposed to take any-body's customers. You had to wait until they called your color. I was out there, and this crackhead started coming up the block. I went down to hit her off and within a few seconds I had her money in my hand. I didn't know she was one of Iron Horse's regular customers. He saw me do this and he went off. He was like, "Yo, yo! What the *fuck* you doin'? Who the fuck is this?"

Big Dave was like, "Yo, that's my man Life."

Iron Horse stepped up in my face all tough and was like, "You can't be doing this. You can't come over and sell to customers ain't yours."

I was like, "Yo, man, I ain't here trying to hustle anybody. Nobody told me about no boundaries. I see a crackhead, I'm gonna hit her off. I'm trying to get this money, man."

He cracked a big smile and laughed. He said, "Shorty, I like your style. You just got here and you don't even know anyone, but you about your money."

Word got back to Prince that I was ambitious, ready to work. I wasn't on 118 for long. They moved me a block over to Baisley Park. Baisley Park could have been a park in a nice suburban neighbor-hood, this big open green space with this pretty pond in the middle of it. It had a real baseball diamond. The only reminder that you were in the ghetto was the homeless crackheads passed out on benches or camped out here or there. I worked on the northwest side, near the field house and the basketball courts. Me and a few other guys were stationed there.

Going over to the South Side was a whole new experience for me. Working for the Supreme Team was like going to work for a Fortune 500 company. There was a hierarchy and strict channels of communi-cation. You worked for this guy who reported to that guy who worked for a guy over him. You'd get your package, work the package, turn in the money, and get paid once a week, on Friday. You worked such and such location, and you worked the same eight-hour shift every day, either the eight to four, the four to twelve, or the graveyard, midnight to morning. They were the same shifts the NYPD worked. Sometimes I worked the graveyard, but usually I worked four to twelve, after school. When my shift was over I had to go to Malik's girlfriend's house. She didn't live far and that was where he stayed. I'd go there, drop the money off, head back to my aunt's for a few hours' sleep, get up, and catch the bus to school. Next day, same thing.

It was hard to get a day off. I couldn't even get off for Theresa's sixteenth birthday to take her out. The operation was round-the-clock, nonstop. Middle of the day, crackheads would be lined up down the block, waiting to buy. It was like zombies over there. We were serving them like the drive-thru at McDonald's. There was that much demand. I would come out with a package of maybe two hundred, three hundred vials on a shift. Go back for at least one re-up if it was busy. That's in one day. I was pulling in $3,000 a shift. Easy. Minimum. And that was just me, one kid on one corner. At the height of the crack era, the Supreme Team was making $200,000 a week. Profit, not gross.

And nobody fucked with them. Nobody dared. Back on 198 and Murdock, I used to carry my .25 for protection. Over in Baisley Park, I didn't even bother. They had shooters protecting the block. I'd be out there, two in the morning, with three hundred vials of crack and $3,000 in my pocket from hustling all day, and never a thought of somebody trying to jack me.

The only thing I wasn't protected from was the Supreme Team itself, and that was the ugly truth underneath it all. They had this Five Percenter talk of peace to Allah and being your brother's keeper, but the Supreme Team was infamous for killing and beating people—its own people—at the drop of a dime. That's how they kept everyone in line. They ruled with fear. You cross us, you're gonna die. You're short with the paper, we'll take it out of your ass.

One night I remember I was out in Baisley Park with this cat Biggs. It wasn't long after I started, late fall, November maybe. It was the graveyard shift, around one in the morning, cold out and pouring rain. Biggs was this short, chubby dude. He was Knowledge's lieutenant, and Knowledge was the guy you did not fuck with. I don't know what had happened. Maybe Biggs had fucked up a package or something. Knowledge came out to the park and was like, "Yo, Biggs. Come here." Biggs walked over, not suspecting anything, real casual like, "Yo, boss, 'sup?" and *Bam!* Knowledge punched him in the face. Dude went reeling and fell back and went down hard.

Knowledge went to work on him, beat the shit out of him, pummeled him. In front of all of us. Biggs didn't swing back. You can't swing back. You take a swing at a guy like Knowledge, your ass is dead. You can't even duck. All you can do is take the beating. That's what Biggs did. Dude stayed there on the sidewalk, taking the punches and the kicks. Then, with Biggs lying there on the ground, Knowledge looked up and was like, "Any of you motherfuckers got something to say about it, I'll fuck you up, too."

He pulled Biggs to his feet, got right in his face, and said, "You stand out here, motherfucker. All night long. You stay out here all motherfucking night. If I fucking find out you left this fucking park, I'll fucking kill you."

Knowledge left. Biggs stood there in the rain, shivering, his fat face all deformed and fucked up and bleeding. He stayed like that for hours. Then the sun came up and we went home.

Welcome to the Supreme Team.

9

Safety Transfer

Newtown High was the place where I could escape my life in the streets. I never missed a day of class. It took me over an hour to get there—one bus, two subway lines, plus a fifteen-minute walk. But I never thought about not making the trip. At school I had a whole different set of friends. My man Reggie. My man Troy. My man Omar. Everything was good over there. It was great.

Newtown was a magnet program, so it was mixed, kids from all over—black, white, Puerto Rican—which made it fun and interesting. The students were focused on school, planning to graduate and go to college. I was playing on the varsity basketball team, so that made me popular. Plus I was interesting to the kids over there because I was like an out-of-towner. Run-DMC and LL Cool J were blowing up. Everybody wanted to be like them, to have that style, and I actually came from that world, from the same neighborhood as those guys. I was coming to school fly, had my swag, my brand-new sneakers. To the girls over there I was the cool guy, so I was messing around with a few of them on the side. I was having a ball.

I never brought drugs to school, didn't sell there, never told anyone I was in the streets. I just let people think I wasn't poor, which was nice. I let them think I had these nice clothes because I could afford it. They were never going to come to where I lived, so they'd never know. I never took a gun to school, either. There was no need. Newtown had a group of tough kids, the hardcases and delinquents, same as every school, but there were no real gangs like the Supreme Team, no rival crews beefing over bullshit. Mostly they were a bunch of normal high school kids.

Everything at school was fine until this one weekend. It was the fall of my senior year, the middle of basketball season. I'd been with the Supreme Team a couple months by this time. We had a basketball game at Newtown. Smooth was home from college. I asked him to come, but I told him, "Don't bring nobody else with you to the game." Smooth had gone to Catholic school. I knew he could handle himself at a place like Newtown. My other friends, I loved them but they were from the hood. I didn't want them coming over to school bringing drama.

That night at the game, the coach had benched me for the first half. I was waiting to go in when Smooth walked in with like nine guys. They were yelling, "Yo, Boo!" "My man, Life! Wassup?!" I was like, Shit, here it comes. They got up in the bleachers and started yelling, "Yo, Coach! Put my man in the game! C'mon, Coach! What's goin' on? Put him in!" I looked at the coach and shrugged my shoulders like, "I have no idea what that's about." Eventually the coach put me in. I played for a few minutes, scored a few baskets. We won. Afterward I was in the shower when people came running into the locker room screaming my name. I stepped out and one guy said, "Man, your friends are out front. They started a riot."

I got dressed, ran out, and there was blood on the floor, people crying and beat the fuck up. I found out later that there was this group of kids in the bleachers near Smooth, Mark, Dre, and those guys. While my crew was cheering me on, a girl who was affiliated with this other crew started running her mouth, talking trash about me during the game. "Your boy ain't shit." That kind of thing. After the game was over, it kept going outside. My guys weren't having it. Somebody disrespects you, disrespects anyone in your crew, there's only one option.

They beat up everybody, the guys and the girls. They punched girls in the face, robbed them, stole their jewelry. It was totally out of control. I remember riding home with them. We stopped at White Castle on the way and ordered something like a hundred burgers and ate them on the bus back to St. Albans, everybody laughing and joking, showing me the gold chains they got, talking about how they hit this motherfucker or that motherfucker. I wanted to be pissed at them, but they were my family, my brothers. It was totally messed up what they did, but they did it out of love, to defend me, so I couldn't be mad.

Then the shit came down. I got suspended for two days. I didn't start the fight—I wasn't even *in* the fight—but they suspended me because it was my friends that did it. I can remember sitting at home for those two days thinking, Damn, this ain't good. I knew I was going to have a problem going to school now. It was a long walk to school from the bus stop where I had to get off. Who knew if these guys were going to jump me or what. But I had to go to school. I needed my education.

The first day I went back, I took my gun and put it in my book bag—just in case. I had it with me in my classes, and I was looking over my shoulder. All of a sudden Newtown didn't feel like this safe place for me to have fun and be a regular kid anymore.

After a few days back my coach called me in. He was upset. I told him, "Coach, I didn't have nothing to do with it. What do you want me to do?"

He said, "You brought those guys over here."

I said, "I told one guy to come. I didn't know all those people would be here."

But he wasn't hearing it. He told me I had to bring my mother in and meet with the principal, Mr. Ross. The next day I brought my mom up to the school for the meeting. I'll never forget that day: riding the bus and the train with my mom, with a gun in my pocket.

At the meeting it was the principal, my coach, my guidance counselor, my mom, and me, with a gun in my pocket. The principal told my mom, "We're concerned for his safety because of what happened at the game. So what we're going to suggest is a safety transfer. He can go to any high school he wants to for a safety transfer. You just have to pick the place."

I thought it was bullshit. I think they'd decided that I was a problem student and so they wanted to get rid of me. I sat there and I begged them. I didn't want to go anywhere else. I was having a great season with the basketball team. I was having fun. I liked Newtown. I hadn't done *anything*. But the principal wasn't having it. He was basically saying that his hands were tied because of this fight. The coach and the counselor didn't speak up for me, either.

I was like, All right. It is what it is. I had to pick a school. I thought about it and I said, "Send me to Andrew Jackson." I knew it was the worst choice. I knew it was the dropout factory. I'd fought so hard to stay out of there. But Theresa was there, and Andrew Jackson had one of the best basketball teams in the city, and I figured at least I'd be able to see her and play ball with my friends. I was like, Fuck it, I'll just go there.

So I transferred. What I didn't realize was that when you change schools in New York City, you have to sit out a year for sports. You lose your eligibility. It's so coaches can't recruit and monopolize the good players. So there I was in the dropout factory, and I couldn't even play ball, which was pretty much the only thing that would have made going there worthwhile. I was pissed. I was angry.

In that moment, I stopped caring. It was exhausting living in two worlds, being two different people. I felt like maybe the dropout factory was where I belonged. If that principal was going to treat me like a thug, maybe I'd be a thug. Looking back, it was stupid to think that way, but that's how your mind works when you're sixteen years old.

I started rebelling, cutting classes. There was this one particular day when I skipped to hang on the block with Mark, Dre, and Smooth, who was home on winter break. They were like, "Hey, let's go up to Flushing and rob some coats." That was the kind of stupid shit we were doing. These leather Triple F.A.T. Goose coats were big at the time. We went up to Flushing High. I didn't have my .25 on me, so Dre gave me this .38 revolver he had. Smooth and I waited outside while Dre and the other guys went inside.

A few minutes later they came running out with these coats, and a dude was chasing after them with a knife. Big fucking knife. Guy was right behind Dre, running fast, swinging at him, trying to stab him. Smooth started screaming, "Yo, yo, yo, he's got a knife! Shoot him!" Smooth and I both started shooting. We were popping off shots. Once the guns started going off, it was chaos. People screaming. Students ducking and running everywhere.

I fired one last shot and the dude with the knife dropped to the ground. Mark and Dre caught up to us, and we took off running until we knew we were in the clear. I was sweating, petrified, worried that I'd killed someone. Did I just murder a guy for a fucking coat? How fucking stupid could I be? Everybody from the neighborhood was talking about the shooting, and eventually word got back to us that the guy was only hit in the leg. He was going to be okay. After that, we went back to the block and hung out, laughing about it all afternoon, like I was a hero for saving Dre's life. The next day the shooting was in the newspaper. I got a copy, cut out the article, and saved it like it was a trophy.

If I'd been in school, I wouldn't have been out there that day, thinking it was cool to go and steal some coats. I could have bought five of those coats with the money I had from selling crack, but we were that dumb. To this day I tell Smooth and them that they ruined my life, starting that fight at the basketball game. If I'd never been kicked out of Newtown, my whole life might have been different. Maybe I'd have graduated on time, gotten that basketball scholarship I was hoping for, been able to go off to college. Maybe I would've never seen the horrible shit that I saw, would've never done the horrible shit that I did. But that's not the way it turned out.

10

Prince

A ndrew Jackson was the opposite of Newtown: no magnet students, almost nobody going to college. It was mostly black kids,
a few Hispanics. Not a white kid in sight. It was an older campus,
overheated in the winter, no air-conditioning in the summer. The
one good thing about that school was that it was hip-hop central, all
the kids sporting Kangols and Cazals, Pumas and Pro-Keds, Mighty
Shirt Kings sweatshirts.

I still went to school every now and then, maybe once a week. It
was mainly a social thing. Andrew Jackson was a cool place to be
seen. My friends from the neighborhood went there, and after all
those years getting bused over to Newtown, it was fun to hang with
them more often. I had a couple of students at Andrew Jackson working for me. That was another reason I'd go, to bring packages to those
guys. I'd wander in late, strapped with my .25, wearing the latest
clothes and all this jewelry, hang out in the cafeteria and the hallway for a while, and then skip out, head back to Baisley Park. By the
spring of '86, I was in the streets full-time. Months away from graduating, and I'd all but dropped out of school.

Since Theresa went to Andrew Jackson, I was labeled her man
upon arrival. That kept most of the girls away, and I couldn't play
around like I'd been doing over at Newtown. That's when I started
seeing more of Tina. Tina was a girl I'd met when I was hiding out
after Spank stabbed those guys. Smooth's girlfriend lived in Brook-

lyn, and one night he asked me to go to a party down there. We went. It was crowded, but me and this one girl kept making eye contact. She was tall, brown-skinned, had this incredible smile with these dimples and a great laugh. She had this intensely sexual vibe to her, too. I asked Smooth to introduce us and we hit it off. Pretty much right away we started fucking. We didn't date. We just had sex. I started going down there a few times a week. I'd get off at midnight, take a cab to Brooklyn, sleep at her house, take a cab back the next morning. Theresa didn't have a clue; she thought I was in the streets every night.

Tina lived at Vanderbilt and Atlantic in Clinton Hill, in a nice brownstone. She had her own bathroom, her own bedroom, with the whole bedroom set and everything. Tina's father was an NYPD detective. He was a real cop, a cop's cop, a guy-you-wouldn't-want-to-fuck-with kind of cop. He even played a cop in the movies. Those 1970s flicks about crime and gangs in New York City, like *The Warriors*, he used to work on the side as an extra playing a cop in those movies. That's how much of a cop this guy was.

He didn't like me. Tina was Daddy's Little Girl, and he knew exactly who I was, some hustler banging his princess. She was eighteen years old, and every single morning he'd come in and kiss her on the cheek good-bye, like she was still nine years old or something. It was weird. I'd have to hide under the bed as soon as I heard him knock. He never caught me.

Most mornings, I'd wake up at Tina's or Theresa's, skip school, and head straight down to the cabstand on Foch and Guy R. Brewer. Even if I wasn't on shift until that afternoon or midnight, I'd go down to hang out. That was the spot. That's where everybody was. Malik. Everlasting. Knowledge. Big Dave. All the dealers wearing flashy clothes, parking their BMWs on the block, blasting Eric B. & Rakim from thousand-dollar stereo systems. At the time, it felt like the Supreme Team was invincible. The whole neighborhood was an open-air drug market, going on in broad daylight.

It was like New York City had surrendered control of the neighborhood. The Queens Narcotics Squad was working to build major cases against the kingpins, but that division was overworked and undermanned. They'd lucked into the big busts against Fat Cat and Supreme, but they still hadn't made a dent in the bigger organization. At the street level, they had nothing. I'll never forget the day I was in Baisley Park. It was broad daylight, middle of the afternoon. I had a bag with maybe three hundred vials of crack in it. I'd taken up my usual spot next to the basketball cages, when this blue-and-white drove right up to me on the sidewalk. Cop rolled down his window and said, "What's in the bag?"

Fuck! This is it. I'm dead. I'm going away forever. I handed the bag to the officer. He looked inside, tossed it back to me, and said, "Tell your boss I did him a favor."

They drove off. I didn't know what had happened. I ran to Malik's house and told him, "Yo, you never gonna believe this shit. Some cop busted me with the whole re-up package and then just let me go."

"Nigga, don't you know?" he said. "They gettin' paid off. Now get your ass back out there."

South Jamaica was patrolled by the 103rd Precinct, and Prince and Supreme had bought off the whole neighborhood. Beat cops were getting ten, fifteen grand a month to ignore the activity on the corners, which meant the narcotics squad had a hard time getting the evidence they needed to build a major case. Supreme was at Rikers awaiting trial, and he had corrections officers over there on the take, bringing him whatever he needed and helping him send orders to the outside. The cops who weren't being paid off were monitored by the Team. If plainclothes cops in an unmarked car were following Prince, he would get the license number and have one of our guys start tailing them round-the-clock and listening in on the police radio, seeing who their contacts were, any informants who might be snitching.

Out on the street, Prince was the man. He controlled everything.

He was out to prove that he could run things as well as Supreme. With him in charge, the Team was more aggressive than it had ever been, locking down any territory that wasn't already claimed. Everything was bigger. Prince drove this brand-new BMW E32, the highest of the high-end luxury cars. Guys said it was tricked out with all this James Bond–type shit, bulletproof plates in the doors. He had his own security team. It was four guys suited up in black fatigues, black hats and boots, with bulletproof vests. They had AR-15s, Mac 10s, 9-millimeter Glocks. They'd drive around in a blacked-out van. Nobody fucked with those dudes.

I was in awe of Prince. After a couple months working for the Team, I finally got to meet him out on the block one day. Malik introduced us. Prince wore Pumas, a brand-new pair every day. Sometimes Adidas, but usually Pumas. He'd pull up in the morning in his BMW, toss one of us the keys, and say, "Yo, shorty, go in my car. Get me a pair of sneakers." I'd go, open his trunk, and he'd have like thirty boxes of new sneakers in there. I'd get him a pair, and he'd take off the old ones that he'd worn for a day, throw them in the garbage, and put the new ones on. Dude was making that much money.

One day Prince waved me over and said, "Yo, shorty, come over here. Get in the car. We goin' to the Ave." I got in and he took me up to Jamaica Avenue. We went to V.I.M., this clothing store where all the hustlers went. Prince bought a couple dozen pairs of sneakers and some fly new outfits. Paid for it in cash. We walked back out onto the Ave. While I loaded up his car, he took off his day-old sneakers, put them in the garbage, and put on the new ones, same as always. Prince made that run every couple weeks, and he started taking me with him whenever he went. I started feeling like, Yo, I'm the fuckin' man. I'm making crazy money. I'm rolling with the Supreme Team. I'm rolling with *Prince*. He's bringing me along.

Life was good. I had the flyest clothes, a fat roll of cash. Everywhere I went I had the respect of being with the most notorious crew in Queens. I'd walk into a club or out on the court and I'd hear people whispering, "Yo, that's Life. He's with the 'Preme Team." I had my girlfriend up at school, my thing with Tina on the side down in Brooklyn. I spent my days in Baisley Park or over at the cabstand. We'd shoot dice, talk shit. The basketball courts for the Baisley projects were right there, and we'd have pickup games going. We did whatever we wanted to do, all day long.

I was spending a lot of time with Malik, too. He was taking me under his wing. There was this cat named David McClary. He was a big-time basketball player. I'd played with him in O'Connell Park growing up. David had a brother who was a big-time dealer with Fat Cat. The McClarys had a house on the South Side not far from where I was staying with my aunt. They'd have underground boxing matches there in this dingy, unfinished basement. Malik started taking me with him to the fights. The room would be filled with dealers, flashing big rolls of cash, placing bets. Two boxers would lace up their gloves and go at it. It was crazy. Guys drinking, smoking weed. Everybody yelling at the fighters. "Knock his ass out!" One night I was down there with Malik, and this dude was like, "Yo, put your man in. Let your man fight my man." There was this other kid there, ready to fight. I actually knew him from school. Malik turned to me and said, "I want you to fight this dude." All right. Whatever. I put on the gloves, went out there for a few rounds. I did okay. I held my own.

Malik also used to let me drive his BMW. I'd take it up to Andrew Jackson in the mornings before school to show it off. Only I didn't know how to drive. I didn't even have a license. One time when I was driving to school with my bodyguard in the passenger seat, he started sniffing the air and got this funny look on his face. He said, "Life, the brakes are smoking." He looked down and saw that I was driving with two feet, one on the gas and the other on the brake. I didn't know you were supposed to drive with one foot. But when I'd drive that BMW to school? Everyone would be looking at me in awe, because they knew who owned it.

I was making money hand over fist. I thought maybe I'd move up, be a lieutenant, run my own crew. I was getting more and more responsibility, but with more responsibility came more pressure. I was working the midnight shift in Baisley Park one night when Malik brought this new guy out, this cat from Hollis. Malik said, "Yo, he's going to work with you tonight. Watch him."

I put the guy on. Since we were both from the North Side I was comfortable with him a little, but I didn't know if I could trust him. I only gave him four or five jumbos to sell at a time. He'd go off with his five vials, come back with $50. I'd give him five more, and he'd go off again. It went like that for a couple hours. At one point he came over, I gave him five, and he said, "Yo, I'm going to the store to go get a sandwich."

I said, "All right, but give me the jumbos to hold while you go."

He said, "No, no, no, I'm good."

I let it go. I said, "Okay, hurry up and get back. This shit don't stop."

He was gone for a bit and then he came back. This fiend came up to buy. I turned to the new guy and said, "Yo, my man. Come hit this guy off."

He went over to the fiend, came back to me. "Yo, he needs two. Gimme two."

I said, "What do you mean, give you two? I just gave you five."

He said "I know, man. But I lost 'em."

I was like, "You *lost* 'em? You fuckin' serious? That's some bullshit. Go home. I ain't fuckin' with you. Get the fuck out of here."

I sent him on and stayed out there, pissed, because now the package was $50 short and I didn't want to put my own money in to make up the difference. That was my own stupid mistake.

Normally, after a shift, first thing I'd do was go to Malik and give him the money I'd made. That morning I decided to go straight to school and make the drop later. I went home to my mom's house, got dressed, went to school. Around lunch somebody was like, "Yo, Malik was up here looking for you." Then this other guy was like, "Malik's looking for you." Malik's sister went to Andrew Jackson. I saw her in the hall. She was like, "Yo, my brother was here looking for you." I was like, "All right, I'll reach him." But I kept putting off going because I didn't want to deal with the fucked up money on the package. After school, I got home and my mother said, "This guy came here three times looking for you."

Finally I decided, okay, let me go deal with this shit. I got in a taxi and took it across town to the cabstand at the corner of Foch and Guy R. Brewer. Everybody was on the block. It was prime time. Malik was there. Big Dave was there. Knowledge. DMC was there, too, hanging out, drinking his 40. Anytime you saw DMC he had a 40 on him.

Malik was waiting. I got out of the cab and went over. "Yo, what up?"

He was like, "Yo, where the fuck is the night shift? Where you been?"

I said, "I was at school."

"I went to school looking for you. I couldn't find you. Where's the money at?"

I gave it to him. I was like, "Here. It's a little short."

"Short?"

"Yeah, man. That motherfucker you put on last night, he went to the store for a sandwich, said he lost five jumbos. I'm pretty sure he stole them. So it's short."

"How much is it?"

"Nine-fifty."

He said, "Oh, all right," and he walked off, didn't say nothing. I thought everything was good. Then my man Big Dave came up behind me. He took a swing at me. I ducked and took a swing back, thinking, What the fuck? He kept punching and I kept hitting back. But Big Dave is just that: big. Dude's like six four. I wasn't much of a match for him. He started pounding me. He grabbed me in a headlock, was punching me in my ribs. Then he pulled me in and whispered in my ear, "Yo, I don't want to do this. Lay down and act like I'm whupping you or it'll only get worse."

I was like, "Fuck that." I kept swinging. Everybody was out on the block, watching me. Girls were out there seeing this shit. I wasn't going to lay down and get my ass kicked. So Big Dave landed a few more punches. After five minutes Malik came over and stopped it. I was pissed off and embarrassed. Malik said, "Get in the car. Let's go."

I was like, "Fuck that. I'm outta here."

"Get in the car. Let's go get something to eat."

"No. I don't want nothing to fucking eat."

"Yo, *get in the fucking car.*"

Finally I got in the car. Me and Big Dave got in the back. Malik drove. DMC got in the front with him. I was pissed. As we pulled off, Malik said, "Yo, Dave was barely hittin' you. You ain't even bleedin'. Just make sure the package is right every time. And you lucky I had Dave do that shit, 'cause you know if I'd had Knowledge do it, your ass would have been in the hospital."

It was true. This was him letting me off easy because he liked me. Guys on the South Side were getting killed for less. But I was still pissed. I slumped down in the back, angry. DMC thought the whole thing was hilarious. He sat in front of me, laughing. I wanted to punch him in the back of his fucking head.

11

Cracked Out

Getting my ass kicked by Big Dave was embarrassing. I never fucked up a package again. I hustled and stayed on point to become one of Malik's best earners. Now that I was in deep with the Supreme Team, I wasn't hanging with my crew on the North Side as often, but every now and then I'd stop by the neighborhood to show off my new gear, flash a wad of cash, show everybody how fly I was.

Back on 198, Smooth was still doing his thing on his breaks and weekends home from college. Mark and Dre had dropped out of school and were dealing full-time. Smiley'd been picked up for selling to that undercover; he was doing a few years on that. A couple of new faces were out there, too. One was this dude Fly. I knew Fly from growing up. He was the coolest brother on the block, hands down. He was selling for this dude, DJ, one of those older guys like Cash and Mack who had a connect. DJ's was down in Brownsville in Brooklyn. He kept a stash house down there.

Guys were making a lot of money on that corner. I kept telling Malik that the Supreme Team should expand, start selling on the North Side, get some of that paper. He'd always say he'd think about it. Then one day, he and Prince took me aside and said, "Yo, let's do it. We want you to go over there and set up shop for us."

I wanted Smooth to help me out. I'd been gone for a minute, and he knew what was happening over there. I said, "Can I bring Smooth in, too?"

Malik said, "Yeah, bring Smooth along. That's cool."

I went to Smooth's house and told him. He was hyped. Right off the bat we were bringing in crazy money. Prince and Malik were happy, but those other guys, they weren't thrilled about us bringing in crack from across town. Things had changed since I'd left. When we started we were a bunch of kids, hanging out, having a party, selling drugs. Now guys' egos started to come out. There was beefing, arguments, fights.

Dudes were getting high now. Cash had a full-blown coke habit, was walking around all jacked up. Mark and Dre were getting fucked up on the regular, smoking woolies, those crack-laced joints. They were jumpy, anxious. Mark especially. Mark and Dre were close, the same way me and Smooth were. But Mark had started smoking, and he was cracked out of his mind. One day Mark and Dre got into an argument over Mark's girlfriend. She was one of those girls that everybody in the neighborhood had had a turn with. Dre had messed with her before Mark, but now Mark was in love with her and he wouldn't hear anything bad about her. Dre said something, they started arguing, and the shit escalated. They were up in each other's faces like they were getting ready to fight. All of a sudden Dre punched Mark in the face, so Mark pulled his gun out of his waistband and shot Dre in the ass. Dre fell down screaming. Everybody was laughing, like it was the funniest thing ever. We got Dre up, put him in a cab, and took him to the hospital. He came through okay.

The neighborhood had been changing for a while, but now the difference was stark. Before crack, there were kids in the park. People in the front yards. Barbecues in the summer. Crack hit, and it just went. Now we'd hear gunshots four or five nights a week. We started seeing flashy cars, guys wearing big medallions and rope chains. But we didn't see everyday people as much. Families stayed indoors, kept their kids at home.

The thing about crack that was different from other hard drugs was people could do it outside. Heroin, freebasing, there's all kinds of gear needed to cook it up. With crack, people could buy it, go around to the alley, and smoke up. Or smoke it right out in the park. Crackheads were everywhere, like pests. Sleeping on the benches, pissing in the playground. If they weren't buying, you wanted to shoo them off, like, "*Go*. Get the fuck out of here."

Fiends were getting brazen, too. In the early days crackheads were desperate, but they knew if they got caught stealing or ripping off a package, they were dead. Fear kept them in line. Now they were so cracked out we couldn't scare them anymore. One day I was out on the block, this fiend rolled up in a car and said he wanted five. I gave him five. The guy sped off, didn't pay, in broad daylight. This fiend was so cracked out he actually came back to me trying to score again. It was maybe two weeks later. I was hanging out with Dre in O'Connell Park, drinking 40s with the guys from the block. This dude pulled up in his car and waved at us to get our attention. Dre was like, "Yo, that's that motherfucker that robbed you!" I got up, walked over. Guy said, "Hey, gimme three." I didn't say anything. I reached in the driver's side window, grabbed the guy's head, took the 40 and smashed it across his face. I opened the door, snatched him out of the car, dragged him onto the sidewalk, and beat his ass, tore him up. Guy was screaming and crying and begging for help.

Shit was getting crazy, violent. Crime was exploding all over New York. Burglaries, robberies, muggings. Fiends were breaking into cars for the stereos, breaking into neighbors' cribs for televisions and VCRs, stealing their mom's jewelry, their kids' record player, anything they could trade for crack. I was like Fred Sanford from *Sanford and Son*. I had everything, shit I didn't even know what to do with. One afternoon I was hanging out on the stoop in front of my apartment on Farmers with this guy from the hood, my man Jimmy. This fiend I knew came over. He was somebody I'd sold to before, this little guy with slicked-back hair and one tooth missing in the front. He saw me, came over, and said he had a thirty-two-inch color TV he wanted to sell me. I asked him how much he wanted for it. He said he'd take five jumbos. I said, "All right. Bring it over." So he went and got the TV and brought it back. He took it upstairs, set it up for me, the whole nine.

Later that day, I was still hanging out with Jimmy, upstairs, watching my new TV. There was a knock on the door. I looked out, and this old lady was standing downstairs. She asked if I could come down. I went down, opened the door, and asked her what she wanted. She said, "My son sold you my TV."

Fuck. Here I was thinking this fiend did a burglary to get this TV. And he had. He took his momma's TV. I said, "Ma'am, I don't have your television." She begged me, even offered to buy it back from me. I wouldn't budge. I couldn't be soft. I said, "Lady, I don't know what you're talking about. Please leave."

She left. Not ten minutes later her son came back around, begging to get his momma's TV back. I was pissed. I was angry that this motherfucker put me in a position where I had to be an asshole to this nice old lady, somebody who probably knew my mother from church. This fiend was begging and pleading, and I didn't want to hear it. I punched him in the face. He went down, and I kept at him. Jimmy joined in and we beat his ass. We fucked him up bad, like kicking a stray dog. We beat him unconscious and left him lying on the sidewalk in front of my house. Eventually an ambulance came and picked him up.

The next day I was at home with Theresa. Some friends stopped by and one of them said, "Yo, what happened to Jimmy?"

"What you talkin' about?"

"Police just came and picked him up."

They didn't know what it was for, but I did. "Shit," I said. "We gotta go down to the precinct."

I got dressed, went down to the one-thirteen on Baisley Boulevard, and went in to check on my man. Place was dirty. Cop precincts weren't nice in those days. When I walked in, Jimmy was standing there in cuffs, right by the desk. Cops were questioning him, and a few feet away was the crackhead we'd beat up. The guy spotted me and said, "Yo, that's him! That's the other one right there." Cops came over, put me in handcuffs, and locked up me and Jimmy on the spot. They charged us with assault in the third degree.

They sent us to central booking. My mother's boyfriend at the time was a corrections officer. He came down to visit me. I gave him my money and jewelry. Jimmy and I spent the night in jail, waiting for a bail hearing with the judge the next morning. Jimmy beat the shit out of this dude in the holding cell so I could sleep on the bench that night. When we saw the judge the next day, she let me go on my own recognizance because it was my first offense. But Jimmy had a rap sheet. She remanded him and he had to make bail. I told him not to worry. I would take care of it, the bail plus his lawyer's fees.

What kind of crackhead actually goes to the cops? I was pissed off, but I wasn't worried. It's not like you have to put a lot of pressure on a crackhead to force him to do something. First thing I did was hire a few goons from the neighborhood to snatch the guy up and put the fear of God in him. "If you testify, we're going to kill you." After that he became an uncooperative witness.

The court assigned me a Legal Aid attorney, this young white guy. I think this might have been his second or third case ever. My first hearing, I had to go to the Queens Criminal Court over on Queens Boulevard. The crackhead didn't show up to testify, but the prosecutor wouldn't drop the case. I wouldn't take a plea, either. So the District Attorney's Office kept filing extensions while they tried to get this guy to come back in and take the stand. The whole thing wound up dragging on for months.

What me and Jimmy did to that crackhead was brutal, but at the time I didn't give a shit. Crackheads weren't people; at least that's what we tried to tell ourselves. In some ways, working on the South Side was easier. Over there I didn't know anybody, didn't care what happened to them. But St. Albans was my neighborhood. I knew most of the people getting cracked out. I grew up with them: There was Tyrone and JJ Bill and his brother Mike. This older dude Willis who did everybody's taxes. These were people from good families with good jobs. They tried not to come down to the corner when we were there. They were embarrassed. They'd stay away for a while, but they'd always be back. They couldn't help themselves.

Soon it wasn't just friends. It was family. I had an uncle and a cousin. They were both cracked out. You couldn't leave them in the house. It was, "You can't stay here. You gotta go. When I go, you go." If they stayed, shit would come up missing.

And the women? Those fine, beautiful girls who were all over us, Yvette and Shan and Niki? Those incredible bodies had shriveled up to skin and bone. A year ago, guys were getting off on the novelty of it, having women throw themselves at us, willing to do anything. Now it had gotten to the point where it made us sick. They stank. They didn't bathe. But they were still coming up to us, five, six times a day, begging us to fuck them, let them suck us off. It was guys, too. They would come up, "Yo, I'll let you fuck me in the ass."

These people were dying in front of us. They were poisoning themselves, and we were selling them the poison. I think that's why Mark and Dre started smoking woolies, so they wouldn't have to think about what they were doing. The people we sold to, we called them fiends, zombies, 'zoids, crackheads. Any name we could use not to think of them as people. It helped us avoid the reality of what we were doing, but sometimes reality got right up in our face and we couldn't look away.

I was out on the block one day when this fiend came up to me. She was dirty. Her hair disheveled, lips ashy, and she was scratching herself. She said, "Corey." Nobody on the block called me Corey. Everybody called me Life. She said, "Corey, it's me. It's Michelle."

I said, "*Michelle?*"

Little Michelle? From third grade? I didn't recognize her. Seventeen years old, and she looked like a ghost. I couldn't believe it. I was friends with her family. I'd always had that little crush on her. I used to ask her mom all the time, "How's Michelle? How she doin'? She good?" Then she comes up to me and she's a fucking zombie. Seeing her like that? It was sad. That shit hurt. I can't lie. But this business, it was cold-blooded. I said, "What you need?"

She said, "I need two."

I sold her two.

12

Dog Years

One night that spring, I was on the block with Smooth. Most nights we wouldn't be out there doing hand-to-hand anymore. We had our guys working while we were inside the candy store, chilling. I remember I was wearing my beige bubble coat with the beige scramble hat, and Smooth was wearing a blue bubble coat with the blue scramble. It was a typical Friday night. Store was packed, everybody hanging out. This guy came in. "Yo, somebody in a car out here asking for Life and Smooth."

Everybody pointed to us. We got up, went out to see who it was. This beat-up, piece-of-shit Cutlass was parked around the side on 198 with the windows down. Smooth recognized the guy in the front passenger seat, this Jamaican gangster, Dinero. Smooth knew who he was from Cash. Another guy sat behind him in the back. We walked over. Smooth said, "Yo, you lookin' for Life and Smooth? Life and Smooth right here."

Dinero was a tall dude, low haircut. Looked hard and mean as fuck. Had this real bad stutter, too. He said, "Y-y-yo, l-l-lemme holler at you, son."

We walked around to the other side, and as we were coming around, the guy in the backseat shoved the barrel of an Uzi in Smooth's stomach. We froze. Dinero said, "Who's b-b-block is this?"

Smooth said, "Ain't nobody's block."

"Where d-do y-y-y'all get y'all w-work from?"

"I ain't tellin' you where we get work from. But this ain't nobody's block. Everybody gettin' money out of here. We all doin' our thing. Y'all wanna get money, y'all come out and get money."

"Y-y-yo, from now on, you all g-g-gonna get y'all work from us. We g-gonna come see you. Y-y-you don't get my work, y'all ain't working, and y-y-you all got to get the f-f-f-uck off this block."

We said okay and we backed off. Had no choice, since he got the drop on us. Dinero pulled away and I said to Smooth, "Yo, let's go." We got in a cab and headed down to Baisley Park to look for Malik. Got there, found him. He said to call Prince. We called Prince. He came down. I told Smooth to hang back while I went up to tell them what had happened. I said, "Yo, this motherfucker Dinero pulled a fucking Uzi on us, told us we had to get our work from him or get off the block."

Prince took it in, thought it over. He said, "Yo, get your man." I called Smooth over and Prince huddled up with us. Whenever Prince talked, he would hunch his shoulders and rub his hands together slowly in front of his face, like he was cold. It could be the middle of summer, and he'd talk like that. He said, "Go back over there, get that money. Don't worry. Y'all gonna see some people. Don't be scared. That's gonna be my guys. You don't gotta worry about nothing."

We caught a cab back to 198 and Murdock. The block was empty. Everybody had vanished after Dinero came through flashing that Uzi. I'd brought my piece with me. Smooth had his, too. But we didn't need them. Across the street from the corner, lying down in the bushes, were four shooters. Prince's security team. They had 9-millimeters, Mac-10s, bulletproof vests, the whole nine. Three houses down from where my aunt and grandmother lived, these guys were lying in the bushes like armed assassins, waiting. Smooth wasn't used to how Prince did things. He couldn't believe it. I said, "Yo, I *told* you the Supreme's shit was real."

We stayed out there and played the block, wondering every second if there was going to be a drive-by. It was a long night.

Dinero didn't come back. I didn't see him again until a few weeks later. I was in the Baisley projects shooting hoops on the court by the cabstand when Dinero walked in. Middle of the afternoon and he just walked in. I was like, Oh, shit.

Dinero said, "Where's P-P-Prince?"

I said, "I'll get him."

I ran to Prince's house a few blocks away. I got over there, told him, "Yo, remember that motherfucker that pulled an Uzi out on me? He's in the park looking for you right now."

Prince said, "Dinero?"

"Yeah."

"All right. Here, put this in your pocket."

He handed me two stacks of cash, at least fifty grand, wrapped up with rubber bands. I put it in my pocket, and we headed back to the cabstand. I was confused so I asked Prince, "What the fuck is going on? We're giving money to the motherfucker that pulled the Uzi out on me?"

Prince said, "Look, shut the fuck up. I told you not to worry about it. So don't worry about it."

We found Dinero, I gave him the two stacks of money, and he left. Two weeks later, I was playing basketball in Baisley Park with some of the crew and one of the guys said to me, "Yo, you hear about Dinero?"

"What about him?"

"He dead."

They'd found the body that morning. I saw Prince later that day. He said, "See, shorty? Didn't I tell you not to worry about that shit?"

———

That whole year, Smooth had been halfway in the game, one foot in, one foot out. He was away at school during the week, home on weekends and breaks to see his kid. Whenever he was home, he'd pick up a package, make a little paper. Even with this chance at college, giving up the hustle was hard. He'd come home, and all his boys were out on the block. He'd want to see us, hang with us. Smooth had started dealing because he wanted to be cool, be fly, be a hustler. That became his rep. He was famous in the neighborhood. He was Smooth from the block. But at college he didn't need that. Over there he was popular just being Mike Russell. Playing sports, going to fraternity parties, whatever. That shit with Dinero rattled him. After that, Smooth came to me and he said, "Yo, I'm out. Can't be doin' this no more." End of that summer, he went back to school and he wasn't around as much. When he was home, he stayed off the block.

Out on the corner, we bragged about how fly we were, flashing our cash and our jewelry. But we knew that dealing crack was a shit alternative to doing something real with our lives. The guys who made it out, who went to college, went on to get a real job, we didn't think of them as being soft. We were excited for them. Once he was out, Smooth would call the pay phone on the block, knowing one of us would be there to pick up. He'd tell us stories about the homecoming games, the girls, the parties. We loved hearing that shit. We'd huddle around the phone to tell him how proud we were that he'd made it. Then we went right back to flashing our cash and our jewelry and talking about how fly we were. But we would have traded places with Smooth, no question.

The go-to-college-and-get-a-good-job route was becoming less and less of an option for me. Even if I finished my senior year, my grades weren't good enough to get an academic scholarship, I wasn't going to get an athletic scholarship after being forced to sit out a year, and my mother had no other way of paying for school. I couldn't see any path but the one I was on. Then one night I went down to see Tina in Brooklyn. She took me in her bedroom and told me she had to tell me something. We sat down on her bed and she said, "I'm pregnant."

Fuck. I was floored. I was like, "Shit shit shit. This is definitely not good." At that moment, all I could think about was how I was going to tell Theresa and how she was going to take it. Tina and I talked for a while longer. I told her to let me know if she was going to keep it, but I already knew she was.

The baby was due in December. I held the news close to my hip for several months. I knew I'd eventually have to tell Theresa, and one afternoon I went to her house and broke it to her. I told her, "Look, I was messing with this girl and she got pregnant, but I still want to be with you. I love you. I want us to live together." She was pissed. She started crying, cursing, hitting me. But eventually we worked through it and she agreed to stay with me.

Then I told my mom. That was rough. I never forgot the day I told my mother I'd never disappoint her again, and for years disappointing her was all I'd done. Dropping out of school, selling drugs. This was the next letdown. I don't think she was even surprised by it. She was like, "I can't believe you, boy. How could you do this?"

Then Theresa got pregnant.

Fuck. Shit shit shit. I couldn't believe it. What was I thinking? What had I done? Why didn't I use condoms? And Theresa's mother was very religious, so she definitely wasn't going to the table. That wasn't an option. I was fucked. Everything was fucked. I was seventeen years old, not even out of high school, a drug dealer who never had a real job, who got two girls pregnant at the same time. Smooth was gone, I was on my own, and the streets were blowing up.

The shit with Dinero was just a taste of what was coming. The violence was escalating. Bodies were dropping. People were disappearing. Guys were getting killed over $100, over $50, over petty insults and bullshit. My friends, the guys I was running with, I'd come out to work and one day they wouldn't be there. It was like here today, gone tomorrow. My man PeeWee got murdered. My man Rahim got murdered. My man Sha-Tiek, he got murdered in Newark. Sometimes we'd find the body. Sometimes the guy just vanished. We didn't know if they died in a robbery, if Prince took them out. We didn't know anything. I'd show up to my shift and say, "Yo, what happened to Rahim?" The other guys would shrug. Don't ask no questions. Keep on moving.

Covering my left shoe to hide the holes for my fifth-grade class photo (bottom row, third from right).

Wearing my sister's too-small jeans in O'Connell Park the summer before I started dealing.

My bodyguard.

Me and Smooth not long after
we started selling weed.

Posing with Smooth outside the candy store.

198 and Murdock. The shirt I'm wearing says "Crack is wack."

The Murdock Ave. crew chilling in O'Connell Park.

I was fashionable, wearing the latest Sergio Tacchini.

"The red and black lumberjack with the hat to match"; I wore it before Biggie rapped about it.

Showing off the .25-caliber pistol I'd just bought from a crackhead.

The Supreme Team uniform.

On the bus with the crew after the brawl at Newtown High School.

Supreme Team soldiers.

Flexing with our fresh gold chains.

With Daryl "DMC" McDaniels at Club Encore.

Theresa and me on our wedding day.

My firstborn child, Corey Jr.

My daughter Tash.

Me and Ma at my high school graduation.

My mother, Eva Jewel Caple.

I was in awe of Prince. I thought he was the man. I couldn't see what he was: a major killer, a psychopath. Violence was his first answer for everything. And where a guy like Knowledge would stomp your head on the pavement, Prince would put a bullet between your eyes. I was always looking over my shoulder, but I still didn't walk away. I couldn't. When you're in that life, you're in it. It's like the worse it gets, the deeper in you go, because you reach a point where you can't see any way out.

There were plenty of nights I wouldn't go home. It was easier to not deal with my mother's disapproving looks. I didn't want to deal with questions from Tina or Theresa, either. Sometimes I'd sleep at the stash houses, on busted old couches in rooms piled with guns, money, and big, clear plastic bags filled with crack vials. I'd sleep with one eye open, tossing and turning and thinking: If the cops come through that door, I'm going to jail forever.

The Supreme Team had crack houses, three or four of them around the north side of the park on 118 and Sutphin, lookouts posted out front, dealers working out of the front room, an armed security guard posted up front to let people in and out. I'd end up crashing at those places, too. They were fucking filthy. Dirty as hell. Gloomy. They reeked of urine and musty old carpets. There was no furniture, just dirty, smelly mattresses spread out on the floor. That's where I'd sleep. No sheet, no blanket, nothing.

The thing that's unnatural about a crack house is the constant movement. People coming, people going. People knocking on the door all night. People fucking in the corner. Guys getting their dicks sucked. Fights breaking out. Some woman getting the shit beat out of her. People passed out over damn near every inch of the floor, passed out on the stairs. You have to kick them to get them to move out of the way. And the whole time that money's comin' in. Guys are gettin' that money, gettin' that money, gettin' that money.

I was killing myself. I could feel myself getting tired, worn out, anxious, paranoid. It's dog years in the streets. Every year is seven years. I'm not talking about guys who come out and deal once in a while. I'm talking about hugging the block the way I was. Being out there twenty-four, forty-eight, seventy-two hours, not changing clothes. If you're in the streets like that, as a teenager, to make it to age twenty-five, that's like being ninety. Nobody makes it that far. You stay out there any length of time, you're going to be dead or in jail. It's inevitable.

There was this guy I worked with in Baisley Park, my man Pac. Pac was real ambitious, hungry for the spotlight. One morning Malik called the two of us over to his girlfriend's house, where we brought the cash from the overnight shift. The safe where Malik kept the money was right next to his bed. As he was putting the cash in the safe, he said, "Yo, it's time for you guys to step up. I'm going to give you the combination to this so you can make the drops yourself."

When Malik offered us the combination, my first thought was, Fuck that. If something goes missing, that shit is going to be my problem, and I don't want no part of it.

That was the moment I took my first step back. I begged off, said I wasn't ready for it. Pac was down. He was eager. He was like, "Yo, I'll take it." After that Malik elevated Pac above me. I wasn't making a conscious move to get out, but I knew that I didn't want to get in deeper with these people than I already had.

I started going to school again. I couldn't change what had happened up to that point, but I knew I could still give my mother the one thing she wanted, to see one of her kids graduate high school. I also knew that, whatever happened with Tina and Theresa and the babies, I wouldn't have any options if I didn't get a diploma. So I decided to get back in school for real. All I needed was a semester's worth of credits, and I knew I could do that with no problem. So I went back to Andrew Jackson, sat my ass in the front row of the classroom, and started trying again.

When Tina was around eight months, I told Malik and Big Dave that I needed to step away from the Supreme Team. I said that I had a baby on the way and needed to go back to freelancing on the North Side, have more flexibility, do my own thing. I went back to 198 and started working packages for the Colombians again. Shit'll be simpler over there, I thought.

I was wrong.

13

I Decided I Would Kill Him Myself

I was on the block late in the afternoon with Dre when I got the beep from Tina. I called her back. She was in labor and headed to Brookdale Hospital in Brooklyn. I told her I'd be there right away. Dre and I jumped in a cab and headed over. When we got there, Tina was set up in a room where they were monitoring her contractions. We waited. She was in labor for a long time.

Dre left after eight hours or so. I stayed by Tina's side all night, holding her hand. She kept begging for ice chips. At one point I fell asleep in the chair next to her bed and woke up to her screaming. The baby was coming. I ran to get the nurses and the doctor. They gave me scrubs, told me to put them on. Tina was screaming at the top of her lungs every time they asked her to push. I grabbed her hand and held it. I thought she was going to break my fingers, she was squeezing them so damn hard. But everything went fine, and that morning, December 12, 1986, she gave birth to our son, Corey Jr. I called him Lil' Life.

For the past nine months, Tina getting pregnant had given me nothing but anxiety and worry. I'd been pissed that she kept the baby. I knew we were too young to be doing this, not to mention Theresa being pregnant at the same time. But the second I saw the baby I was so happy. I was the proud poppa of a new baby boy. I held him in my arms. He was so small. I stayed with Tina and the baby the rest of the day, then left to go home that night. From the hospital I took the bus back to Queens, right to the bus stop at 198 and Murdock.

I stepped off the bus and saw my man Nashaun walking toward me. Nashaun was a couple years older than me, a real street legend in the neighborhood. Short guy, but rough-looking, with a big fucking head. He was a Five Percenter, just back from prison, where he'd done a few years for being involved with a robbery where a female cop got shot in the chest. Our families were tight going way back. We used to play Little League together. We'd never had any beef. When I saw him, I thought he'd heard about the baby and was coming to say congratulations. But he pulled a pistol out and cracked me in the head. I crumpled and fell to the ground. He stood over me and said "Yo, get the *fuck* off the block! You can't work here no more!"

I scrambled, got up, and ran. I didn't have a choice. I'd come from the hospital, didn't have my gun, was totally caught off guard. I ran home and holed up there, pissed off and confused. Over the next two days, my friends were coming by. "Yo, how you want to do this? Let's handle it."

I had to respond. On the block, everything is about street cred. Nashaun was fresh out of prison; his street cred was solid. If I didn't get him back, I was done. I could have paid someone to take him out, but that wouldn't have had the dramatic effect I wanted. I had to let people know I couldn't be fucked with. I decided I would kill him myself.

I planned the whole thing out so I could get the maximum impact. I figured I'd go down around five in the evening when everyone was out of school and there would be people hanging out. I didn't go down there thinking I was going to get away with it. The whole point was to be noticed. Before I did it I even told myself, "Yeah, I'm gonna do five or six years on this. Whatever. It is what it is." That's the mentality in the street. When you're living that life, you don't care. Even with my newborn son sleeping in the hospital a few miles away, even knowing it would destroy my mother, I decided to murder somebody because he'd swung a pistol at me.

Two days later I went down to the block. I had my .25, tucked in the pocket of my red corduroy jacket. I hadn't been out for a couple of days, so everyone was waiting to see what I was going to do. I walked down, my hands in my pockets, everybody watching me. Sure enough, as soon as I got out there Nashaun ran up on me, got right in my face. "Yo, didn't I tell you to get the fuck out of here?"

I pulled the gun out. It all happened fast. Two, three seconds. I was totally calm the whole time I was doing it, too. No hesitation. I pulled the gun out, stuck it in his chest, and pulled the trigger twice. *Click, click.* Nothing. Gun didn't work. I froze. As soon as Nashaun saw that my gun didn't go off, he reached for his. *Oh shit.* I turned and I ran. Nashaun started popping off shots behind me. I could hear them whizzing by.

As fate would have it, at that exact moment my man DJ was coming around the corner in his car. He saw what was going down. He jumped out of his car with his pistol and started shooting at Nashaun. So now Nashaun turned and ran and we started chasing him back the other way. Nashaun ran up 198 halfway down the block, into Smiley's house. Me and DJ ran up to the front yard and we stood out there yelling, "Get that motherfucker out this house! Get him out here!" Finally Smiley's momma came to the door. She knew me. She opened the door and said, "Boo, please don't do this. Please don't do this at my house." Those old ladies from the neighborhood, they were still the only ones who could get to me. DJ and I walked away. That was the end of it. Nashaun never bothered me again after that.

The fact that my gun didn't fire that day was the luckiest thing that's ever happened to me in my life. If it had gone the other way, if those shots had fired, I'd still be locked up today, a convicted murderer. What happened was that I didn't know how to fire a gun. There was no bullet in the chamber. The only gun I'd ever fired was Dre's .38 revolver. With a revolver, you just pull the trigger. My .25 had a clip. After that shit went down with Nashaun, one of the guys from the block was like, "Yo, what happened?" I gave him the gun and he racked the slide and said, "Yo, dumb ass. You gotta drop one in the chamber. Don't you know that?"

I didn't. All I knew about guns was you had a gun, you walked around flashing it, and if somebody bothered you, you pulled the trigger and shot them. It was the same with so many of us. We were out there, carrying guns, flashing big rolls of cash—and we didn't know what the fuck we were doing. Nashaun had fired a half dozen shots at me from ten feet away and didn't hit me once. We weren't trained killers. We were a bunch of clowns.

Before crack, getting a reliable connect for cocaine or heroin wasn't easy, which limited the number of serious players. Only career criminals, the mafia, or guys connected to the mafia had access to real weight. Now that the Colombians were flooding New York and Queens with cheap cocaine, anybody could get in the drug game. You could set up a full-scale drug lab in your girlfriend's kitchen. There were more crews, more guns, more beefing over turf.

We'd hear guns popping off in the middle of the day and it wouldn't shock us anymore. We'd hear the shots, wait a few minutes, then head in that direction to see what had happened. One afternoon, we were out hustling and heard five shots, real quick, coming from up Murdock. We ran to 201st Street, where we saw this kid, maybe seventeen, eighteen, slumped over in his car with bullet holes in his head and chest. He had a bunch of jewelry on, so it wasn't a robbery. It was an execution.

Outside of the Supreme Team and a few other organized gangs, the crack game was nothing but petty crooks acting like kingpins. Guys like Dinero and Nashaun, who probably couldn't get a job at McDonald's, were going around with Uzis and running their mouths like they were the biggest shit since Nicky Barnes. My man DJ, he was a wannabe kingpin, too. He was around five eight. He never smiled, was always in business mode. He'd been after me to work for him for a while. After he bailed me out of that situation with Nashaun, he asked me to start getting work from him instead of the Colombians. I felt like I owed him, and I was tired of going uptown, so I said yes. I started getting packages from him on consignment. DJ would deliver the work to me on the block, or sometimes I'd ride with him in his old Cadillac Seville to his stash house in Brownsville to get the re-up.

At that point, DJ's two main guys on the corner were me and Fly. Fly worked as much as I did. He was out there hugging the block day and night. We never went more than a day or two without seeing each other. Then all of a sudden he went missing. He was gone for like a week. Everybody was asking for him. "Yo, where's Fly? Where's Fly?" His brother was coming around, "Yo, you seen Fly?" Even DJ was saying he didn't know where he was, and Fly was one of his top earners.

Then one day DJ was like, "Yo, take a ride to Brooklyn with me." We got in his car and headed down. While we were driving, DJ started going off, saying, "Yo, I hate it when motherfuckers cross me. Anybody crosses me, takes something from me, I'll kill the motherfucker." I sat there and listened. I'd never crossed him, so I wondered why was he telling this to me.

We pulled up to the stash house, this shitty, dilapidated building that had probably been condemned. We went in, headed down to this dark basement. We came to a door, DJ went to get his keys, and from the other side I could hear a guy screaming, crying in pain. DJ opened the door. It was Fly. His hands were tied to a pipe in the ceiling. He was hanging there, and two guys were beating the shit out of him, torturing him. His face was bloody, swollen. Blood dripping on the floor, his clothes soaked in it.

I could feel DJ staring at me, trying to gauge my reaction. Fly looked up. He saw me and gave me this look: "Help me."

I was like, *Damn.* I didn't do anything, didn't say anything. I turned and walked out of the room. That was my man in there. Fly was a good friend, but whatever this was about, I wasn't getting involved. DJ followed me out. He said, "Yo, that motherfucker started smokin' that shit. He was fuckin' my package up. But don't worry. I ain't gonna kill him. I'm just teaching him a lesson."

DJ was trying to make sure I learned that lesson, too. We handled our business and left. A couple days later, Fly came back on the block. He was all fucked up, but he was out there and he was working. He didn't talk to me much after that. I don't think he liked me anymore. But what was I going to do? It's the code of the street: You fuck up, you pay for it.

I'd bailed on the Supreme Team, thinking shit would be better over here. It wasn't. It was worse. The money was coming too fast, and guys were losing their minds. I didn't want to deal with DJ's bullshit. I didn't want to wait for the next Nashaun to come around the corner. So I did the only thing I could think to do—I went back to the Supreme Team. It was the only move that made sense. I had to work. I had hospital bills to pay: Tina's delivery, Theresa's doctor's visits. Over in Baisley Park the money was good. The cops were paid off. Nashaun would never have come at me like he did if I'd still been running with Malik and Prince. It felt like the safer place to be while I figured things out. I went and talked to Malik and got my old job back.

For years I'd been fooling myself, thinking I was smarter than the other clowns on the block, that I was about my money and none of the bullshit. But I'd put a gun to Nashaun's chest and pulled the trigger, and over what? Because he hurt my rep? I couldn't pretend anymore. I had to look myself in the face and admit that what I was doing was wrong. I hadn't killed anyone, but I'd put a lot of poison in people's veins. Out of the thousands of vials I sold, was one of them somebody's last hit? I didn't know. I'll never know, but the guilt was keeping me up at night. I wasn't sleeping. My conscience was catching up to me. My mind was constantly racing: "I can't do this no more. I can't take this no more. I gotta get out of here."

I had to make a decision: Do I want to be a street legend, or do I want to be a hero to my children? I started thinking about my own father, how he wasn't there for us, how he never told us he loved us. I carried that pain with me for years. I didn't want that for my kids. I wanted to be someone they could look up to and be proud of. I never wanted them to have to come and visit me in jail, or see me in a casket before my time. I didn't know how I'd make that happen. I didn't have any idea how to get out.

Then I met this cop.

There was a police officer assigned to Andrew Jackson High School. He'd patrol the campus during the day. He was an older guy with an Afro, in his forties maybe. He had some time on the job, twenty years maybe. Andrew Jackson was probably an easy post for him to hang out and wait for retirement. He was friendly, would always say good morning, how's it going? The students liked him. He always had girls around him, too. Drug dealers got plenty of girls, but the nice girls, the girls in school, they liked that uniform, I could tell. I saw those girls and was like, Fuck, that's the kind of job I need.

I'd never wanted to be a police officer, had never even thought about it. But I started talking to this cop more and more. I'd stop for a few minutes, we'd have chats in the hall. He knew I was in the streets, but he encouraged me to straighten up, stay out of trouble. One day I asked him about being a cop. He said, "It's a good job. Good benefits. Good pay. You go down, fill out an application, and take a test. They'll call you." I told him I'd think about it. He said. "You'd be good at it. Take the test. You could change your life."

Being a cop seemed crazy at first, but after a while it wasn't crazy at all. It gave me a way out. If this guy liked me and thought I could do it, maybe I could. They wouldn't take me if I had a criminal record, but my record was clean. Five years in the streets, and I'd never been convicted of anything. The only thing hanging over my head was the assault charge from beating up that crackhead with my man Jimmy. But that guy wasn't going to testify, and the case was shaky. If I could get it thrown out, I'd be free to apply. I decided to sign up for the test. No one could know what I was doing. I kept my head down, kept working my shifts for the Supreme Team, but every day I was thinking: I'm done with this. I'm out.

Then late one afternoon in Baisley Park, I was chilling on one of the benches next to the handball court, about to start my shift. Prince and Malik rolled up in Prince's black BMW. Malik got out. He came over to me and said, "Yo, come on. Get in the car. We gotta go somewhere."

I jumped in the back. Malik got in the front passenger side, closed the door, and Prince pulled off. Malik reached back and handed me a shiny black 9-millimeter pistol and said, "Here, hold this."

I was nervous. I took the gun and said, "Wassup?"

He said, "We're going to take you someplace. When we get there we're gonna point somebody out to you, and when we do you're gonna shoot him in the head."

14

Please, Please, God, Please

We pulled away from Baisley Park. Prince cut over to Sutphin Boulevard and headed north. The whole time we drove I kept up this tough-guy attitude. I sat there in the backseat saying, "Yo, let's *get* this motherfucker. Shit, I'm ready." I wasn't ready. I was terrified. I wasn't a murderer. I wasn't like these people. All I did in that car was pray. *Please let this not happen. Please get me out of this. Please, please, God, please. I'm just a kid.*

We pulled into the parking lot of this pool hall at 112th and Sutphin. It was a spot where Jamaicans hung out. We went inside. It was a big room that only had one pool table. It seemed like a front for a drug operation. The air was thick with smoke. The smell of weed practically knocked us over as we walked in. It was dark, hard to make people out, but there must have been thirty guys in there. Prince went up to every single person, looking them right in the eye to see who they were. I had the gun in my pocket, hand on the trigger, waiting for the word. I felt sick to my stomach. Every guy he went up to I kept praying, *Please let that not be him. Please let that not be him.* Because I knew: If I got a body on me, I'd never get out. No matter where I went, what I did, I'd have that hanging over my head. But if they pointed the guy out and I didn't kill him, I was afraid they'd kill me.

I waited and waited. Prince went through the whole club, to the last man. Finally he came back and said, "He ain't here. Let's go."

We went out and got in the car. Malik took the gun back and started laughing. He said, "Nigga, you wasn't gonna shoot no motherfuckin' body." Prince busted out laughing, too. They made it like the whole thing was a joke.

Was it? The whole ride back to the park they were laughing at me. I laughed along, too, so they'd think I was cool with it. Because that's how much of a psychopath Prince was: it could have been a joke, his idea of some funny shit to pull. That scared me more than the fact that he might have wanted me to murder someone.

The whole thing might have been a loyalty test, too. They did that all the time. "Let's do a trial run. Let's take him and see if he's going to clam up, see if we can count on him. If he shows he can do it, we'll put the next one on him." The real murder might happen next week, or the week after that.

Were they fucking with me? Was it a test? Or was there actually somebody in there they wanted me to kill? To this day I don't know. All I knew was that I had to get away from Prince, from Malik, from everybody. They dropped me off back at the park. I said nothing to no one. I quietly worked the rest of my shift, thinking about how badly I wanted out.

I needed an exit plan, and I needed to move on it fast. I talked to my guidance counselor at school, who told me that applying for the NYPD wasn't like applying for other municipal service jobs. It takes a long time. After signing up to take the test, I might not get called for a year. Then they'd run a background check on me. After that, they might not call me for another year, or they might not call me at all.

I was in deep with one of the most notorious drug gangs in America. If I stopped dealing cold, I was broke. I needed a real job, something with benefits for my kids. Bagging groceries at Pathmark for $4.25 an hour wasn't going to cut it. And no way could I get out and stay in Queens. I couldn't keep hanging around guys like Mark and Dre and not get pulled back in. I needed to vanish off the face of the Earth. I needed a way to leave quick, get gone, and stay gone.

The army. It was perfect. It was brilliant. They'd pick me up, take me away to basic training, give me three meals a day, put a roof over my head, and six months later I'd be on the other side of the world, off to California or South Korea or wherever else. There was a military recruiting station on Jamaica Avenue. I went in and talked to the recruiter. I told him straight up, "I need to get out of here as quickly as possible. How soon can I enlist?"

The recruiter explained everything. He told me about life in the military, took me through the process, what I had to do, what the parameters were. Same as the NYPD, applicants had to take a test, be a high school graduate, and had to have a clean record: no felony convictions.

I went down and took the entrance exam at Fort Hamilton, which is on the Belt Parkway near the Verrazano Bridge in Brooklyn. I wanted to be gone right then, but it doesn't happen overnight. It was going to take a few weeks to get my enlistment date, and my actual departure would be a few months after that. In the meantime I still had to eat, take care of my son. I'd paid the hospital bills on his delivery and was paying for all kinds of baby gear that Tina needed. I was about to start doing the same for Theresa. She was already eight and a half months pregnant and ready to give birth any day. So I stayed in the streets. I kept hustling, and I told no one. I didn't want anyone thinking I was disloyal, or that I might be a snitch. I didn't want anybody to suspect anything, so I kept it to myself. I didn't even tell Theresa or my mom. I was waiting to make sure everything worked out first.

Summer came. I was busting my ass to make sure I passed my final exams so I could graduate. On June 14, I was home studying when Theresa's mom called to say she was in labor. They were driving to the hospital. They'd stop by and pick me up. I ran downstairs, and they pulled up a few minutes later in Momma Willis's black Ford Escort. Theresa was in the backseat screaming. I jumped in to try to soothe her. Momma Willis took off, heading for La Guardia Hospital on the other side of Queens. Once we got there, I jumped out, grabbed a wheelchair, and took Theresa in through the emergency room while her mother parked the car. Fortunately, this time the labor wasn't too long, and everything went fine for both Theresa and the baby, our daughter, Natasha. We nicknamed her Tash. I called my mom to give her the good news.

Right after Tash was born, I got a call from the army recruiter with my enlistment date: October 18. It was still the middle of June. Four months I had to wait. Up to that point I still hadn't told anyone, but once I had the enlistment date and Tash was here, I confided in Theresa. I wanted her to know I was making a plan for the baby's future.

Two weeks later I made good on the promise I'd made to my mother: I graduated from high school. The day of the ceremony I went down to Harry's Barbershop and got a fresh cut. On a normal day my waves were spinning, but this day they were really spinning. I was the sharpest dude at graduation. Everyone else was wearing whatever their mother ordered for them from Sears, but I was killing it in a silk shirt, brand-new slacks, suede Bally shoes, a big diamond ring, and a big rope chain with a huge gold medallion that had my name "Boo" in diamonds on it.

My mom, all my sisters, aunts, and uncles, Theresa and our new baby came to watch me graduate from Andrew Jackson. Smooth was there, too, with some of the boys from the corner. As soon as our class walked into the auditorium and took our seats, I craned my neck around to make sure I knew where my mother was sitting. She was in the top right balcony.

The ceremony started. One by one I watched my friends cross the stage while I waited. Finally my row was ordered to line up against the wall. The principal called out "Corey Pegues." She mispronounced it, of course, but I didn't care. Smooth and the other guys, they were cheering and calling my name. I walked up, took the diploma, and shook the principal's hand. Before I left the stage I turned and looked out to my mother, held the diploma up over my head, and mouthed,

"This is for you." I could see her crying up there. I was choked up my-self, but I wasn't about to be up there crying in front of everybody. I was too cool for that.

After the ceremony Ma and I found each other. She hugged me close in this long, warm embrace. All I could think about was the heartbreak and disappointment she'd had in her life, all the times I'd let her down, all the times she told me I was going to be dead or in jail. I was so proud that I had given her that moment. It was one of the last moments we would ever share. One month later my mother was dead.

15

I Have to Do Right. I Have to Do Good.

It was ovarian cancer. She'd known for months, but had kept it from everyone. The doctors had caught it too late, and nothing could be done, so she'd decided not to burden the rest of us with it. She'd been losing weight, but nothing dramatic. Nobody had a clue. About a month after I graduated, my older sister Linda came to the house. It was late. My mother wasn't home. I'd assumed she was over at one of my aunts' houses or something, which she did sometimes. Tawn and I had already gone to bed when Linda came in and woke us up. "Hurry, we have to go the hospital to see Ma."

"What's the matter?"

"She's sick."

We rushed to the hospital and went up to her room. She'd gone in earlier that day for a checkup. She'd collapsed and was admitted. She looked terrible. She kept saying her feet were cold. I touched them and they were freezing, ice cold in the middle of summer. We kept her covered with blankets. She couldn't talk much; they had her on all kinds of drugs and painkillers. She mostly slept. I stayed by her side the whole next day. That night I went home to catch some rest and get a bite to eat. Before I left, I hugged her and said, "I love you." I left to go home. As soon as I got there I got a call from Linda at the hospital. Ma was dead.

It was crazy. It happened so quick. She was here and then she was gone. The whole wake and funeral were a blur. I don't remember any of it. Linda moved in to look after Tawn for her last two years of school, but I was eighteen and a new father. I was on my own. Without Ma I knew I had to step up and be a man, take responsibility for my own family. My mother died thinking her son was a crack dealer, but I knew she'd be watching me from up above and I wanted to make her proud. I wanted her to know that the life she gave me, the years she spent raising me, weren't going to be a waste. I said to myself, "Everything from here on, I have to do right. I have to do good."

———

There was only one thing left standing in my way: the assault charge. I had a hearing scheduled for the second week in August. It'd been dragging on for a year by that point, different motions, continuances. Basically they were stalling, waiting for this guy to change his mind and testify, which he never did. Without him as a witness, the prosecution didn't have much of a case. Still, if the judge didn't like me or wanted to make an example of me, there was a chance I might pick up a conviction and my whole plan would be derailed.

When I showed up for the hearing, I didn't wait for the proceedings to begin. I leaned over to my Legal Aid attorney and I told him, "Yo, tell the judge I'm going into the army."

"The army?"

"Yeah, I already enlisted. Tell the judge. Maybe it'll help."

So the attorney told that to the judge, and the judge asked me if it was true. I said it was. I told him I'd made some bad choices but that I was determined to turn my life around. I already had my enlistment date coming up, and if he gave me a second chance, I wouldn't make him sorry.

The judge and the prosecutor and my attorney conferred. The judge took a minute. Then he announced that he was dismissing the charge. "But if I see you in my courtroom again," he said, "no matter what the charge, you're going to jail."

I let out the biggest sigh of relief. I said, "Thank you, Your Honor. Thank you, thank you. I won't let you down, I promise."

I was free to go. My guardian angel was looking out for me that day. The same guardian angel who was looking over my shoulder when my gun didn't fire on Nashaun, when the cop busted me with three hundred vials of crack and let me go, when the cops raided the block and grabbed Smiley instead of me—all those times I could have been shot, killed, caught with a gun at school, thrown in jail, who knows what. I'd made it through with a clean record and a chance to make things right. That alone was a miracle. Nobody makes it five years in the street with that kind of luck, but somehow I had.

That August Supreme got out of prison. He was supposed to be in twenty-to-life, but his lawyer argued him out on a technicality, and now he was back on the block at Foch and Guy R. Brewer. I'd see him. He was an unassuming, soft-talking guy. Nothing like Prince. If I'd seen him a year before, I probably would have been in awe of him. Seeing him now, it was just another reminder that I didn't want to be going down that path. I didn't want people celebrating because I was coming out of prison, or bragging about my street cred because I'd done my time like a man.

With Supreme back, everybody was excited, talking about how the Team was going to be in full effect, banging and hustling harder than before. I kept my head down. I showed up, worked my shift, and went home. I started making excuses for not being around as much. When guys would start up a dice game, or go off to do stupid shit like stealing bikes, I made myself scarce. With two babies, I could get myself out of whatever was happening. I'd pretend to get a page on my beeper. "Yo, man, Tina all over me about this shit with the baby." Then I'd skip out. I stayed home, spent time with Theresa and Tash, and talked about the future. For the first time I felt like I had a future.

The first week of October I asked the recruiter what I had to do to bring Theresa and the baby with me after basic training. He said the only way they could join me was if we were married. He also told me if I was married with a dependent, I'd get an extra $250 a month in pay. Theresa and I knew we wanted to be together, but we'd never actually discussed marriage. Now it made sense. There was no romantic proposal. I went home and said, "Let's get married." When I asked her, she smiled from ear to ear. She started screaming and we were both laughing. Her mom came down and we told her the news, about getting married, me going into the army. Momma Willis was so happy she cried. She was proud of me for stepping up to do the right thing.

Now came the hard part. I had to break the news to Tina. I hadn't even told her that I was leaving to go into the army. I went down to her house in Brooklyn. Lil' Life was ten months old, just getting to the age where he'd react to me with cute facial expressions. We ate dinner and I held him in my arms until he fell asleep. I put him to bed in his crib with his favorite teddy bear. Then it was time to break the news. Tina was glad that I was enlisting. She knew it made sense even if I'd be leaving for a while. Then I told her I was marrying Theresa, and she went berserk. She started yelling, crying, taking swings at me. It was bad. She told me to leave. On my way out she said, "You'll never see your son again."

Theresa and I were married a few days later, on October 9, by a justice of the peace at the Queens County court. Momma Willis and Theresa's godmother were there as witnesses. We went back to her house, where her mom had made us a cake and a nice meal. Some of Theresa's family and friends were there, too. I ceremoniously carried her through the front door as a joke; there hadn't been anything old-fashioned about how we got together.

Nine days left. I was ringing Tina every day, trying to get her to see me, to let me see Corey Jr., but she wasn't taking my calls. Finally, with two days to go, she let me come for one last visit. I went over, played with him, and held him close for as long as I could before saying good-bye. Before I left, I gave Tina a roll of cash, a few grand, and told her I'd send more when I could. That same evening I worked my last shift for the Supreme Team. I sold my last vial of crack, turned in my money, and went home.

My last night in town I had a going away party at my house. In the past couple of days, I'd been telling my sisters, the rest of my family, and a couple of close friends that I'd enlisted. They came over and we spent the night drinking, taking pictures, and having fun. After everyone went home, I packed up the last few things in my room and Theresa and I went back to her house, where the recruiter was scheduled to pick me up. We stayed up late, hugging and kissing, talking about what was to come. I gave her the rest of the money I'd saved. I didn't want any of it. I only kept $40 for myself for the road.

At 5 a.m., the recruiter pulled up out front in this Chevy sedan. It was still dark out. I grabbed my bag and went outside. Theresa and her mom stood in the doorway crying as I hugged them good-bye. I walked down to the car, threw my bag in the back, and climbed in. The car pulled away, and I disappeared. From Theresa's street we turned onto Farmers and headed down to Baisley Boulevard. The streets were empty. We crossed Guy R. Brewer, and Baisley Park was there on my right as we went by. It was too dark to see, but I knew that over on the far side of that park, past the baseball field, near the handball courts, there was a young guy out there, maybe fifteen years old, hustling, holding down the graveyard shift, thinking he was the man with the fly clothes and the fat roll of bills in his pocket, and I knew that would never be me again.

At the bottom of Baisley Boulevard, we took a left and merged onto the Belt Parkway. The car sped up. South Jamaica disappeared in the rearview. I could feel this weight lifting. I had the biggest, fattest smile on my face. The park, the block, the drugs, the life, it was all behind me now. I was gone. I was flying. I was free.

PART TWO

Cop

16

Old Habits

When I climbed into that army recruiter's car and left the streets behind, I was still a kid. All I knew was that I wanted to change my life. I had no idea what it would take, but I was determined to never give up, no matter what.

My first stop that morning was Fort Hamilton in Brooklyn. I spent a day there, filling out paperwork. The next day they put a bunch of us on a bus headed to Fort Dix in New Jersey for basic training. The minute I stepped off that bus, I was in a completely different world from anything I'd ever known. They herded us into a barbershop and shaved everyone bald, took off everyone's facial hair, stripped us down to nothing. We were treated like cattle at every turn, people yelling and screaming at us. When it was time to get assigned bunks in the sleeping quarters, my name was called and I was way in the back with this huge duffel bag of gear. I was slow getting to the front, and they were screaming my name and telling me to double-time it. I tripped and fell and dropped my bag trying to run up to the front of the line.

I wasn't ready for any of it. With my mother dead and my father gone, I was basically an orphan. The apartment on Farmers Boulevard was gone. I didn't have a home to speak of. It was just me, alone in this army barracks, wondering how I was going to make a life for my wife and my two kids.

I adapted quickly. I actually enjoyed the discipline. I was ready for it. I needed it. All those years hugging the block, sleeping in crack houses, I was always on my own. I never had a strong father figure telling me what to do, where to go, how to be. Now I had that, and I loved it. It allowed me to take my energy and my mind and focus on positive things. One of the best parts of basic training was actually learning how to shoot a gun properly. I'd been running around the streets, popping off my .25, pretending to be a gangster. Now I realized what a bunch of clowns we were, how little we actually knew.

The only thing I didn't like was going out into the field. We had to go out and spend days at a time surviving in the woods, living in tents, eating MREs. I was a city kid. I hated it, never got used to it. The other part of me that never adapted to military life was my walk. During my days as a hustler I'd developed a bit of a ditty-bop in my step, and the army couldn't break me of it. They couldn't drill me out of it, couldn't punish me out of it. Whenever we marched and it was my turn to carry the platoon flag, the flag would bop up and down a half step out of time with the rest of the unit. The drill sergeant would yell, *"Pegues, stop moving my flag!"* They'd pull me out of formation and scream at me. But I couldn't help it. Even in the army, shaved and stripped down like everyone else, I never lost that hip-hop part of me that came from growing up on the streets of Queens with LL Cool J and Run-DMC.

After three months in New Jersey, I graduated from basic training and the army transferred me down to Fort Sam Houston outside San Antonio for my advanced individual training (AIT) as a combat medic. Compared to basic, AIT was easy, routine physical conditioning in the morning and classroom work and tests the rest of the day. I talked to Theresa on the phone every day and we exchanged letters, and those three months passed pretty quickly.

At the end of AIT, I learned that I was going to be stationed at Fort Drum in upstate New York, assigned to work in the base medical clinic. I was thrilled. It's a ways from the city, up in the mountains near the Canadian border, five and a half hours by car. But it was close enough that I'd be able to visit family from time to time. As soon as I relocated, I applied for family housing so that Theresa and Tash could join me. A few months later, they did. The army rented us this drafty old farmhouse way out in the sticks with cows and horses and everything. I didn't even own a car at that point; another soldier had to drive me out to look at the house. The army paid to move Theresa and Tash up from Queens. I learned how to drive, got my license, and financed my first car, a brand-new Isuzu I-Mark sedan. Theresa was pretty lonely and cut off for the first few months, but I convinced her to go into town on weeknights to take classes for her GED. She started doing that, and we both felt good about our situation. We were starting our family.

We didn't have much. Most weeks we barely had enough money for groceries. I'd gone from making $3,000 a day to making $600 a month, but I didn't care. I was so happy. It was the best money I ever earned, the first honest money I'd ever earned. Things were especially tight because on top of everything I was paying child support to Tina for Corey Jr. I was always thinking of ways to make a little extra. I went to the PX and bought clippers and started charging guys $10 to cut their hair. I'd never cut hair a day in my life, but I watched the barbers at the barbershop on base, learned a few tricks, and eventually convinced a bunch of guys to start letting me trim their cuts instead.

The other thing I had that the guys on the base wanted was my connection to the rap scene back in Queens. Hip-hop was blowing up all over the country now, and my friends who were DJs back in the city had the latest cuts and singles. They'd put them on mix tapes and sell them on the streets for five, ten dollars a piece. Nobody at Fort Drum had that kind of music. I'd go back home, pick up a bunch of these tapes, copy them over and over again, and sell as many as I could. I made enough from the tapes to cover everything I was sending Tina each month for Corey Jr.

Only a year after leaving the streets, I'd turned my life around 180 degrees. I was earning an honest living, learning a trade, serving my country, and supporting my family. The best thing the military did for me was it got my mind right. I wasn't walking around in fear anymore. My rough edge had been honed down. I learned to trust people again. Gangsters put up this big front about being tough and having street cred, but they're really driven by fear, the fear of being seen as weak. So much of hustling was about proving you were better or tougher or flashier than the next guy. Which is why the violence and the drama, it all escalates. In the army there's none of that. Everyone's stripped down to the same level. Everyone starts at the bottom, and everybody learns to depend on everybody else and to have real camaraderie.

The army taught me how to be the person my mother had wanted me to be. The lessons she tried to teach me in Sunday school, about right and wrong and how to treat other people, I'd always wanted to be that person. I was finally in an environment where I could see those principles at work and do better for myself. By the end of that first year I was a completely different person.

Almost.

Old habits die hard. Going home was difficult for me. I missed being with my aunts and uncles and cousins, but being home meant being back in the hood. It meant the lure of the streets was right there. After that first year away, right after Halloween, I was home on weekend leave. I was hanging with Smooth and some other guys from the block, my boy Jimbo and this other dude, Rakim. We went out in my new Isuzu and hit the bars. We were drinking, having fun, and somebody said, "Yo, let's go to the Rock."

The Rock is this big red, black, and green boulder on Farmers Boulevard where folks hang out, drink, play dice. We went over there and they had a Cee-lo game going on and we started rolling dice with these guys. We played and drank and got wasted and lost all our money. After the last game, my man Rakim gave me this look and nodded toward the car, like, Yo, let's get these dudes. I knew what he meant. We gave everyone a pound, and the four of us took off.

We got back in the car and Rakim said exactly what I thought he was going to say. He was like, "Man, let's rob these motherfuckers. Get our money back." Everybody was drunk as hell and we thought it sounded like a great idea. We drove back to Rakim's house. He got a gun. Smooth got a gun. I said, "Yo, we need masks. Let's go to my house. I got masks." So we went by Theresa's mother's house, where I was staying. We had these kids' masks from Halloween. I had this pumpkin mask from my daughter, and Rakim got a Cinderella mask that Smooth's little girl had worn. I said, "Okay, Jimbo, you're the driver, and Smooth, you're the lookout." Smooth gave me his pistol, and we drove back to the Rock, looking for the guys who took our money.

We parked around the corner and went creeping back around looking for these dudes to do the stickup, me in this pumpkin mask and Rakim in this Cinderella mask, both with these pistols at our sides. People must have thought we were out of our minds. We went around the corner onto Farmers Boulevard, and the dudes were gone. We ran back to the car and jumped inside. I said, "Yo, man. They're gone. It's not happening."

Jimbo went to back out, but he was so drunk he put the car in drive when he meant to do reverse. He slammed on the gas and slammed into the car in front of us. Everybody yelled, "Oh, fuck!" He panicked and jammed it in reverse, floored the gas, pulled off, and ripped the whole front bumper off my brand-new car. We were hanging halfway out of this parking spot, with my bumper lying in the middle of the street, wearing Halloween masks and laughing like a bunch of idiots, like it was the funniest thing we'd ever seen. We got out, grabbed the bumper, put it in the trunk, and took off.

The next morning my hangover was killing me. I sat there at the breakfast table looking at my wife and my daughter, thinking, What's the matter with me? Was I really stupid enough to try to rob some dice game? Jimbo took my car and went and paid to get it fixed, and I knew I needed to get back upstate as soon as I could. I couldn't be around this environment anymore. Later that afternoon, Rakim came by all excited. He had a plan. He was like, "Yo, since you're away in the army, every time you come home on leave, we go and stick up some drug dealers. They ain't gonna tell the police, and you leave with the money. It's untraceable, man! Ain't nobody ever going to know!"

Rakim was still in the streets. To him this sounded like a genius idea. I said, "Yeah, that sounds like a plan." Then I took my wife and my daughter and I got in my patched-up car and I drove out of there, and I never called Rakim again.

17

TNT

I left for the army on October 18, 1987. On November 6, less than three weeks later, a small army of FBI agents and cops from Queens Narcotics raided the Baisley Park Houses and took out the Supreme Team. They destroyed it. They hit the cabstand, the stash houses, the corners, everything. It was chaos. People panicking, running. Guys throwing bricks of cocaine out of the tower windows, flushing the stuff down toilets. The cops got Prince. They got Supreme. They got everyone. If I'd been there, they'd have got me, too.

For years, crack gangs had had free rein on the South Side of Queens. Whether it was the big crews like the Supreme Team or Fat Cat's organization, or the freelance crews like we had on 198 and Murdock, we rarely worried about the police. A lot of them were on the take, and the undercovers who tried to buy from us were a joke. Guys got pinched, but it was usually because they did something stupid. Every now and then narcotics squads got lucky with big raids, like the one they did on the Baisley projects, but for the most part the cops were slow to catch on to how the crack game had changed. The NYPD was too corrupt and too lazy to launch an effective counterattack. And to be honest, if a bunch of black kids in the ghetto wanted to kill each other over jewelry and bullshit, cops didn't care.

All that was about to change. On February 26, 1988, a twenty-two-year-old rookie cop named Eddie Byrne was sitting in his patrol car in front of a witness's house in Jamaica. The witness, a Guyanese immigrant named Arjune, had been complaining to police about the nonstop drug activity taking place on his block. He'd agreed to testify against the dealers, and he'd started receiving death threats. His house had been bombed, so the 103rd Precinct had put a patrol car out front. At three thirty in the morning, the night Byrne was on watch, four guys crept up behind the patrol car. One of them put five bullets in the back of Byrne's head with a .38.

The hit had been ordered by a guy named Pappy Mason, a lieutenant under Fat Cat. He wanted to "send a message" to the cops to back off. That's how arrogant these gangsters had become. But you don't assassinate a cop in uniform to show who's boss. It don't work. The public was outraged. Not just in New York, but across the whole country. President Reagan called Eddie Byrne's family to offer his personal condolences. Vice President Bush was campaigning for president at the time, and Byrne's murder gave him the perfect opportunity to look tough on crime. He gave a big speech up in Westchester, calling for the death penalty for all drug-related murders. Byrne's parents gave Bush their son's badge, and he carried it with him on the campaign trail, pulling it out and using it to talk about escalating the fight against illegal drugs.

The year before Eddie Byrne's murder, as the crack trade had escalated, New York's murder rate had gone up 5.8 percent. In Queens it had gone up 25 percent. In the 103rd Precinct in Jamaica, it had gone up 33 percent. Before Eddie Byrne, a lot of cops looked the other way. Now they were pissed off. Days after the murder, Mayor Ed Koch announced the formation of a new Tactical Narcotics Team, the TNT squad: 118 special officers in bulletproof vests, with shotguns, flooded into a one-square-mile area in Jamaica. They started busting down doors of crack houses, storming into bars and pool halls that served as fronts for the gangs. The fire department was brought in, too; they targeted all the known drug houses, hit them up with inspections, hit landlords with code violations, confiscated whole buildings. The TNT squads did massive sweeps of the corners, picked up hundreds of guys. The Queens district attorney set up a special narcotics court in the neighborhood to process all the people being arrested.

It was a national story. I followed it in the newspapers from Fort Sam Houston in San Antonio. I can remember reading the headlines, watching it go down on the same streets where I'd been hustling a couple months before. Every week I'd call home and I'd hear about friends getting picked up, friends getting shot. I was so happy to be gone. I couldn't believe my own luck.

I tried not to pay too much attention to it while it was happening. I wanted to leave it alone and focus on getting my life in order. One thing I couldn't ignore was the story in the paper the day they caught the shooter: David McClary. I couldn't believe it. A guy I used to ball with in O'Connell Park. The guy whose basement I used to go to with Malik to watch the underground boxing matches. Of the four guys who crept up on Byrne that night, they were saying he was the one who'd actually pulled the trigger. If I needed any more confirmation that I'd made the right choice with my life, that was it. David McClary chose to be a street legend, and now he was going to spend every day of the rest of his life in jail. I chose a better life for my kids. Now all I had to do was not screw it up.

The shooting of Eddie Byrne was a turning point in the history of the War on Drugs and the NYPD. Before that, politicians always talked the talk about getting tough on crime but never did anything. Now it was war. After cracking down on south Queens, Koch expanded the TNT squads to cover all the city: in Harlem, in the Bronx, in East New York. But getting "tough on crime" was mostly for show. It didn't fix the problem. Koch allocated $116 million for more cops, but only $10 million for new prosecutors and Legal Aid attorneys, which meant the cops were out arresting people the system had no way to process. Drug arrests more than doubled. The district attorneys were carrying thousands of felony drug cases with a handful of assistant DAs to handle them. Judges' dockets were backed up for months. In the municipal courthouses, empty storage rooms were being turned into makeshift courtrooms to handle the overflow. The jails were beyond capacity, too. From 1985 to 1989, the city's jail population doubled, from 9,815 to 18,630. There was no way to try all the cases, and no place to put the defendants while they waited to be tried.

The only solution was to plead everyone out on lesser charges. Guys were getting picked up on felony drug possession and weapons charges, and they were back on the streets nine months later. And in the nine months they were gone, what had happened? Some other young crew had taken their corner, and now there was going to be some kind of beef over it. There'd be a gunfight, somebody'd get shot, probably killed. Then those guys would go back into the system and a different crew would come along. There was no justice being served; black bodies were being cycled through the system to satisfy the public's demand to "do something."

There was no doubt that black neighborhoods and housing projects needed to be saved from the crack trade. But without guys like Supreme and Prince and Fat Cat keeping some kind of order, the streets actually got *more* violent as rookie crews fought to try to take control in the middle of the chaos. The TNT squads were destabilizing the crack business without dismantling it. They weren't making minority neighborhoods safer; they were turning minority neighborhoods into war zones. After a year of the TNT program, New York's murder rate went up another 10.4 percent, from 1,691 homicides to 1,867; 38 percent of them were drug related. It would go up again the year after that.

But, hey: if it's not working, do it more. Going after black thugs and crack dealers was politically convenient, even if it wasn't accomplishing anything. After campaigning with Eddie Byrne's badge for a year, George Bush got elected, and in September of '89 he gave the first prime-time public address of his presidency. He held up a plastic Baggie of crack and declared he was finally going to win the War on Drugs, but the policies he announced were more of the same: hundreds of millions of dollars for more prisons, more police, more street enforcement.

That fall, the candidates for mayor of New York were out on the campaign trail, and it was more of the same there, too. Every candidate tried to out-tough the other on the issue of drugs and crime. Manhattan Borough President David Dinkins won, the first black mayor in the history of New York. His first big legislative push was the "Safe Streets, Safe City" plan, a $1.8 billion anticrime program that was supposed to finally bring crime under control. It passed in Albany in February of 1991. "Safe Streets" was going to put thirty-five hundred new cops on the streets of New York over the next six years. I would be one of them.

18

#900570

At the end of my first year at Fort Drum, I got the letter inviting me to take the test for the NYPD. Me and one of my army buddies took a leave and drove down to the city to take it. It was your basic aptitude test—some reading comprehension, some math. I felt like I did fine. After that I started getting calls from the city, wanting me to bring in my high school transcript, telling me to meet with an investigator. But I couldn't take leave and pop down to the city every time they needed me to do something. Then I learned that there's a special list for people serving in the military. You can put the application process on hold and then, once you're discharged, they pick your case back up and you're already at the front of the line. So that's what I did.

In March of 1991 I was honorably discharged from the United States Army. I would have been out the previous October, after three years, but they kept me an extra six months because of the First Gulf War. There was a chance I'd need to be deployed to Iraq, but then the whole thing was over in less than a month and they let me go. So I could keep making some extra money and work toward a military pension, I stayed enlisted in the New York National Guard and was assigned to the 105th Infantry as a combat medic. We had drills one weekend a month at Camp Smith up in the Hudson Valley and for two weeks every summer back up at Fort Drum.

Theresa had taken Tash and moved back to the city a few months earlier to look for a job. She moved into her grandmother's basement, which was where we were going to be living until we figured everything out. While I was away in the army, Tina had enlisted in the military, too, and Corey Jr. had gone to live with her where she was stationed, so unfortunately I wouldn't get to see much of him.

I came home and contacted the city to let them know I was ready to start the application process up again. While I waited, I got a job at this factory out in Lynbrook, Long Island. It was an assembly line–type job, standing on the line all day, putting these widgets in a box, labeling them, packing them up.

After a few months I got a letter from the police department saying this guy Jeffery Harp would be my liaison and investigator, the guy conducting my background check and helping me navigate the application process. Lucky for me Harp was a black guy. I felt comfortable talking with him, and he was enthusiastic about helping more young blacks get into the department. When I started the process, I told him straight up that I'd been arrested for assault when I was sixteen, but that the charges had been dismissed when I went into the army. I didn't want it to come out later and have it look like I was trying to hide something. He told me to write up the incident as it had happened because he had to inform his captain, who'd have to sign off on it. He said, "Just be honest. Don't lie about anything, and it'll all work out the way it's meant to."

I wrote up the statement on the assault, and I said that a guy had sold me a stolen television and I'd gotten pissed off and beat him up—which was the truth. Maybe it wasn't the *whole* truth, but it wasn't a lie. I didn't tell a single lie on my NYPD application. I didn't have to. Nobody thought to ask me if I'd ever been a crack dealer. Coming out of the military helped me a lot with that. I'd been honorably discharged and was an active National Guardsman, so nobody raised any red flags about my past or my character. The arrest for assault looked like a youthful indiscretion from growing up in a rough neighborhood.

It was the same with my background check. While I was working every day at that factory, boxing up those widgets, I knew they were going around St. Albans, talking to friends, former classmates, my aunts, uncles, and cousins. People would tell me, "The cops were here asking about you." Everybody knew I'd been in the streets. It was no secret. Any one of them could have killed my application cold, but that didn't happen. They looked out for me. Back on 198 and Murdock, the old ladies like Ms. Smith were always telling me, "Baby, get off this corner." Ms. Smith was happy that I'd made it off, so she wasn't going to screw that up for me.

That whole fall and winter while they did the background check I was working my little factory job and praying I'd make the next academy class. On my breaks I'd slip into the restroom and do two, three hundred push-ups to keep in shape. I was completely focused on this one thing. I didn't have a backup plan. I didn't apply to work at the post office or to take tolls for the MTA or anything else. I wanted to be a cop. If it didn't work out, I didn't know what I was going to do.

There was one thing I knew I had to do when I moved back to Queens. I was putting my life together, building a family, and that meant my whole family. I wanted to reconnect with my father. It wasn't hard to find him. I called his sister, my aunt. She told me he was renting a room in a house in Hollis. That whole time he'd been gone from my life, missing my childhood, missing my birthdays, missing Christmas, he'd never been more than a mile or two away.

I went over to see him one afternoon. He was disheveled and reeked of alcohol. This room he was renting had a bed, a desk, and a dresser. Nothing else. It was messy. He was still on disability, and he would sit at home drinking, every day, waiting for that check to arrive. That's what his life had become. He was fifty-five years old, and he was drinking himself to death.

We didn't talk much the first time I visited. He was never one to say much. This was a man who never told me he loved me, never hugged his children. I suppose I had every reason to be mad at him. I could have yelled at him for leaving, for not being there, but I wasn't interested in doing any of that. I wanted to find a way to have a relationship with him. I wanted to spend as much time with him as I could, because I knew the way he was going he wasn't going to be around for long.

I started taking him to his doctor's appointments. Every night, when Theresa made dinner, I started asking her to make up an extra plate. I'd take it over to him to make sure he was eating something. I brought Tash over to meet him, because I wanted her to know him. I begged him to stop drinking and clean himself up, but there wasn't much point. It was what it was.

Harp had told me to call him once a week to check in, so I did. Late that December, before I'd received my letter from the department, I called him and he said, "You made it. You're going in the first class starting in January. The letter is coming later this week." I was thrilled, and relieved. Here I was raising a family with no benefits, no medical, no dental. Now I was going to have a real career, a real opportunity. Harp told me, "Shut your life down. Stay home. Don't go out. Don't drive anywhere. You don't want to get a speeding ticket, get in a traffic accident, get a court summons—you don't want anything to happen that might derail you." I took his advice and laid low. A few days later the official letter came.

The swearing-in for my police academy class was on January 13, 1992. The ceremony was at Brooklyn College. It's a big orientation event. They gave us uniforms, name tags. You fill out a ton of paperwork. They also give you an ID number. Nobody has that number but you. You keep it until you die. Mine is #900570.

We had a huge class, over a thousand of us coming in under the "Safe Streets, Safe City" program, everybody packed into this huge auditorium. Very few of them looked like me. Even the other black recruits, none of them had my style. I was wearing slacks, a button-up shirt, and a big gold chain hanging around my neck—I was becoming a cop, but I wasn't going to lose my swag entirely. At one point I got up to go use the bathroom and I walked past one of the academy instructors. He saw the ditty-bop in my step and he pulled me aside and was like, "Look, if you want to make it through here, you might want to do something about that walk."

I smiled and said, "All due respect, sir, I just spent three and a half years in the army. If they couldn't change my walk, I don't think a few months in the police academy is going to do it. But I'm going to be fine, don't worry."

I kept going on toward the bathroom, and when I turned down this corridor to go in I ran smack into this guy from my old neighborhood, my man Rocky. I knew Rocky from the streets back in the day. He wasn't part of the 198 and Murdock crew; he was from up on Hollis Avenue. But he'd been a freelancer like me, hustling, selling drugs, stealing cars.

I said, "Rocky? What the fuck are you doing here?"

He said, "What the fuck am *I* doing here? What the fuck are *you* doing here?"

I said, "I'm changing my life."

He said, "Me too!"

We both cracked up laughing. It was especially funny to me because my man Smooth was on the right side of the law now, too; after graduating from Morgan State, he moved back to Queens and became a corrections officer. It makes you stop and wonder how many guys, black or white or whatever, move from one side to the other. It's probably more than people think.

The academy lasts six months. There's a physical training component, a lot of classroom training, teaching you the law, the criminal code, some political science. Coming out of the army, the physical aspect was easy; I breezed right through that. The academic part of it wasn't hard, either. The handbook you have to learn, what they call the patrol guide, it's pretty basic. This is the code for a robbery, this is the code for a domestic disturbance, so on. It's written on an eighth-grade level.

You don't have to be a rocket scientist to be a cop, and I don't say that as an insult to cops. I say it because book smarts aren't necessarily what make you good at the job. Some of the best police officers you'll ever meet, all they've got is a high school diploma. What I would come to learn on the job is that the thing that makes a great cop is the ability to deal with people, to understand them and empathize with them in the heat of tense, difficult situations. That's what the job is, and that's the one thing they can't teach you in the academy. You learn everything in the book, and then you get out and you realize the job has almost nothing to do with what you learned in the book.

At the end of six months, I passed my physical and written exams with no problems. Graduation was July 3, 1992. The night before the big day I was so excited I couldn't sleep. I was climbing up and down the stairs to the kitchen all night, raiding the refrigerator and cabinets, eating anything I could get my hands on—cookies, crackers, PB&J. I was full of nervous energy. I'd had a lot of sleepless nights in my life, always because of something bad—wondering if I was going to get shot, afraid of going to jail. This was the first time I could remember not being able to sleep because of something good.

I finally went to bed for maybe an hour or two, got up, grabbed a shower, and took my dress uniform out of the plastic bag from the cleaners. I started ironing it. Theresa looked at me like I was crazy, ironing a perfectly pressed suit straight from the cleaners. But I insisted. I said, "I want to stand out. I want to have the sharpest looking uniform in the class."

Before getting dressed I went and picked up my father. When I arrived he was standing in the doorway wearing slacks, a dress shirt, and a tie. I'd never seen him that dressed up for something. I said, "You look great, Poppa. Thanks for being here today."

He said, "I wouldn't miss this for the world."

We ran back home. I went back down to the basement and put my uniform on, carefully and deliberately, one piece at a time. The pants, the socks, the shirt and tie and shoes. Then the dress jacket. I adjusted my shield to make sure it was perfectly straight. I carefully fitted my eight-point hat on my head. I took my gun and put it in my holster to complete the look. I stood there looking in the mirror, doing my best to look like a tough cop. I made quick-draw moves with my right hand, saying, "Freeze! Don't move!" Like I was a cop in the movies or something.

I heard Theresa laughing and I turned around and saw she was behind me, holding Tash. She was in stitches, watching me trying to act cool. But wearing that uniform, seeing my wife and my daughter laughing and having fun, I was so happy I didn't care how silly I looked.

Before we left, Theresa's grandma gathered everyone in the living room and had us hold hands for a prayer. Grandma Bryant was an ordained minister, the assistant pastor at a local church. As she started leading the prayer, asking God to look over me and the other recruits, all I could think of was my mother. When she died, I was still in the streets. I wanted her to see what I'd made of myself, and I believed she was there in spirit, that she knew what I'd accomplished. Thinking of her looking down on me from Heaven, I broke down and cried.

But I was lucky to have at least one parent with me that day. After we prayed, I got ready to go and walked out to the car. From behind me I heard Poppa call out. He came over and he stopped me and grabbed me and said, "I love you, son. Good luck."

One year later my father was dead.

19

The Most Racist Thing I've Ever Seen in My Life

Five days after my graduation, an angry mob of Dominican protestors burned a police officer in effigy at 172nd Street and Audubon Avenue in Washington Heights.

I'd picked an interesting time to become a cop.

The graduation itself was incredible. There was a sea of blue uniforms in the auditorium at St. John's, one of the largest classes in the department's history thanks to the "Safe Streets, Safe City" program, all of us with our chests puffed out. Our parents and friends in the audience, cheering us on. Mayor Dinkins gave the commencement speech. I was walking on air the whole day. But the euphoria was brief.

When Dinkins was elected, there was actually a lot of hope that as a black mayor he'd be able to do something about crime. He would reach out and connect with minority communities. Dinkins had even brought in the city's second black commissioner, Lee Brown. Dinkins and Brown talked a lot about getting tough, putting thousands of new cops on the street, expanding social services, restoring trust. They talked about community policing, too. They were going to bring back Officer Friendly to walk the beat and build relationships. But Dinkins didn't have an aggressive, take-charge personality; he was more of a calm, reserved type of guy, which made him look passive. His reforms were slow to take effect, and in the meantime the crime rate kept going up and up and up. Crack wasn't going away. Kids were dropping from stray bullets. Tourists were getting shot and stabbed on the subway. After this one especially grisly murder, the *New York Post* ran a headline that screamed DAVE, DO SOMETHING. A lot of people felt that way.

Then came the riots in Crown Heights. On August 19, 1991, a motorcade for the Grand Rebbe of the Lubavitchers, a sect of Hasidic Jews living in Crown Heights, sped through a red light at Utica Avenue and struck and killed Gavin Cato, a seven-year-old black kid. The tension between the black and Lubavitcher communities in Crown Heights had been bad for years. The Lubavitchers complained that the city did nothing about black crime; the black community complained that their needs were ignored while the Lubavitchers got special treatment from the city—the motorcade that killed Gavin Cato had a special police escort.

It was a hot summer night. All you needed was a spark to set everything off. People gathered around the scene of the accident. They started getting angry. Folks started yelling, and pretty soon it was chaos: people throwing rocks and bottles at the cop cars, smashing windows. A few blocks away, a gang of angry black kids assaulted and stabbed a Hasidic student, Yankel Rosenbaum. Rosenbaum died that night at the same hospital as Gavin Cato.

Over the next three days, the violence spread. News crews were attacked, cars overturned. To everyone in the city it looked like the cops weren't doing anything. They weren't. There hadn't been a major riot in New York in twenty years. Nobody was prepared. The top brass failed to see how serious the situation was getting. Rather than mobilizing the whole force citywide, the NYPD left the local precinct commanders to handle it. At one point the cops were so outnumbered by protestors that a whole platoon actually had to turn and run away and retreat back to their precinct. Without enough cops and the right plan to deploy them, the whole thing raged on for days, until the city was finally able to step in and shut it down.

The truth is that the NYPD blew it. They were slow and disorganized and ineffective. But the perception was that Dinkins let the riot get out of control because he was scared to come down hard on the black community—the black mayor was soft on black criminals. That was the death blow for Dinkins. His reputation never recovered. Protests and marches went on well into the fall and winter.

The following April, I was barely halfway through the academy when the Los Angeles Riots broke out. Four white officers were acquitted in the beating of Rodney King, and the city went up in flames. Fifty-three people killed, a billion dollars in damages. It didn't involve us directly, but it didn't reflect well on cops in general, and coming so soon after Crown Heights it made everyone nervous about another long, hot summer in New York.

One week later, the fires in LA had barely died down when the NYPD was hit by its biggest corruption scandal in years. Six New York City cops were arrested in Suffolk County out on Long Island. A bunch of guys from the 75th Precinct in East New York had been stealing drugs off of dealers in the city and selling them out in the suburbs. It was a huge embarrassment that they'd been caught by these suburban cops out on Long Island and not by the NYPD's own Internal Affairs Bureau, but it was hardly surprising. People in the department knew what was happening, but the leadership had been turning a blind eye for years. The main guy who got busted, this cop named Michael Dowd, there'd been complaints about him filed with IAB going back to 1986. But every time somebody complained, he'd get transferred to another unit. When Suffolk County picked him up, he was driving around in a brand-new red Corvette and he owned four houses, one of them worth over $300,000.

The whole thing was brazen and out in the open. The department tried to play it off like it was a few bad apples, but people weren't buying it. It was one of those scandals that leaves a taint on everybody. It dredged up all the old stories about Frank Serpico and the Knapp Commission hearings from the 1970s. The last week in June, right before the academy graduation, Dinkins tried to get control of the issue by announcing an independent panel, the Mollen Commission, to investigate corruption in the department. Brown, his own commissioner, publicly opposed him on it, which fed people's impressions that the department was unaccountable and nobody was in charge. The public was turning on the cops. The cops were turning on the mayor. It was ugly. As our class was graduating, the media wasn't writing about the positive impact the new "Safe Streets" recruits were supposed to have. They were talking about how dirty the cops were and how ineffective the mayor was. In the *New York Times*, the headline of the article covering our graduation was: CLOUD LOOMS OVER POLICE AS ROOKIES JOIN THE FORCE.

That same night, Friday July 3, while we were out celebrating with our families, the tension and bad blood finally boiled over. Three cops from the anticrime unit of the 34th Precinct in Washington Heights were on patrol in an unmarked car on St. Nicholas Avenue at 162nd Street when they saw this young Dominican guy, Jose "Kiko" Garcia. They said he had a suspicious bulge in his waistband. One of the officers, Michael O'Keefe, got out to stop and question him. According to the police, what happened next was O'Keefe confronted Garcia in the lobby of his building. Garcia tried to get away; they struggled. Garcia went for his gun, a .38, and O'Keefe pulled his revolver and shot him.

Two Dominican women who lived across the street claimed different. They said O'Keefe approached Garcia, unprovoked, started calling him racial slurs, dragged him into the building lobby, and began beating him. According to them, Garcia didn't resist at all. He was curled up, crying for his mother while O'Keefe beat him. Then, with Garcia pinned on the lobby floor, the cop pulled out his gun and shot him.

As the sun came up Saturday morning, word started to spread through the neighborhood: the cops killed an innocent man. People started pouring into the streets, throwing rocks at the patrol cars on the scene. It escalated from there. Two completely different stories took off. In the newspapers, Garcia was a low-level drug dealer who'd tried to shoot a cop. He was an illegal immigrant, a petty thug with a prior arrest for possession. On the streets of Washington Heights, Garcia was an innocent bystander, not a drug dealer but a quiet kid who never bothered anyone, who worked selling clothes as a street peddler, the victim of the same abuse Dominicans endured at the hands of the police every day. In that story, O'Keefe was the bad guy, a cop who already had a reputation for being aggressive and a history of shaking down drug dealers and making suspicious arrests.

By Sunday, organized protests had broken down into angry mobs raging all over the neighborhood, looting stores, turning over cars, setting buildings on fire. There were cordons of cops in riot gear getting pelted with bottles, going after people with nightsticks. On Monday night at the corner of 172nd and Audubon Avenue, a twenty-eight-year-old Dominican guy, Dagoberto Pichardo, was killed after plummeting from the roof of a building. Witnesses said the cops pushed him. The cops said Pichardo fell. The next night, a mob was out on that corner, hanging and burning a police officer in effigy.

After what happened in Crown Heights, the NYPD wasn't taking any chances. They flooded the neighborhood with two thousand cops. That was my first detail as a New York City police officer. They loaded sixteen of us into a van, drove us up there, and stationed us in teams on every single corner in the neighborhood. I was nervous. My first time in uniform, and here I was in the middle of a city about to blow up.

Everything turned out fine. Once we deployed in those massive numbers, the chaos died down pretty quick. But now it was time for the political storm to blow up, and it blew up right in Dinkins's face. During the riot, for three days straight, Mayor Dinkins had been out in the streets, being visible, calling for peace and calm. He also went and met with Garcia's family to express his condolences. He even went so far as to invite them to Gracie Mansion. The cops were furious. A lot of them took it as the mayor siding with the rioters over the police, like he had more sympathy for a drug dealer who tried to kill a cop than he did for a cop who, allegedly, almost got killed. Cops were savaging him in the press. They called him out to his face when he addressed an afternoon roll call at the 34th.

Two months later, on September 10, the grand jury findings in the case came back, and the DA announced that the shooting was justified and O'Keefe wouldn't be indicted. The physical evidence was consistent with O'Keefe's account of the shooting and directly contradicted what the two Dominican women claimed to have seen. They'd said that Garcia was shot in the back while O'Keefe had him pinned facedown on the floor; the autopsy showed Garcia was shot standing up, with the first bullet hitting him from the front, as the cop had said. An independent pathologist hired by the family to examine the autopsy results said the same thing. There was also a tape recording of O'Keefe crying for help over the radio before the shots were fired.

It was a disaster for the mayor. Dinkins had fought for over a billion dollars in state and federal funding to implement the "Safe Streets" program, but because he blew it in Crown Heights and Washington Heights, his opponents were able to make him look soft on crime. He was "anti-cop," a man who coddled the families of drug dealers.

Six days later, it was the cops' turn to start a riot. A rally had been planned for a while. The police were going to march on city hall to protest the mayor's plans to create an independent civilian review board to monitor the police, but once the Washington Heights thing happened it became more about that. The police union, the Patrolmen's Benevolent Association, made this big push for the rally. The PBA wielded a lot of power in the city, even more so than today. I'd been assigned to the 114th Precinct in Astoria, Queens, and was on my training rotation there. At every roll call the PBA delegates were talking about this rally, telling us to come down. They were putting up posters all over the precinct.

For PBA-sponsored events, the city gives cops time off. The people with the most seniority are first in line, so it was left to the younger guys to police the rally, which was how I got assigned to work it. I was posted right on the steps to city hall. There were ten thousand cops packed into the park and the streets, waving signs: NO MORE SYMPATHY FOR DRUG DEALERS; DINKINS SOLD OUT THE NYPD; NO JUSTICE. NO POLICE. Everybody was chanting "Dinkins must go! Dinkins must go!"

They were drinking, too, a lot of them. I mean, we're talking *drunk*. Whenever cops get together, there's liquor and beer involved. That's what they do. Guys had coolers of Budweiser in the trunks of cars, like they were tailgating. They were sitting around before it started, going, "C'mon, drink up. Let's go."

It was bad. It wasn't a political protest. It was a bunch of shit-faced white cops in the streets. It was easily the most racist thing I've ever seen in my life. In the papers, when they called Dinkins soft on crime or said he coddled drug dealers, everybody knew what that was code for: the black mayor sides with the black hoodlums and the Dominican thugs and not the honest, law-abiding white people. But out there at that rally, nobody was talking in code. They didn't care. They were yelling, "Fuck Dinkins." They were calling him a coon, a nigger. They called him a washroom attendant. There were a couple of black cops out there protesting. Not many, but a few. I was like, *"Really? You're a part of this."* But that's how strong the peer pressure is to fit in. Some guys fold.

A bunch of people made speeches. The worst was Rudy Giuliani, our future mayor, who'd lost to Dinkins in 1989 as the Republican nominee. Giuliani was up there at the microphone, cursing, trashing Dinkins, race-baiting. It was ugly. And that was the peaceful part of the day. After hours of getting whipped into a frenzy, a bunch of cops finally lost it and started going nuts. It turned into a full-on riot. They started trampling the barricades, jumping on the roofs of cars. And there was nothing we could do to stop them. There were only around three hundred patrolmen assigned to the rally. What were we supposed to do? Some drunk lieutenant shoves past me, what am I going to do, arrest him? Arrest a superior officer? I'm a trainee barely two months out of the academy. Police can't police police. It don't work. The cops doing crowd control weren't in control of anything. We had to stand back and watch it happen.

It was easily the saddest day I've ever had as a cop. They trampled the barricades and stormed up the steps to city hall. From city hall, they swarmed over to the Brooklyn Bridge and took over the bridge and blocked traffic for over an hour, pissed off, pissy drunk, waving their angry signs and yelling horrible racist shit at the top of their lungs.

Welcome to the NYPD.

20

Not Exactly
Starsky & Hutch

When I joined the 114th Precinct in Astoria, I was in a class of fifteen guys. Our training sergeant was this guy named Hasselbeck. The training sergeant gives you lectures, teaches you procedures, educates you about the area you'll be patrolling. The rookies take turns going out with him on tours every couple weeks. Hasselbeck was a real throwback, a no-nonsense guy, very German, not a guy you'd sit and joke around with. He had some serious time on the job, was highly decorated. I was driving with him one day, and we were talking. He asked me where I was from. I told him South Queens. He said, "Oh, yeah? When I was in Queens Narcotics I locked up a lot of guys down there."

"Really?"

"Yeah. I was with the operation that took down the Supreme Team."

The hair on the back of my neck stood up. He started talking about the operation, where the stash houses were, how they took it down. He knew everything. He started naming names: Prince, Malik, Born Justice. I nodded along, played it off like I knew them from growing up in the hood. I said, "Yeah, yeah. I know those guys. I seen 'em around."

He said, "Oh, I know 'em, too. Those guys know me *well.*"

Cops and criminals have a strange relationship, something I would eventually learn for myself. Joining the NYPD had been my ticket out of the streets, a way to get a good job and take care of my family. But the truth of it was I got out of the streets just to go right back in, back to the same world, only on the other side. I was going to have to be extra careful to make sure no one ever found out.

Hasselbeck was a good training sergeant. He was tough, but I liked him. He taught me a lot about what the job is actually like. In the academy, we learned "This is the crime, this is the charge, here's what you do." Nothing in the streets is that black-and-white. There's a lot of improvising, a lot of ad-libbing. The police have a great deal of discretion. They have the power to arrest someone, but more important than that, they have the power *not* to arrest someone. Cops get called to a bar fight: was it an assault or a couple of hot tempers that need to cool off? Cops catch a teenager with a loose joint: do they haul her in or take her home and trust her parents to handle it?

Most people go through their lives and their only interaction with the criminal justice system is maybe a speeding ticket. But for people who actually get arrested, even if they're completely innocent and never convicted, that experience impacts their lives forever. They get fingerprinted, get their mug shot taken, spend the night in jail. Their family has to borrow to come up with collateral for a bond, to pay for an attorney. They'll have to answer questions on job applications.

It's an experience that marks them, especially if they're black or Hispanic. Once the cops know who they are, once the system knows who they are, that's the first step down a road that goes nowhere good. Cops have the power to prevent that from happening. Once someone is arrested, they get a lawyer, there's a judge. There are people and checks and balances that play a role in deciding what happens to that person. But the power not to arrest someone, that power lies 100 percent with the police officer—and that's a lot of power for one person to have.

I spent many nights in the army barracks dreaming of being a cop, and I had this idea of what the job was going to be like. I grew up watching *Starsky & Hutch* and *Hill Street Blues*. I thought I was going to be in the middle of the action, charging into gun battles. During the application process, I told my investigator that I wanted to go SWAT. I wanted to be rappelling out of helicopters on ropes, scaling down walls in tactical riot gear. He turned and made a joke to the other guys in the office, like, "Hey, this kid thinks he's going to be jumping out of helicopters!" They laughed, but that's how I felt. I wanted to go out and conquer the world.

When I got out of the academy, it was like someone slammed a foot on the brakes. It's not cops and robbers 24/7. There's a lot of downtime. Days can go by where nothing remotely interesting happens—and that's a good thing. The one-fourteen was not a high-crime area. It's one of the nicest areas in Queens. It's a large precinct. There were a couple of high-crime pockets, mostly around the housing projects. There were the Ravenswood Houses, the Astoria Houses, and the Queensbridge Houses, which is the largest public housing development in the city, right where the 59th Street Bridge comes over from Manhattan. Those were low-income families, almost all black and Hispanic, but the rest of the area is middle class, a lot of Greek families, East Indian families, some Middle Eastern pockets. Soccer is huge in those neighborhoods. During the World Cup it's always crazy. There's a commercial strip on Steinway Street where people go to shop and eat. If you like Greek or Middle Eastern food, you'll find the best restaurants in the city there. There's also an affluent section north of the Brooklyn Queens Expressway, near Rikers Island, with half-a-million-dollar homes. The one-fourteen also covered Silvercup Studios, where they filmed *The Cosby Show* and lots of big movies. We'd see celebrities here and there, filming in the streets around the neighborhood.

Inside the precinct, it was lily white. There were around three hundred patrolmen there at the time. Out of that, there were only twenty-eight black cops in the whole place. There was only one black supervisor, Sergeant Lee. He worked the midnight shift, and I was on the four-to-twelve. I literally never saw the guy.

The NYPD was a real old boys' club. Guys looked after each other, bent the rules for each other. If a cop got involved in something off-duty, if there was a domestic incident, a DUI, his buddies would take care of it, make it go away. They couldn't cover up a DUI where a civilian got injured, but if a cop tried to drive home drunk and he bounced off a telephone pole and hit a couple parked cars, guys would pick him up, drive him home, call a pal to come get the car.

One of the top chiefs in the department lived in the nice area by Rikers. There was a bar on Ditmars Boulevard where he'd drink. He'd be in there in full uniform, drunk out of his mind, getting loud, causing a scene. The bartender would call the precinct and we'd get sent over to pick up him and drive him home. I remember one time me and my partner had to drive him. He was in the backseat wasted, screaming, cussing us out for dragging him out of the bar. This was a two-star chief, and we were a couple of rookies. What do you do? You go along with it. That's the culture. Either you were part of it, or you didn't fit in.

The one-fourteen was like any other place people work. There were some truly good people, guys like Sergeant Hasselbeck, who cared about the job and excelled at what he did. Then there were the people in the middle, punching the clock. They'd show up, do the job, and go home. If an officer stays with the NYPD for twenty years, he can retire with a full pension. Twenty-and-out, they call it. A lot of guys were there for that.

Then there was the bottom of the barrel. I'll never forget Patrol Officer Burke, the biggest drunk in the precinct. The guy would come to work smelling like a whole bottle of Calvin Klein cologne trying to mask the smell of alcohol. He'd be walking around, sweating profusely, slurring his speech. Burke had been to what we called "the farm." The NYPD has this farm upstate where they send alcoholics to detox. Some guys had been there three, four, five times. They'd send an officer up, dry him out, put him back on the job. We carried our .38s in a swivel holster, which spins all the way around on your belt. Burke would always be walking through, trying to look sober, spinning his .38 around on his belt. It was crazy. I was like, Nobody sees this? But they would turn him out on patrol like that. I had to work with him a couple of times. I was scared to go out with the guy.

Cops like Burke never got fired. They'd hang around the department for years. Same with PO Greeley, maybe the worst guy I've ever worked with. Greeley was 100 percent Irish cop. Six-foot-four, big handlebar mustache. He had about twenty years on the job. If a cop's got twenty years and he's still on patrol, that means he's either got zero ambition or he's too stupid to pass the sergeant's exam. Or both. Which was probably the case with Greeley. He was a real asshole. He always came to work smelling of liquor. Not as bad as Burke, but bad.

Greeley was a jerk with everyone, but with black cops his thing was that he wouldn't even talk to you. He'd look right through you, ignore anything you said. His attitude was "You're not even supposed to have this job, nigger," and he didn't try to hide it. There were a lot of cops like that. I'd walk into a room and say, "Hey, guys. What's going on?" And nobody would say anything. They wouldn't look up. It was like I didn't exist.

Burke and Greeley were the worst of the worst: lazy cops who couldn't care less about the job or the community. I'd say at least 25, 30 percent of the cops in the precinct fell into that category. That estimate might even be low. There was so much deadweight on the force. There's cronyism in the department today, but nothing like it was. Cops like Burke and Greeley would get in, probably had a brother or an uncle who came before them, and from then on there was no accountability whatsoever. The union would protect them no matter what they did.

It was bad enough having those cops with me on patrol, but it was worse with the sergeants and lieutenants above me, because they had actual power to make my life miserable. There was one sergeant in particular: Sergeant O'Rourke. From day one in my training he had it in for me, was on me about every little thing: "Your tie isn't straight." "Why didn't you salute me?" As a patrol officer, I had my memo book, which is where I'd keep a log of everything that happened on my shift: where I went, calls I answered, who I stopped. Superior officers are supposed to do spot checks. Scratch your book, it's called. O'Rourke would always scratch my book. Every shift. He'd flip through and find something to call me out on. White rookies would be standing right next to me, making the same mistakes, and O'Rourke would never scratch their books.

O'Rourke also gave me the worst assignments. My first day on patrol, once I was done training and part of the regular squad, O'Rourke came into roll call and started handing out assignments. When he came to me he said, "Pegues, Queens Plaza North, Twenty-Fifth to Twenty-Sixth Street." I didn't even know where that was. The guys around me were shaking their heads, because they knew. They were like, "*Damn.* What did this guy do to get sent down there?"

It was late November by that point. Cold out. Queens Plaza North was this abandoned industrial zone down where the 59th Street Bridge comes in on the Queens side, a forty-minute walk from the precinct. Back then there was nothing there. It was deserted. The other cops got posts on Steinway Street, on Ditmars Boulevard, places with shops, restaurants, people. O'Rourke put me in the middle of nowhere. Thirty degrees out, and there wasn't even a place to use the bathroom. Just empty warehouses and vacant lots. I had to walk that beat, by myself, from four to midnight. He sent me down there a few times.

Every time there was an assignment at roll call nobody wanted, it went to me. If there's a hospitalized prisoner, somebody's got to sit and watch the room. You literally do nothing but sit in a chair in the hallway of a hospital for eight hours, bored out of your mind. Every time we had a hospitalized prisoner, O'Rourke called my name. It was the same with the DOAs—dead on arrivals. Anytime there's a dead body, when an old person dies in his sleep and the neighbors report a smell, someone has to go and sit on the body and wait for the medical examiner to come and pick it up. Sometimes these people have been dead in their apartments for weeks. The stench is foul. If the ME is backed up, you could be there for hours. DOAs are probably the worst job in the NYPD. Nobody wants to work them. I worked them all the time.

It wasn't exactly *Starsky & Hutch*. Never mind jumping out of helicopters and scaling down walls. They didn't even want me being a regular cop on the beat. Whatever the worst assignment for the day was, I would hear my name. "Pegues, you got the DOA." It was automatic, like clockwork. I'd gather up my gear, head to the house or the apartment, and set up for the day, nothing to do but stare at the walls and try to ignore the smell.

21

The Biggest Gang in New York

Richard Perry was one of the other rookies in my platoon. We hit it off during the training sessions at the one-fourteen. Once training was over, people were looking to partner up. Richard and I got along, so I said, "Yo, man, let's partner up."

I was learning my way around, but Richard knew about the force. He'd grown up in a cop house. His dad was a detective first grade with Manhattan homicide, one of the most prestigious jobs in the NYPD. They lived in Bayside, where I'd been bused to middle school; Richard's friends were probably the guys who chased me and tried to beat me up back in the day. He wasn't like that at all. So that was a plus. Richard was a mild-mannered type of guy. He was smart, but he knew nothing about the streets. Everything he knew about the projects or the hood, he probably saw it on TV. So I brought that knowledge to the team, and he helped me understand the culture of the department better. We balanced each other well.

We were working a movie set when I made my first arrest. Robert De Niro was filming *A Bronx Tale* at Silvercup Studios. They were shooting a scene on location in Astoria, and I was assigned to do crowd control. It was the middle of the day. I was standing at my post. All of a sudden there was a commotion outside this bodega on the corner. These three dudes jumped this other guy. Somebody ran up to me, yelling "Officer! Officer! There's a fight! They're fighting!"

I said, "No, no. Calm down. It's just a movie. They're filming a movie."

He said, "No. This guy's really getting beat up."

I went over, and there's the star of the movie, this kid Lillo Brancato. He was being assaulted outside this bodega. He'd had words with these three kids or something. I stepped in and broke it up. I arrested the three guys and cuffed them and got the Brancato kid back to the set in one piece. De Niro came over to see what had happened. He thanked me, gave me this signed eight-by-ten photo from *Raging Bull*. It was a pretty great way to make your first arrest.

My second arrest was a completely different experience. I was on foot patrol, and I caught this young black kid stealing a bike. I cuffed him, sat him on the sidewalk, and called for a patrol car to come and take him in to be processed. The patrol car showed up. It was two white cops. I was doing my paperwork, and they were watching the prisoner. I don't know if the kid mouthed off to them or what, but they started kicking him. He was cuffed, on the pavement, and they started beating him up. I ran over, going "Yo, what are you doing? He's got cuffs on."

You can't hit a prisoner once he's cuffed—or you're not supposed to at least. That's textbook. That's Rule #1 of police brutality. And these guys were violating it like they didn't even care. When the sergeant showed up on the scene, he said, "Pegues, what you got?"

I told him, "Sir, I don't have anything, because I'm not taking this collar. I had this guy cuffed, and those two started beating him up. So I don't have anything to do with this. You see those injuries? I don't have anything to do with those. I'm not taking this arrest. They can have it. And the next time I see something like that I'm calling IAB."

Some of the black cops in the one-fourteen wanted to fit in to the culture, felt like they *had* to fit in. I never did. Every precinct had a precinct club. It was a social thing, but it was also a big part of advancing your career, getting to know the other guys, getting friendly with everyone. You paid $50 a year to join and once a month they had "meetings," which were usually a party at an Irish bar, everybody getting drunk and loud. I went to one, and I never went again.

At this party there was a ton of that fake-friendly, hey-I'm-just-kidding kind of racism that I can't stand. Somebody straight-up hates me because I'm black, okay, I can handle that. But those guys who crack jokes about fried chicken and watermelon while they're smiling and buying you a round, expecting you to laugh and play it off? That's what these parties were. A lot of the black cops would go along. They'd go to the parties, drink, laugh, pretend like it was nothing. I couldn't do it. On the job, guys would make cracks, racial jokes, and I would be like, "Who do you think you're talking to? Don't play that with me. You talk to those other guys like that. Don't talk to me like that."

They'd go, "Aw, there you go with your bullshit, Pegues." But eventually they stopped bothering me. It made me something of an outcast, but I was fine with that. I knew what my purpose was. I was out of the streets and living a different life. I was there for myself, not to be a part of their club.

I made it clear I wasn't going to play along, but I didn't let them get to me, either. That's the fine line you have to walk. I respected the rank and the uniform. I was always "Yes, sir" and "No, sir" no matter what kind of hassle they were giving me. In fact, the more racist you were to me, the nicer I was to you. They hated it. Sergeant O'Rourke would be in the break room, and I'd say, "Hey, Sarge. I'm going out for a bite, you want me to get you something?"

"No."

"You sure? Sandwich? Cup of coffee?"

"No."

"Snickers bar? Bag of chips?"

"No."

"It's really not a problem, sir."

"Fuck you, Pegues. I don't want no fuckin' food."

They hated when I was nice to them.

The racism directed at me, I learned how to adapt and deal with it. But the racism directed at the black community, out in the streets, that was harder to swallow. I could refuse to participate in it, but I didn't have the leverage to change anything. I'd be in the precinct, some cop would come in with a collar, and you could tell the kid had been tuned up. That's the jargon for it: tune somebody up, rough 'em up. The suspect would be cuffed, his face all bruised and bleeding, cursing and yelling, "Yo, fuckin' cops fucked me up! Fuckin' cops fucked me up!" Cop would say the kid resisted arrest, and as a rookie you can't challenge a veteran officer's account. He says that's what happened, that's what happened.

We had this one plainclothes cop, this big, thick-necked Irish guy. Crazy. Messed-up attitude. I'd swear he was on steroids. He rarely brought in a suspect who wasn't black and blue. A lot of times he'd bring in guys wearing a turban. That's what cops call it when a guy comes in with the gauze wrapped around his head from an injury, meaning the guy was so messed up they had to take him to the hospital to get him patched before bringing him into the station. Wearing the turban—it happened so often there was a name for it.

I call the NYPD the biggest gang in New York. I know a little about gangs; I joined one. You join a gang because you feel insecure being on your own. You join the Supreme Team and you can walk around with your chest puffed out a bit, knowing that if somebody steps to you, you've got a whole crew of guys right behind you to back you up. Joining a gang makes you a tough guy, even if you're not one.

If an NYPD officer gets in trouble—or if he starts some trouble himself—he can get on the radio and have three hundred officers there in two minutes, all of them with the authority to use lethal force. There's not a single gang out there that can match that kind of power—not the Bloods, not the Crips, none of them. That's what pissed me off so much. Most of these cops, without the badge, they'd be middle-management geeks at a desk job somewhere. But they get that shield and they think they're Superman. Without the uniform, they'd be scared to walk down the street where I come from. With the uniform, they'll walk right into the projects and start messing with people for no reason, slamming kids against the wall for talking smack to them. Legally, you *can* talk back to a cop. You can say anything you want to a cop. It's the First Amendment. You can call a cop a pig and an asshole, and technically, he's not allowed to do anything. That's how it's supposed to work with the police, but that's not how it works with a gang.

The other thing that's true about a gang is that once the culture or mentality is set, that's it. It's almost impossible to change it. Everyone adopts it. Everyone is scared to challenge it. And the culture of the NYPD reflects the country we live in. In white neighborhoods we were there to protect and serve. In minority neighborhoods and the projects, we were there to maintain order. It was like you had two different jobs with two different job descriptions. From day one on patrol, the mentality was: If you're looking for an arrest, go to the projects. That was automatic. That was the default.

There have always been quotas in the NYPD. They don't call them quotas, but that's what they are. They want you to write so many citations per month, make so many arrests per month, and so on. Nobody cared if you met them. There was no accountability. Some guys were content to sit in the patrol car and wait for a call to come in. But Richard and I, we were young and ambitious. We were hunters, out looking for the action, looking to put up big numbers. If you're on patrol in a nice neighborhood, like the affluent area up by Rikers, you have to hunt for crime. There isn't much. Everyone's indoors. You've got to go up and down the block for hours, looking for people peering through windows or pulling car doors. But you go to the projects, everyone's out and about, hanging on the corners. For poor people, time and money are scarce, and they often find themselves committing infractions they can't avoid. Maybe they can't afford to get a brake light fixed. Maybe they can't get off work to go do their vehicle inspection. Maybe they're out on the corner drinking because there's a difficult situation at home. So if it's the end of the month and you need to write citations or you're looking to make a collar, that's where you go.

When people talk about the problems between minorities and the cops, the beatings and the shootings get the headlines. But those are the incidents that spiral out of control. The real problem, the real frustration, is the day to day. There's an arrogance about the way a lot of cops treat minorities—all minorities, not just blacks. I was on patrol one afternoon, not with Richard but with this other guy, and we got a call about a disturbance at a local mosque. We drove over. It wasn't a grand cathedral-type mosque; it was more like a regular building, like someone's house, that had been made into a mosque. We walked up, the imam came to the door, and we said, "We got a call. What's going on? May we come in?" The imam said sure but we had to take our shoes off. So I sat down and started unbuckling my boots. I turned to my white partner and he was just standing there. He said, "I'm not taking my shoes off."

"What do you mean, you're not taking your shoes off?"

"Exactly what I said. I'm not taking them off."

"You have to take them off."

"I'm not taking them off."

"Take them off."

"Fuck that. I'm not taking my fucking shoes off."

I pointed to the pile of shoes by the door. I said, "You see that pile of shoes? You see those guys praying in there? Those are their shoes. You can't go in with your shoes on, and I can't go in without backup. You're going to let me go in by myself?"

We argued for at least ten minutes. Finally I said, "Look, I'm going in, and if something happens to me, you can explain to the captain why you violated procedure and didn't back up your partner." He gave in and took his shoes off. Something like that never would have happened at a Catholic church or a synagogue. It would have been "Yes, Father" or "Yes, Rabbi" to whatever they needed. But at a mosque, this officer couldn't be bothered. He was totally disrespectful of the people there.

That attitude was routine among a lot of the cops I worked with.

There was almost no effort to change or improve it, and the efforts the department did make were pathetic. After nine months on the job, the first week of March in 1993, we had to go to the academy for a mandatory cultural awareness training class. It was a complete joke. First off, the NYPD is a paramilitary organization. What the top brass says, goes. What the chiefs want to get done, gets done. In a paramilitary organization, change doesn't happen from the bottom up. It comes from the top down. But the guy they had teaching the class was some low-level instructor from the academy. You had sergeants, lieutenants, and captains forced to sit in on this class. You can't have a junior staffer telling ranking officers what to do. It don't work. That right there told me the class wasn't a priority. It was an obligatory thing the department was doing to say it had been done, to cover its ass.

The instructor was this white guy. He actually started off the class by saying, "Look, I'm sorry you guys have to sit through this..." That was how he set it up. For the rest of the class he just read things off a lesson plan that we were supposed to know about different ethnicities—like how you're supposed to take your shoes off at a mosque. Nobody paid any attention. Guys were reading the newspaper, checking their beepers. The only time people actually engaged with the material was to crack jokes about it. Cops were making racist jokes *in* the cultural awareness seminar, and even the instructor was laughing along. Halfway through the class I looked around and there were at least a half a dozen cops with their heads down on their desks, asleep. One of them was snoring.

My army intake photo.

In the field during basic training.

Me and my father on the day I graduated
from the police academy.

My father, Richard Russell Sloan.

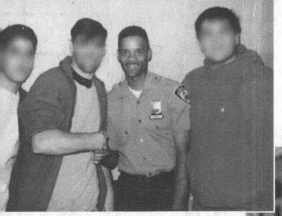

The perps from my first arrest.

With LL Cool J at a youth event at the Astoria Houses.

The cornrows had to go when I was promoted to lieutenant at the eight-one in Bed-Stuy.

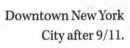

Downtown New York City after 9/11.

Meeting then Senator Hillary Clinton at a church in Brooklyn.

My family and Ray Kelly celebrating my promotion to lieutenant (left to right: Natasha, Brendale, me, Diquan, and Kenyetta).

With Mary J. Blige at a store opening in Harlem.

My family and then Chief of Department Joseph Esposito
celebrating my promotion to deputy inspector.

My staff at the
six-seven.

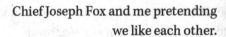

Chief Joseph Fox and me pretending
we like each other.

Addressing the troops at J'Ouvert.

Speaking at a conference for NOBLE (National Organization of Black Law Enforcement Executives) inside the Compstat war room.

Meeting President Barack Obama at the one hundredth annual NAACP convention.

Ray Kelly playing the drums at a community event in the six-seven.

With then Mayor Michael Bloomberg at a reception in honor of the 2009 West Indian American Day Carnival.

My two youngest kids, daughter Cori (left) and son Cordale (right).

22

That Cool Cop

After a year on the force, I was playing in a police basketball tournament at the Milbank Center in Harlem. The NYPD has intramural sports and games between the precincts; it's one of the social parts of the job that I actually enjoyed. There was this cop on the team I was playing against, a young black guy named Alex Brown. During the game he kept saying to me, "Yo, man. I know you from somewhere. Where I know you from?" I shrugged. We kept playing. He couldn't let it go. "Yo, I *know* you. Where I know you from?"

I played it off, said he must have me confused with someone else. But I knew exactly where he knew me from. I knew it as soon as he opened his mouth: He was the undercover who'd tried to buy from me back on 198 and Murdock, the guy who came over acting all cracked out but who was obviously in great shape under his ratty, messed-up outfit. I told him to get lost. Then I filed away his face and never forgot it, just in case he came around again. So when he started talking to me on the court that day, years later, I knew who he was immediately. He and I actually became great friends. We studied for the captain's exam together. To this day he doesn't know.

Once I left the streets, I left them forever. I wanted to be a good cop. Most cops are good cops, but because I'd been on the other side I had an even greater sense of the need to do right. I regretted the crimes I'd committed growing up, the people I hurt, the poison

I sold. So I was the most straight-edge, by-the-book cop in the one-fourteen. On patrol, we'd stop and eat lunch at these great restaurants and diners on Steinway Street. The owners would never let us pay. You'd eat and no bill would come, or they'd only charge you for your coffee. Sometimes you'd get a huge plate of shrimp for two dollars, and they'd say, "Thanks, officers! Make sure you look out for us. We like to see you guys come around." It's a tradition that's been passed down. My partners would enjoy the free food. I was afraid to take it. I thought IAB would be watching or people would think I was doing wrong. I wanted to be on the up-and-up. I'd try to give the waitresses money. Usually they wouldn't take it. Sometimes I'd give a dollar and ask for four quarters so it would at least look like I was paying in case someone was watching.

When you're a cop, temptation is everywhere. People want to give you a free lunch, a free TV. Especially with drugs, the money that's lying around for the taking is insane. Late one night I was out on patrol on Astoria Boulevard, and me and this other cop pulled this guy over, a white guy in a sedan. It was for a broken taillight or something like that. We walked up alongside the car, me on the driver's side and my partner on the other. There was this big duffel bag in the backseat. I said, "Sir, what's in the bag?"

He said, "I don't know."

"You don't know? That's not your bag?"

"That ain't mine, officer. That's yours."

I said, "That's *my* bag? Well, I guess you won't mind if I check to see what's in it."

We searched the bag. It was full of money, stacks of cash bundled up in rubber bands. The other cop looked at me with these raised eyebrows, like, "*Yo*, we *got* this. Jackpot."

I shook my head: "Hell, no." IAB runs sting operations on cops all the time. No way was I getting in that kind of trouble. We took the guy in. When they counted the money, it was something like $30,000. I'm going to throw away a career for half of thirty grand? Not a chance.

I'd seen so many of my friends go to jail, I couldn't bring myself to break the rules. I didn't even want to bend them.

The irony is that, even though I was the most by-the-book cop out there, most of the guys I worked with thought I was a thug. I'd changed who I was on the inside, but in terms of my style and my appearance, I stayed true to where I came from. Cops don't wear uniforms to work; we show up in street clothes, go to the locker room, and dress out. I came to work with the hat to the back, the gold chain, the Adidas tracksuit or the saggy jeans. Whatever the current hip-hop style was, that's what I had on when I arrived. The other officers were always cracking jokes. "Hey, how'd this thug get in here?" "I thought you were a cop, Pegues. Why you dress like a criminal?"

That was their perception. I can remember being on patrol with Richard. We'd be out, there'd be a group of kids hanging out on the corner, and Richard would say, "Hey, check them out."

"What about 'em?"

"Look at 'em. They look like they're in a gang. Let's toss 'em. I bet we find something."

I'd say, "Man, that's the same shit I wore to work this morning. Did you not see me come in? Not everyone who dresses that way is a thug. It's *fashion*."

The thing is, I would still say that Richard Perry was a good cop. He was a decent person, but he didn't understand the culture of the place he was being asked to police. We'd walk through the projects on patrol, folks would be hanging out, and I'd be like, "Yo, wassup? What's good? Everybody a'ight?" I'd look over at Richard and he'd be tense, looking around suspiciously, not talking to anybody. I'd say to him, "Yo, you got to calm down. Relax. These people are cool. You're not going to develop any relationships with them coming through here like a tightwad." I understood the projects. Those were my people. That was my world.

Kids in the ghetto hang out on the corner because there's simply nothing else to do. Not every corner is a drug corner, and even on a drug corner, like back on 198 and Murdock, not every kid out there is involved in what's going down. Because I'd been in the streets, I could look at the corners and I knew exactly what I was looking at: This guy was in charge, this guy was the runner, that guy was the lookout, those kids are the wannabes trying to hang out and look cool. Police work came easy to me; I already knew everything the bad guys were doing.

There were a lot of drugs moving through the projects in the one-fourteen. There was a narcotics unit for the precinct. As a patrol officer, if you saw something go down in front of you you'd make an arrest, but otherwise narcotics did the surveillance and the buy-and-busts. Still, I wanted to keep things on my watch as quiet as possible. I started patrolling this one particular block around the Queensbridge Houses on the regular. I could tell pretty quickly who the crews were and who was doing what. I'd go up to them and talk to them and say, "Look, guys. From four to twelve this is my block. What you do after that is none of my business. You be cool with me, and I'll be cool with you. Just don't do anything in front of me, okay? I want us to be good, but I actually am a cop and I will send you to jail."

There was this one kid, a total hard case, wouldn't listen to me. He wanted to be the big man on the block. He was like, "Fuck that cop. I'm gonna do what I wanna do." He kept hustling. So one night I called for backup. While they were on their way, I walked over to stop and question him. Once I heard the sirens coming in the distance I started hassling him in front of his crew. Because I knew what he'd do. He had to be the tough guy, showing off for his boys. I kept on baiting him, and then finally he blew up at me right as the patrol car arrived. I arrested him for disorderly conduct, and they hauled him off. After that everybody on the corner knew: Officer Pegues ain't playing. The rest of the crew fell in line, and I was able to keep the block quiet.

At the same time, I knew that not every kid on the corner was the same as that hard case. I tried to use discretion, good judgment. One night I was patting this kid down. It was a routine stop and frisk. I was looking for a gun. He didn't have a gun, but I could tell patting him down he had five vials of crack in his pocket. Kid knew he was busted. He was sweating. I had to look at this kid and decide: Is he a hard case or a kid like I used to be, a guy making bad choices who deserves a second chance? I let him go. I didn't even confiscate the crack. I said, "I see you out here again, you're going to prison for a long time." I never saw him again.

It didn't take me long to develop good relationships in the community, especially in the projects. I was approachable. I was fair. I also never looked down on them, because I was only a couple of years removed from living where they were. People started coming to me with their problems. How to get their car back after it was towed, how to navigate the courts, what to do if their kid was in trouble—things you're supposed to be able to call the cops for, but that black people never do because they're afraid.

I had a strong connection with them through hip-hop, too. I'd grown up with Run-DMC and LL Cool J in Hollis and St. Albans. Queensbridge was the other big spot for hip-hop in the borough. A lot of famous rappers and DJs came out of there—Marley Marl, MC Shan, Roxanne Shante, Tragedy Khadafi, Nas. That was their turf, and now it was my beat. It was fun. I developed relationships with them. I knew them to say "Hi" around the hood. They'd be like, "Yo, that's that cool cop." Everyone knew I was the cool cop because I could fit in. Hip-hop culture was my culture, and I never left it.

I had this old friend Brian who was LL Cool J's manager; he also managed Nas for a while. Nas was coming up at the time, had just bought himself a Lexus 300. I'd see him driving around in it. He came by the precinct a few times, because this or that friend had been picked up. He'd find me and we'd chat and I'd help him with whatever he was there for. Eric B. had a recording studio in Astoria. I'd stop in whenever I was on patrol over there. The same way the white cops would stop in the diner, I'd go by the studio, drop in to say, "What's up? Everything good?"

That first year I was on the beat, LL Cool J was in town working on *14 Shots to the Dome*, his follow-up to *Mama Said Knock You Out*. He asked me to come in on my off hours to do security at the studio for him. I even got to be on the album. While they were recording the track "God Bless," Todd asked me to step in and ad-lib something on the record. The line in the third verse, "I thought you fell off, kid!" That's me. That's my hip-hop claim to fame.

There was a group that did youth programs in the Astoria projects. The youth officer from the one-fourteen knew that I was friendly with LL Cool J. She reached out and asked me if I could set something up for him to come and speak. So I helped her do that. He came down, met with the kids, which was a huge deal for them. I was like the official hip-hop liaison of the one-fourteen, probably one of the only cops in New York reaching out to have a positive relationship with the hip-hop community.

Outside of my hip-hop connection, my first two years on patrol were pretty typical: a couple of DUIs, a breaking and entering, a grand theft auto, lots of domestic disturbances. Domestics take up nearly half your time as a cop, sadly. Guys beating their wives, spouses yelling at each other until the neighbors call the cops.

There were some crazy calls. One was an EDP, an emotionally disturbed person. A husband had called in his wife. She was in the backyard freaking out, having an episode. She had a knife to her stomach and was threatening to kill herself. I managed to talk her down and she surrendered. February of '93 was the first World Trade Center attack, a truck bomb parked in the underground garage of the North Tower. It's hard to imagine now, post 9/11, but there was no change in policy after that first attack, no mandate to go out and look for terrorists. Everyone saw it as a onetime thing.

After a couple years, Richard and I were both looking to get promoted. There are a few ways you can move up from patrol officer. You can study for the sergeant's exam and move up through the ranks. You can try to make detective in a special division like homicide or narcotics, get your gold shield and move up there. But the assignment everybody wanted was the Street Crime Unit. If you went there, it was a big thing.

Every precinct has an Anti-Crime Unit, a team of plainclothes cops tasked with making major felony arrests and getting illegal guns off the streets; Michael O'Keefe, the cop who shot Kiko Garcia in Washington Heights, was part of the Anti-Crime Unit for the three-four. The Street Crime Unit was the citywide version of that, only way more prestigious. It was an elite squad of around 140 plainclothes officers. They had their own headquarters on Randall's Island, separate from any precinct. To get in you had to have perfect recommendations from your commanding officer, no civilian complaints against you, and no prior shootings. They called themselves "The Best of the Finest." Their slogan was "We Own the Night."

Richard and I were young, eager, and we wanted to get the bad guys. So we applied. What I didn't know was that less than 3 percent of the cops in Street Crime were black. At that point, Richard and I both had the exact same amount of time on the job, two years. A couple months after we applied, we were heading to roll call and I checked my mailbox. I had a letter. It was my application, returned. It had writing on it in big red letters saying I needed at least three years to apply. I showed the letter to Richard and said, "Look, we need three years to get in."

We both shrugged and said "Oh, well" and went in and sat down. Minutes later, at that exact same roll call, the sergeant called out, "Perry, you've got twenty minutes to get over to Randall's Island for your interview for Street Crime."

I was like, "You've gotta be kidding me." I don't know why I was surprised. I shouldn't have been. Richard didn't know what to say. He looked at me like, "Uh . . . Corey, man, I'm—I'm sorry . . ."

I said, "Yo, don't sweat it. Good luck on your interview."

23

Doing Something

In November of 1993, New York City went to the polls to vote for mayor: Another four years of David Dinkins, or Rudy Giuliani. During that police rally in front of city hall in '92, when I heard Giuliani out there on the loudspeakers race-baiting the crowd, I can remember clearly thinking, *This* guy wants to be the mayor? What a clown. He'll never win. Then Dinkins blew it.

The city's murder rate peaked in 1990: 2,245 bodies, six homicides a day. The press hammered Dinkins on it. He never delivered on his plan for community policing. He talked about replacing the heavy-handed TNT squads with Officer Friendly walking the beat, but the high-crime areas were in the black and Hispanic neighborhoods, and the NYPD went and recruited thousands of white cops from the suburbs and Staten Island, guys like Richard Perry. The department needed more black and Hispanic cops to reach out and build relationships in those communities, but they were not only failing to recruit us, they were actively weeding us out. A black recruit with one traffic summons would be disqualified while a white recruit with a stack of speeding tickets was getting in because he knew somebody. The rollout of "Safe Streets" was also too slow. Most of the new cops paid for by the program didn't get out of the academy until 1994. By then Dinkins was gone.

Dinkins's biggest problem was that he thought he could please everyone. He didn't want to ruffle anybody's feathers. With the riots in Crown Heights and in Washington Heights, he wanted to stand by the cops and support the protestors at the same time. You can't do that. People say they want consensus and bipartisanship, but what they really want is for you to pick a side and fight for it. That's what people respect. Rudy Giuliani gave that to people. He made a play for the angry white vote by promising to crack down on all the unruly black and brown folk. And he kept his promise.

Cops were crazy for Giuliani. They liked him because he was a prosecutor, a crime fighter. He was pro-cop. The Patrolman's Benevolent Association might as well have been an official part of the Giuliani campaign. They were putting up signs and stickers everywhere. After Giuliani won, the big question was who he was going to put at commissioner. Lee Brown had stepped down in August of '92, right after the Washington Heights riot. His wife had cancer. That was the official reason, but it was also true that a lot of the rank and file had lost confidence in him. Ray Kelly was Brown's number two, and Dinkins promoted him to take Brown's place.

I liked Kelly. He was a cop's cop. Thirty years on the job. He knew the culture and the institution inside and out. Under Kelly, crime actually leveled off and things cooled down a bit. He handled the police response to the first World Trade Center bombing. He eased some of the tensions with the black community by going and speaking at black churches and reaching out for more black recruits. But Kelly was Dinkins's man, and that alone meant Giuliani was never going to keep him in the job.

Back then New York had three separate police forces: housing, transit, and the city. Each was its own completely separate bureaucracy. The division never made any sense from a policing perspective. The only reason for it was money. City cops worked for the city. Transit and housing were state and federal; having transit cops and housing cops made New York eligible for extra funding from Albany and DC to operate those programs.

City cops considered themselves the real cops. Housing and transit were looked down on, and transit was probably the lowest of the three. Transit cops were glorified security guards rousting homeless people for pissing on the subway; it wasn't real police work. Then, in 1990, Bill Bratton took over as chief of transit, and everything changed. Bratton was a cop from Boston. He came off like your average Irish cop in his demeanor, but his thinking about law enforcement was 180 degrees from what anyone else was doing at the time. The NYPD ran itself like a club. Bratton ran his department like a corporation, with him as the CEO. He would talk about team-building and efficiency and managerial strategy. Bratton was also a big believer in the "Broken Windows" theory: that the failure to police minor offenses like graffiti, loud music, and open containers encouraged a lawless atmosphere that led to larger, more violent crimes. Deploy a policy of zero tolerance on small problems, he believed, and you prevent bigger ones.

When Bratton took over, the subways were horrible. They stank like a toilet, were covered in graffiti, panhandlers bothering you nonstop. Getting mugged on the subway was like a rite of passage for New Yorkers, something people accepted as a part of life in the city. Bratton started his reforms by turning transit cops into real cops. He gave them new uniforms, dark blue sweaters that looked more professional. He upgraded the entire transit force to 9-millimeter handguns. At the time, the NYPD still used .38 revolvers, and the PBA had been petitioning city hall for years to upgrade to the 9-millimeter. The argument for them was simple: The bad guys had them, so the cops needed them, too. Dinkins balked at making the change, but over at transit Bratton had his own separate budget and he answered to the MTA, not Dinkins. So transit cops got the upgrade.

Then Bratton sent his cops out to be cops. Over 170,000 people a day were jumping the turnstiles without paying, costing the city over $80 million a year. He stationed plainclothes officers at the turnstiles, and they started hauling fare-jumpers out of the subway twenty at a time. Anytime a cop detains someone, that cop is off the streets for the next several hours; he's got to go back to the precinct, process the arrest, do the paperwork. Bratton started parking buses outside the subway stations to process the arrests. He called it the "bust bus." They'd handle the paperwork right there, and the cops would be back on patrol in less than an hour.

Bratton also had a lieutenant, Jack Maple, who was head of transit's central robbery division. Both Maple and Bratton were obsessed with finding new ways to tackle policing. Maple started putting up these huge maps and charts on the walls of his office. They showed the whole subway system. Maple would use colored pins and markers and crayons to track where every robbery, assault, and violent crime was happening. He tracked which ones were solved versus unsolved, what time of day they happened, who the victims were. Any piece of information he could quantify, he'd pin it to the maps and track it.

Crime isn't random. Criminals have habits. They're also not very smart. Something works once, they do it again. By tracking this information, Maple and Bratton were learning the habits of the criminals in the subways and deploying their resources accordingly. It worked. Crime in the subways fell for the first time in a decade. In Bratton's first year there was a 13 percent drop in fare-beating. There was also a 40 percent drop in robberies. As it turned out, going after turnstile-jumpers had a huge effect: One in seven fare-beaters had an outstanding warrant for a more serious offense, and one in twenty was carrying a weapon. Catching these guys at the turnstiles was preventing them from committing more crimes on the trains. Bratton and Maple were hailed as geniuses.

In April of '92 Bratton left transit to take a job back in Boston, but he was already a legend in the department: the guy who'd made transit cops into real cops. For the first time ever, guys actually wanted to go work in transit. Morale over there was way up. After his election, Giuliani announced that Bratton was coming back from Boston to be the commissioner of the NYPD. Here was a guy who was going to be good for the department. We were all amped up.

Bratton was sworn in in January of '94. Crime in the city had leveled off under Kelly, but it was still bad. In 1993, the year before Bratton took over, New York City had 86,000 robberies, 112,000 car thefts, and 1,946 homicides. On top of that, there were 5,861 people injured in shootings; a shooting is just a homicide where the victim got lucky. Bratton came in promising a 40 percent reduction of crime in three years, which was the equivalent of Babe Ruth calling his shot from home plate. Nobody had ever talked like that before.

Like the corporate-minded guy he was, Bratton had management consultants come in to evaluate the culture and the practices of the NYPD. They shined a light on how messed up and dysfunctional the department was. There was no coordination between the organized crime bureau and patrol, no communication between patrol and the detectives. The warrant squad, responsible for serving outstanding warrants to people wanted for arrest, that whole division only worked Monday to Friday, nine to five, not on nights and weekends when people might actually be home to get served.

Bratton started clearing out the cobwebs. Down at One Police Plaza, he cleaned house. New head of internal affairs, new chief of staff, new chief of department, new chief of patrol. He visited roll calls at individual precincts and gave these big motivational talks. Same as with transit, he gave us new uniforms. We'd been wearing light blue shirts with dark pants, which made us look like mall cops. Bratton brought back the dark shirts that looked more professional. He put computers in the patrol cars. He authorized the 9-millimeter pistols with the fifteen-shot clip that the patrolman's union had been asking for. It felt like a new day. Morale was at an all-time high.

Just as Bratton came on the job, the Mollen Commission came out with its findings. They weren't good. Thanks to Frank Serpico and the movie Al Pacino made about him, the NYPD was famous for corruption in the 1970s. The mob was running drugs and numbers rackets all over the city, and they'd pay off the local precincts to look the other way. The payoffs went all the way up to One Police Plaza, and nearly everybody got a taste. By the 1990s, that kind of widespread corruption had been rooted out. What was left were these deep, isolated pockets of corruption in certain precincts where the drug trade was big. Cops in those precincts weren't just on the take; they'd crossed over and become full-blown criminals. The worst of the worst was the 30th Precinct in West Harlem—the Dirty Thirty. There was so much money in crack, and the temptation was too much for some guys to handle. Cops were taking drugs off of dealers and re-selling them. Cops were breaking into drug dealers' homes to steal drugs and cash.

Bratton had enough goodwill among the rank and file that he could take on corruption in the department and still be considered pro-cop. He also had the benefit of coming in from the outside; the corruption documented in the Mollen Report had taken place before his watch, so he could challenge it without going after his own peo-ple. That April, Bratton made a surprise raid on the three-oh at mid-night. He tipped off the news cameras to be there, walked into the precinct, and marched out with dirty cops in handcuffs. The next day he held a press conference where he threw their badges into a gar-bage can. Thirty-three cops were convicted on corruption charges. Two of them committed suicide.

The single biggest change Bratton made in the NYPD was intro-ducing the crime-tracking system he and Jack Maple had developed at transit. Only now it wasn't colored pins and crayons on the wall. It was a sophisticated, computerized program for collecting and ana-lyzing data across the entire city. They called it the Computer Sta-tistical Analysis System: Compstat. Prior to Compstat, statistics on crime in New York City were only collected and submitted once every quarter, and even then it was only for record-keeping. Amazing as it sounds, nobody was using the data for anything. Under Bratton, the numbers had to be collected and turned in weekly. Every Thursday, meetings were now held in a massive war room on the eighth floor of One Police Plaza. The boroughs would rotate. One week it was Brooklyn North, the next week Queens South, the next week Staten Island, etc. At these meetings, every precinct commander would be called up to stand at a podium in front of a bank of screens and computer monitors. The crime stats from that precinct would be projected up for everyone to see. The higher-ups would grill the commanders, and they had to be able to analyze the data, draw conclusions from it, and formulate strategies to address it.

Compstat was like a firing squad. A lot of the old guard couldn't hack it. They'd never been held accountable, and they had no capacity for critical thinking. Guys would lose it and break down stammering and stuttering in the room. Some of them lost their jobs on the spot; they'd be relieved of their command right there in front of their peers. Bratton didn't care what connections you had or who your uncle in the department was—if you couldn't deliver results, you were out.

Before Compstat, as a patrolman, you never saw the precinct commander at roll call. Never. He'd be in his office reading the newspaper—or, depending on the time of day, out at a bar drinking. Now we saw him there all the time, screaming and yelling about the numbers, because he knew his job was on the line. The days of these old Irish cops rolling in late, drunk, sleeping at their desks—those days were over.

For the first time in the history of the NYPD there was real accountability. There had always been targets, monthly quotas, for what you were supposed to do as a patrolman. You had to do one arrest, twenty-five parking summonses, ten moving summonses, three red lights, and one quality-of-life summons, which is for a violation like drinking in public or playing a boom box too loud. But nobody ever checked to see if you were making the quota, and a lot of guys didn't care. There were cops in the one-fourteen who'd go six months without making a single arrest. They were riding around in their patrol cars, whistling at girls. Bratton's attitude was, No, that's not how it works. Being a cop, you don't have a job, you have a purpose. You're a public servant. Many of the older guys couldn't adapt. They washed out, took early retirement.

With Bratton the NYPD transformed itself from a reactive department into a proactive department. For years we'd never tried to prevent crime; we responded to crime as it happened. If someone got shot, we'd show up, ask questions, bag the evidence, and look for suspects. Now we were looking at the data and trying to get a jump on where there was likely to be another shooting. If we arrested someone with an illegal gun, we could look at the Compstat data and see that it was coming from an area with a lot of illegal gun activity, connect the dots, and find the person selling the guns. Before, when we arrested someone, we only ever questioned them about the crime they'd committed. Now, if we caught someone for robbery, we'd grill them about every robbery in the area, find connections, identify repeat offenders. It was such a simple change, yet nobody had thought to do it before. Having the data gave us the tools we needed to go after criminals, and having accountability on the job made sure people were using those tools the best they could.

At the end of 1994, after one year, overall crime was down 12.3 percent. Burglaries were down 9 percent. Car thefts were down 14 percent. Shootings were down 16.4 percent. Homicides fell from 1,946 to 1,561—a drop of 18.8 percent. The next year homicides fell to 1,177. The year after that, to 983. In 1995, overall crime fell another 16 percent. In 1996, another 14 percent. Bratton promised a 40 percent reduction in crime in three years, and he delivered.

Of course Bratton wasn't the only one responsible. There were other variables involved: the economy getting better, the crack epidemic tapering off. And there was one other factor in there that rarely gets mentioned. The Mollen Commission Report that gave Bratton his big win against corruption? That commission was started by Mayor Dinkins. And the reason Bratton could clear out the deadweight and replace so many people? That was because he had thousands of new officers coming into the pipeline from "Safe Streets," the program that Dinkins had pushed through the state legislature. The money for the new uniforms and the 9-millimeters and the computers in the patrol cars? All that funding came from "Safe Streets" as well.

For all the anti-cop, soft-on-crime attacks people lobbed at the first black mayor of New York, he was the one who made the turnaround possible. David Dinkins put the chess pieces in place. Bill Bratton had the strategy to use those pieces to run the board. And Rudy Giuliani took all the credit.

24

Climbing the Ladder

Practically overnight the NYPD—as lazy, bloated, corrupt as it was—transformed itself into a well-oiled machine. For me it was a real lesson in how leadership works. Change can come from the bottom, but it tends to take a long, long time. When change comes from the top, like it did with Bratton, things happen fast.

Sadly, the other lesson I learned was that it's easier to make lazy people more efficient than it is to make racist people less racist. The brand new 9-millimeters we were issued? I was one of the last guys in the precinct to get one. Rookies who came on after me got theirs weeks before I got mine. I was still getting the worst assignments, too, the DOAs and the hospital watches. The petty harassment and the daily insults never let up, not for a minute.

Richard Perry passed his interview and got accepted to the Street Crime Unit. After he left, I paired up with a new partner, Bob Russo. An Italian guy, great guy, love him like a brother. Richard never used to tell me what other cops said about me; he didn't feel comfortable doing that. Bob didn't have a filter. He'd tell me straight up.

If I have one major flaw, it's that I'm always late. No matter where I'm going, what I'm doing, meeting my wife, showing up to work, I'm twenty minutes behind. Like the ditty-bop in my walk, I've tried to fix it, but I can't. Bob used to catch hell from the sergeants over my being late. They'd ream him out. "You tell that fuckin' nigger that he'd better get his ass here on time." Or "If that nigger don't straighten his ass out, we're going to start taking it out on you, Russo. You're going to be on the fuckin' foot post." Bob would come to me saying, "Corey, please, you're killin' me. I can't keep defending you."

The sergeants would hassle me constantly. You're supposed to get an hour for dinner, but technically you're not guaranteed the whole sixty minutes. If there's an emergency, your commanding officer can send you back out. I would come in for my dinner break, and like clockwork, O'Rourke would step into the lounge after twenty minutes and say, "You need to get back out." No emergency. Just a regular Thursday night. I'd think, Really? But I'd never say that. I'd say, "No problem, sir." And I'd go.

I only lost it one time. I was in the lounge eating lunch one day, watching TV, probably sports or something. PO Greeley came in, put his food down, walked over, and without saying anything, turned off the TV I was watching, sat down, and started eating. He didn't even acknowledge me. I sat there like, You've got to be kidding me. I stood up, grabbed the edge of the table, and flipped it over, yelling, "You *motherfucker*. Who the fuck you think you are? I was fuckin' watching that."

Greeley got in my face and we went at it, screaming at each other. People came running in to break us up. People probably thought I was crazy, only three years on the job and here I was big-talking a twenty-year veteran. If the senior officer wants to pick what's on the TV in the break room, fine, I get that. But you have to treat me with respect. At least acknowledge that I exist.

I had to deal with crap out on patrol, too, and with the public you had to smile and take it. One night Bob and I answered a call about a disturbance over in the mostly white part of Astoria. I was at the door, ringing the bell. I kept ringing and ringing. No answer. I got on the radio to the dispatcher, "Central, this is 4-Adam, we're here and there's no answer."

The dispatcher came back, "4-Adam, the woman called again. She says there's a black man at her door impersonating a police officer."

I rolled my eyes. I said, "Central, you can let her know that we have these jobs, too." I could hear everybody on the radio laughing. That happened on more than one occasion.

For a black or Hispanic officer who's frustrated and wants to get promoted out of patrol, the fastest way to do it is to become a detective in narcotics. The department is always looking for black and brown faces to do undercover buy-and-bust operations in the projects. If you go that route, in eighteen months you've got a gold shield. It's a short path to a good promotion, a good pay bump, and you can bank a lot of overtime, but it's a dead end.

The command hierarchy on the NYPD goes like this: patrol officer, sergeant, lieutenant, captain, deputy inspector, inspector, chief, and from there on up to commissioner. Promotions for sergeant, lieutenant, and captain are strictly merit-based. You take a test, pass the test, and you move up. Above that promotions are discretionary. Which means they're political. Who likes you, who you know. The detective squad is its own unit, separate from the hierarchy of the department. Detectives can get promoted from third-grade to second-grade to first-grade. Detectives come off as cool on TV shows like *Law & Order*, but they don't have a lot of power. They don't have authority over anyone but themselves.

At that time, on a police force of more than thirty thousand uniformed officers, there were fewer than twenty blacks with the rank of captain or above. If you look at where blacks are in the department today, it hasn't improved much. There are tons of us clustered in the lower ranks of the detective squad, almost all third-grade, very few first- or second-grade. There are very few blacks in the elite squads, like counterterrorism, and there's only a handful of us in the command structure. It's a problem that's become self-perpetuating: Because it's so hard for black officers to climb the ladder, a lot of us go for the shortcut to detective, which means there are fewer of us to climb the ladder.

After three years on patrol, I was offered a spot working under-cover with narcotics. This old white sergeant came to me and said, "Hey, you wanna do this? You can make a lot of money."

He wanted me to work undercover *in* the one-fourteen. I told him he was crazy. I said, "I've been working these streets for three years, practically the only black face out here, and you want me to go and try to work undercover in the same precinct I've been patrolling in uniform? Are you trying to kill me?" I told him, "No, thanks. What I want is to do your job. How do I get to be sergeant?"

He said, "This job? Nah, you don't want to do this."

I said, "No, I do want to do that." I'd been in the military. I knew how the power structure worked, and I wanted to go where the power was.

You have to have three years on the job before you can take the sergeant's exam. I'd passed the three-year mark, so I started study-ing. All the crap I'd been through with O'Rourke and Greeley, I used it as motivation to succeed. I figured if I could be their boss, they'd have to speak to me. They'd have to respect the rank, even if they didn't respect me.

NYPD promotion tests are like the bar exam. There's a ton of memorization. You have to know the entire New York City crim-inal code backward and forward, same with NYPD policies and procedures. So all the terrible assignments I was getting, I started using them to my advantage. Every time they sent me to the hospi-tal or to sit on a dead body, I'd bring my books to study. If I had to be there for eight hours, that was going to be eight hours of time well spent.

On the DOAs, I learned a trick from one of the old-timers: When you arrive on the scene you burn coffee grounds on the stove, and that takes the smell out of the air, makes it tolerable. I actually started volunteering for DOAs, which nobody does. The sergeants would be like, "You *want* the dead body? What's wrong with you, Pegues?" But they didn't realize what I was doing. They thought they were punishing me, but they were giving me the time I needed to prepare myself to take their job.

While studying for the sergeant's exam, I also went back to school. You only need sixty-four college credits to make sergeant, but I wanted a bachelor's degree and maybe a master's. I enrolled at St. Joseph's College in Brooklyn for a degree in organizational management. I worked day tours when I had a night class, night tours when I had a day class. I moved things around to do whatever I had to do.

Theresa and I separated. This was early in 1996, around January. I was working so much, and we'd married so young. It was mutual. We stayed on good terms when it came to sharing custody of Tash, but it was time for both of us to move on. My sister Tawn was working at the post office and living in this one-bedroom apartment in Queens. I moved in with her and slept on her couch for a few months.

I started seeing a female cop who worked for the housing police in Astoria. Ever since Michelle got me expelled over the pushing match in third grade, women had always been my downfall. Sure enough, a couple months later: "Corey, I'm pregnant."

The crazy thing was the same week she told me that, I met my future wife. When I got kicked out of third grade and had to transfer to PS 36, there was another girl over there I had a huge crush on, Brendale. We were in third, fourth, fifth, and sixth grade together. We actually walked each other down the aisle at the sixth-grade graduation ceremony, her in a white dress and me in a dark blue suit, holding hands. After that our paths went different ways. She became an accountant, worked for a bank. I'd ask about her when I ran into friends we both knew, and I'd joke, "You know I'm going to marry her one day."

Then we ran into each other one night at Proper Cafe, a bar in the old neighborhood, on 219th Street at Linden Boulevard. We were both there with old friends. I didn't recognize her at first. I started flirting with her like she was a stranger at the bar. I was like, "Hey, how you doin'?"

She said, "Corey, it's Brendale."

"*Brendale?* What's goin' on? Did you know I was always in love with you?"

We both laughed and we started talking and that was that, like it was fated from the day we walked down the aisle in sixth grade. There was only one wrinkle. I had to tell her: "Look, I was seeing this woman. She's five months along. She says it's mine . . ."

Brendale took me anyway, and we moved in together in a housing development in Jamaica called Rochdale Village, a couple blocks from Baisley Park, my old stomping grounds. It was a two-bedroom place, Brendale and I in one room and the kids in the other. We were high up in this tower with a small terrace looking out over JFK, and you could sit there and watch planes land every five minutes.

Brendale had a daughter from a previous relationship, Kenyetta, whose father wasn't in the picture. From that day I raised her as my own. Corey Jr. was away with Tina in the military, but I got to see him from time to time. I had Tash on weekends. Later that year, the cop I'd been seeing gave birth to our son, Diquan. Since then, Brendale and I have had two kids of our own, Cordale and Cori. It isn't what you'd call a conventional family, but it's worked. I've been happy and settled ever since.

————

That same year I got a new boss—a black boss. The day Lieutenant Clarence Drummond walked into the one-fourteen, my whole world changed. Drummond was older, had joined the NYPD in the late 1960s, early 1970s. I thought I'd seen racism, but he was there when the real shit went down: the corruption, the department trying to infiltrate the Black Panthers, white cops leaving him stranded when he called for backup. He'd tell me stories.

Drummond had a presence. He was tall, around six five, had a deep voice, long dreadlocks in a ponytail. He wore glasses just like Malcolm X's, and he had the attitude to match, a real no-nonsense guy. Very spiritual. Very knowledgable. He had been on Mayor Dinkins's personal security detail, and now he was running the platoon on the four-to-twelve shift at the one-fourteen. When he came in, O'Rourke and Greeley and all the other racists had to answer to a black LT. They had to say, "Yes, sir," every time he spoke. They hated it. I loved it.

Drummond was the highest-ranking black officer in the precinct, and the black patrolmen looked up to him—all twenty-eight of us. He started getting us together for meetings. It wasn't anything official. We'd meet at people's houses once a month or so, eat food, have a few drinks, talk about issues we faced on the job. Drummond would give us advice, share his experiences. If there were things he felt we should change, he could take our complaints to the commander.

It was also a good way for us to network. The one thing black cops can't do at work is go sit at the black cafeteria table and talk among ourselves, because that makes the white cops nervous. It was at Drummond's meetings that I got to know Mike Williams. Mike was a city kid like me, from Queens. He'd been in the military, was doing the National Guard thing same as I was. He was on the midnight shift, so we'd only see each other in passing. Once we got to know each other, we were like peas in a pod. It helped both of us, having someone close we could count on for support. A lot of young black cops had come in under the "Safe Streets" program, but we felt isolated because we were spread out across different shifts and precincts. Once we started to connect and network with each other, we felt like we were part of a new generation that was going to come in and, hopefully, make a difference.

Lieutenants don't go out on patrol that often. Most of the time they sit at the desk. When they did decide to go on patrol, they'll have a driver take them. Shortly after Drummond arrived, his driver left, and he asked me to take over. Once I started driving for him, he took me under his wing. We'd talk, not just about the job, but about family, kids, marriage. He became a real father figure to me, the father I never had. He knew I was gunning for sergeant, and he knew how hard it was going to be for me. He'd encourage me, nurture me, but he'd also ride me hard, give me the big speeches about working twice as hard, sticking it out when I got down. Drummond was cool, even-keeled. I'd come into his office worked up about O'Rourke and Greeley. "Fucking O'Rourke. You don't know what I go through when you're not here."

He'd say, "Corey, you know those guys are racist. You know they don't like black people. So why stress about it? You just do what you've got to do."

With the sergeant's exam, he pushed me harder than I'd been pushing myself. He'd say, "Corey, you have to ace that test. It's the only way. You can't effect change down here. You have to go to the top where the decisions you make truly matter." As his driver, I was on call my whole shift. Being on call means sitting around and waiting— and Drummond made sure I had lots of time to sit around and wait. Every day I'd come in to work, and he'd say, "I'm not going out for a few hours." That meant "Go down to the locker room and study." And I would.

Drummond would quiz me, hit me with random questions. If I got one wrong, he'd send me back down to study some more. I started getting them wrong on purpose. He'd hit me with three or four questions, I'd flub the fourth, and he'd send me back down. I'd study, study, study, take Drummond out on a round of patrols, come back, and study some more. If I was out on patrol with Richard or Bob, anytime it was slow I'd say, "Pull the car over," and I'd get out my books. I studied at work. I studied at home. "No talking at the dinner table, Daddy's reading." I took all my vacation days and spent them studying, too.

I did that every day for nine months. In the spring of 1996 I took the exam at Springfield Gardens High School in Queens. It's a six-, seven-hour test, but I blew through it. My answers were flying off the page. When I finished, I didn't even have to double-check my work. I knew the second I put my pencil down and walked out of there: I crushed it.

25

The Worst Thing I Ever Did as a Cop

While I was waiting for my promotion to come through, Richard Perry came back to the one-fourteen. He left the most elite posting in the NYPD, the Street Crime Unit, to come back to patrol, the bottom of the pile, and he did it voluntarily. That's unheard of. He told me, "Corey, I couldn't take it anymore. All we do is drive around violating people's rights. All night. Every night."

Crime is always going to exist. It can only go down so much. When Bill Bratton took over, the city had been under-policed for so long that there were a lot of bad guys walking around. There was a lot of meat on the bone. All you had to do was walk out your front door to start catching criminals. That's one reason the drop in crime was so dramatic. The problem is, for a politician, especially for a guy like Rudy Giuliani, it can never go down enough. Even after the massive turnaround, Giuliani wanted more arrests and bigger headlines.

Bratton liked the spotlight of being the top cop in New York. He ate dinner with celebrities at Elaine's on the Upper East Side. He was a colorful guy, and the media loved him. He got full-page spreads in the *New York Times*. A reporter from the *New Yorker* followed him around and wrote a huge profile for the magazine: "The CEO Cop." Bratton signed a book deal for $300,000, and in January of '96 *Time* magazine put him on the cover, making him the poster boy for falling crime nationwide.

It drove Giuliani crazy. He wanted the credit for himself. He tried to set it up so that announcements about major arrests and new policies would come from city hall instead of One Police Plaza. Those two guys and their egos got into an epic pissing match. But no matter how much clout and popularity Bratton had, the mayor of New York is the mayor of New York. Two months after the *Time* cover, Bratton resigned.

Giuliani appointed Howard Safir to replace him. Safir wasn't a cop. He was the commissioner of the fire department. He'd been a US Marshall way back in the day, but he wasn't a cop the way Bratton was a cop. Safir's main qualification for the job was that he was Giuliani's boy. He was a yes-man. Which meant that for all intents and purposes, Rudy Giuliani was now running the NYPD. Everyone was pissed. For the rank-and-file cops on the job, Bratton was our guy. He ran the department the way we liked it. Black cops liked Bratton. There were plenty of black cops in transit, and they were some of the first to embrace him. The black community liked Bratton, too, even if they didn't love Giuliani. Most of the initial reduction in crime had been in black and Hispanic neighborhoods, and people were happy with the results. Ray Kelly had done a lot of outreach to the black community, and I felt like Bratton would have done the same if Giuliani had let him.

It was completely different under Safir. On the job, the change in morale was night and day. Out in the communities, a lot of the goodwill went sour. Giuliani and Safir wanted to keep getting Bratton-level reductions in crime. They wanted to keep ramping up enforcement at a time when most of the bad guys had already been locked up. Every year they wanted to do more and more, and every year there was less and less meat on the bone, which meant the people being targeted were less and less likely to be criminals. We'd done good work to reform the department, and that good work was now about to go too far.

In 1997, Giuliani and Safir declared that they were going to get illegal guns out of circulation through a massive expansion of the Street Crime Unit. They tripled it in size, from 138 cops to 438 cops. To get that many officers they had to dramatically lower the standards it took to join. If that wasn't bad enough, the cops they recruited were still virtually all white. The neighborhoods they worked were not.

Any fool could see how this was going to play out. The head of Street Crime resigned over it. He wouldn't stay and implement Safir's plan. He said it was a recipe for disaster. That's when Richard Perry quit, too. He said the pressure on them to get guns was becoming unbearable. The year Street Crime expanded, the unit took 1,139 guns off the street, a 59 percent increase over the year before, but you can't put up numbers like that without going to extreme measures to get them.

Street Crime would go out in teams of three, and Richard told me the pressure on each officer was to bring back at least one gun per night. You might have to toss forty people to come up with a single gun, so this one car could be out there tossing 120 guys a night. Multiply that by twenty, twenty-five cars on each tour. There's *no way* you've got probable cause to search that many random people in a single eight-hour shift. It's not possible. Not unless you're making things up: You saw a bulge, a guy made a suspicious movement. These teams would literally drive through the ghetto and go hunting: run up on a corner, jump out of their car, throw twenty guys against the wall, rough them up, pat them down, head on to the next corner and do it again. Next night, same thing.

I saw them do it. Russo and I would be on patrol, parked near the housing projects, a bunch of black or Hispanic guys hanging out on the corner. A team of Street Crime guys would roll up, get out, throw everybody against the wall. The cops didn't show badges, didn't give their names. No probable cause. No reports filed. It was unlawful search after unlawful search. And if the guys on the corner mouthed off or refused to submit, it was "Fuck you, spic" and "Fuck you, nigger" and arms twisted and bodies slammed on the pavement. Everything you see with cops roughing people up on these cell phone videos today? It's *mild* compared to what happened back then, because back then nobody was watching. Richard Perry decided he couldn't do it anymore. It wore on his conscience, turned his stomach, so he quit. Richard was a good cop. He saw himself crossing over to a dark place and he had the awareness to pull himself back.

It's easy to go over that line, a lot easier than most people think. The guys on Street Crime, driving around cracking skulls and violating the Constitution every night? I guarantee you they didn't start out like that. Most of them signed up out of a genuine desire to protect and serve. The culture of the department and the nature of the job made them that way. Being a cop, you deal with the worst elements of humanity. Especially if you're working that midnight-to-eight shift. On the day tours you're drinking coffee and chatting with the hostess at the diner. At four in the morning it's thieves, murderers, freaky sex crimes, guys who beat their wives, guys who beat their kids—night after night after night, that's literally all you see.

Every cop can tell you about the worst night he ever spent on the job. For me it was June 8, 1997. The Ravenswood Houses. This guy Richard Lyle Timmons killed his wife, Annita, their seven-year-old son, Aaron, and his thirteen-year-old stepson, Sharron. Timmons was a monster. He had a long history of violent, abusive behavior. He would stalk his wife, follow her around. He would hold her captive in the apartment at knifepoint. At one point he beat her so bad he shattered her eye socket.

Earlier that year, he'd been picked up on the most recent charges of abuse. The prosecutor had more than enough to convict, but Annita wouldn't testify against him. She was too scared—too scared to fight back and too scared to leave. The judge let Timmons out on a plea deal, and Annita let him come home. That night, he heard one of the boys say something about Mommy having a friend over while dad was away. He flipped out, went into a jealous rage, lost his mind. He took a hatchet and a kitchen knife and cut off his wife's head. Then he did the same to his seven-year-old son. The older boy, the thirteen-year-old, called 911 and was screaming for help on the phone when he was killed. Timmons tried to decapitate him, too, but he didn't get his head all the way off; he left it hanging off the boy's neck. When the police responded, they found the wife's head resting on a pillow on their bed and Timmons sitting on the couch with these superficial slits on his wrists, like he'd tried to kill himself but not really.

I wasn't with the team that took the call, but the whole precinct responded. It was a big, big deal. They played the 911 tape for us at the precinct. You could hear it: the chopping in the background as Timmons hacked off the heads of his wife and his little boy. You could hear the older son screaming "Daddy! Daddy! Stop! Stop!" as his mother and his brother got sliced up in front of him. The boy kept screaming and screaming until there was a loud *thwack!* and his voice went silent on the call.

Once you've heard that kind of thing you can't un-hear it. It stays with you. Every call you're on edge, because you know in the back of your mind what human beings are capable of. Even though you know 99.9 percent of the people in the world aren't monsters like Timmons, it still changes how you think. Soldiers in war zones deal with the same levels of stress, and they get rotated out on a regular basis. There are cops who stay on midnights their whole careers. And we wonder why some of them turn into monsters, too. I know how easy it is to slip over the line, because one time I let myself do it.

A lot of this friction between cops and the public stems from the fact that we ask too much of cops to begin with. The social safety net in America is practically nonexisitent. Public health services, mental health services, child welfare services, they're all underfunded, and the police are left to deal with the consequences of that. You have to separate a child from an abusive parent, so now you're a social worker. You get to a job and somebody's been stabbed and they need medical aid, so now you're an EMS worker. You've got a domestic disturbance, so now you're a marriage counselor. You have to handle an emotionally disturbed person, so now you're a psychiatrist. It's too much.

In a psych ward, orderlies break up fights with emotionally disturbed people without using firearms, and they do it every day, because they've been trained. Cops go into the same situations, they're frazzled, scared, and somebody gets shot. Guys reach for their gun or go for the chokehold as a primary instinct because they don't know what else to do. People get PhDs to deal with those situations. With cops, it's six months of training and they're in the streets. We're telling them to wing it.

My biggest mistake as a patrol officer came from my getting involved in a domestic dispute. It was late one night, almost midnight, right before the shift change, and Bob and I got a call for a domestic. We got to this apartment building in Astoria right before twelve. It was this young Hispanic couple in an all-out brawl. They were screaming, throwing dishes at each other, waking up the whole building. This old grandmother was living with them, cowering in a corner while they fought. Bob and I went in and got them separated. Bob took the wife into the other room to get her statement; she was the one who'd called the police. I took the husband aside and tried to get him to calm down, but he was all in my face, mouthing off, "*Fuck you, police,*" and this and that. At first I let him vent. "*Fuck you, cop. Fuck your punk ass. Fuckin' punk-ass cop motherfucker.*" But he wouldn't stop. Finally I got fed up. I said, "Yo, you see a punk, hit a punk."

He did. *Bam!* Coldcocked me right in my face. He got me good. I went down and I hit the floor and I was like, Oh, *shit*! Motherfucker hit me! Guy dove down and tackled me and kept on punching. I was wrestling with him, fighting back. Bob heard us and came running in. He went to try to break us up, but the wife flipped out and started yelling in Spanish and she jumped on Bob's back, was punching him, pulling his hair. She was the one who'd called us, but now she was switching sides, defending her man.

Finally I got my hand on the radio and called for a ten-thirteen—officer needs assistance. But we were right on the shift change, so there was literally no one to answer. The whole thing dragged on for an eternity while we waited: me on the ground, fighting this guy, trying to protect my gun, afraid he was going to go for it; Bob running around with this crazy woman scratching and clawing on his back; that old grandmother in the corner, yelling and screaming in Spanish at the top of her lungs. It was chaos.

Eventually something like a hundred cops showed up. By the time they pulled the guy off of me, I was hot. I was seeing red. I was covered in cuts and scrapes, this guy's blood all over me. We cuffed him, and I went to walk him out to the patrol car. At the top of the stairs, he stumbled and slipped out of my hand. I didn't push him, but I didn't try to catch him, either. I let him fall, and he went down the stairs handcuffed, head first: *boom boom boom boom boom.*

For that split second, I didn't care. The only thought going through my mind was: Fuck him. At that moment, he wasn't a citizen with rights. He was the asshole who punched me in the face. I let a man in handcuffs fall headfirst down a flight of stairs. He could have broken his neck. He could have died. Hands down the worst thing I ever did as a cop.

For years, police have used resisting arrest as a blanket cover-up for brutality, but the fact is that people do resist arrest. They do attack cops. It does happen. You're stepping into situations that are already volatile. People are drunk, angry, their adrenaline pumping. Tempers are going to blow, and every now and then some guy is going to coldcock you in the face because you were stupid enough to ask for it. Standard procedure is when a cop and a suspect get into an altercation, as soon as the prisoner is restrained, that cop is to be separated from the prisoner in order to de-escalate the situation. A neutral officer steps in and handles all prisoner contact from that point forward, taking the prisoner back to the precinct, processing the arrest, everything. But standard procedure is almost never followed. Somebody takes a shot at you, your fellow cops aren't going to separate you. They're going to look the other way while you take a shot back. That's the culture: eye for an eye.

That night in Queens, I never should have been allowed to walk that prisoner back to the patrol car. The senior officer on the scene should have said, "Corey, step aside. Cool off. I got this." When that didn't happen, I should have had the presence of mind to remove myself. But I didn't. I let my temper get the better of me, and I was lucky I wasn't responsible for a man being killed in custody.

If that wasn't bad enough: Once we got back to the precinct, an EMS team came to check out our injuries from the fight. Hispanic guy told the medic, "I'm HIV positive." And there I was, all cut up and spattered with his blood. It turned out okay in the end, but I had to go to the hospital for a bunch of tests and get re-tested again and again over the next year or so.

I knew what I did was wrong. I knew it the second I saw the guy tumble down the stairs. I swore I'd never let it happen again. From that day, anytime I had a difficult arrest, a perp taking swings at me, I'd get the cuffs on him and walk away, let another officer handle it. Unfortunately, not all cops are willing to do the same.

———

At four in the morning on August 9, 1997, a fight broke out outside Club Rendezvous, a Haitian nightclub in Brooklyn. A cop got punched trying to break it up, and the officers on the scene grabbed the guy they thought did it, but they grabbed the wrong guy. The man they grabbed was Abner Louima, whose only crime was being in the crowd outside of the club. They dragged him back to the 70th Precinct, stopping along the way to beat him before they got there, saying they were going to teach him a lesson about respecting cops.

When they got him back to the seven-oh, they dragged him past the front desk, in full view of the cops on duty, into the bathroom. There they beat him some more and shoved the handle of a bathroom plunger up his rectum. They perforated his colon and he started hemorrhaging internally. Then they took the shit-covered plunger and shoved it in his mouth, breaking his teeth. Then they took him to Coney Island Hospital. To cover up the abuse, they charged him with disorderly conduct, saying his injuries had come from the club.

No one at the precinct reported anything unusual that night. It was only because of an anonymous tip to the *Daily News* that the story got out. The cop who beat Louima was this young hothead Justin Volpe; it came out later that he was jacked up on steroids. Three other officers were charged as accomplices, but because of conflicting testimony none of them were ever convicted.

At the one-fourteen, we heard about it the minute the story broke. It was all over the news. It was bad. I remember talking to Richard on the phone. He said his father, who had over thirty years on the force, had told him, "I've seen some wild shit in my time, racial shit, all kinds of shit, but nothing like this." The cops in the one-fourteen, even the guys like O'Rourke and Greeley who were the biggest racists around, they couldn't believe it, either. It was that crazy.

It was also totally preventable. In every precinct, everybody knows the hothead. You just know. He's the cop who's always bringing in suspects beat up black and blue with the turban on. Volpe came in that night all sweaty and red-faced and 'roided out—and somebody let him take this tiny Haitian guy into the bathroom to strip-search him? Are you kidding me? Who was the sergeant on the desk? Where was the lieutenant? Who let Volpe leave the scene with Louima in the first place? Who failed to put a leash on Volpe years before that night?

That scandal destroyed nearly every ounce of goodwill the NYPD had built up in the past three years. We went from being heroes on the cover of *Time* to being villains on the cover of the *Daily News*. For months, everywhere you went, people were like, "Yo, cop? You gonna put that nightstick up my ass?"

What happened to Abner Louima was a failure of leadership. Volpe led the attack, but the culpability was with the whole institution around him. The seven-oh is a violent precinct, and the mentality in the department is "It's a violent precinct, so the cops have to be violent back." Which isn't the case. When you're a cop, just because they take a shot at you doesn't mean you get to take a shot back. You have a higher responsibility, but that sense of responsibility only gets instilled in you if it comes from the top, the people who set the tone and dictate the policies.

What Volpe did was horrible. Unfortunately, it was so horrible that the mayor and the commissioner were able to paint it as a case of one deranged cop acting out, and not something related to the culture of the department. Volpe got thirty years, a bunch of cops from the seven-oh got fired, the city and the PBA paid out a settlement for $8.75 million. But none of that had any effect on the day to day. Giuliani set up some community-relations task force that didn't have any real authority to do anything. Other than that, there was no meaningful change in department policy, no serious soul-searching about what had happened. Once the headlines died down, it was back to business as usual.

26

Yo, I'm the New Sergeant

Passing the sergeant's test doesn't get you promoted right away. You're ranked based on your raw score, seniority, and a few other factors. Every couple of months they promote fifty or sixty guys from the list and assign them where they're needed. You sit and watch the list tick down and wait for your turn. It can take months, sometimes years.

I took the exam in the spring of '96, and got my results a few months after that. I'd passed with flying colors. I only missed sixteen answers on the whole test. But I was young, so there were plenty of officers with my same score who had more time on the job, which meant they ranked higher. I was halfway down the list, around a thousand out of the two thousand who passed. I had a while to wait.

In the meantime, Lieutenant Drummond left the one-fourteen. He was promoted to serve as an executive officer in the 101st Precinct in Queens South. My mentor and protector was gone, and I was back on patrol, pulling hospital watches and DOAs. I'd go out with Bob or Richard and we'd catch the usual: DUIs, domestics, noise complaints. Other than the whole scandal surrounding Louima, it was a whole lot of hurry up and wait. By the spring of 1998, my number was coming up on the list. I was sitting at the switchboard when it came over the teletype: I was to report to the sergeant's school downtown on Gold Street for four weeks of training. Sergeant's school was a breeze, and at the end of four weeks, I got my assignment. I was going back to the hood: the 81st Precinct in Bedford-Stuyvesant, Brooklyn. Bed-Stuy, Do or Die. Home of Radio Raheem and Mookie and Buggin' Out. I was stoked.

The day before I officially reported for the job, I had to move my gear from the locker room at the one-fourteen over to the eight-one. Smooth helped me get it done. I had a new BMW X5 SUV. I picked up Smooth, we loaded up my gear in Astoria, and we headed down to Bed-Stuy.

I was always about the latest styles. This was back when Allen Iverson was killing it over in Philly with the 76ers, and everybody was getting cornrows. I had them with the doo-rag on top, and the Yankee hat to the back. Gold chain. The Champion sweat suit with one leg down, one leg rolled up to my knee. I imagine Smooth was dressed the same. We pulled into the parking lot at the eight-one, hip-hop blasting. I parked and we went in and walked up to the desk.

I was young to make sergeant. Most cops take ten, twelve years to do it. I made it in five and a half years—a five-year wonder, they call it. I also looked young for my age. When I rolled up to the desk all hip-hopped out, the desk sergeant, this young Irish guy my age, he stared at me, like, "What the fuck is this perp doing in the precinct?"

I said, "Yo, I'm the new sergeant. Can you tell me where the locker room is?"

There was this awkward pause. He didn't say anything. He stood there looking at me like I had two heads.

I said it again. "I'm the new sergeant. The locker room. Where do I go?"

The lieutenant, this other Irish guy, was standing behind the desk sergeant. He reached over, tapped him on the shoulder, and said, "Hey, you hear what he said? He's the new sergeant. Get up and go show him the locker room."

Smooth busted out laughing. He was crying he was laughing so hard. Finally the sergeant snapped out of it and took me to the locker room. I put my gear away, Smooth and I went back and climbed in the car, music blasting, and we drove out. Smooth was still cracking up over it. He loves telling that story to this day.

The eight-one was a night-and-day change from the one-fourteen. In Bed-Stuy in 1998, there wasn't a hint of gentrification in sight. It was a 99 percent African-American community. Low-income. High crime. People getting shot, people getting mugged, people getting raped. Drugs were everywhere. It was exactly where I wanted to be. I wanted to be in a community like the one where I grew up, a place where the relationships between cops and minorities needed all the help they could get. I wanted to go there and protect and serve the same way we do in the middle-class white communities.

As a sergeant, you oversee a squad of eight or so patrol officers and you have some responsibilities—giving out assignments, managing their shift changes and vacation requests, running a crime scene until a ranking officer shows up—but for the most part you're still one of the troops. The single biggest responsibility you have is that every arrest made by one of your officers has to go through you. Two cops answer a call for a burglary, catch the guy crawling out the window, put the cuffs on him. The next thing that happens is the sergeant comes and signs off on the arrest: Did the officers follow procedure? Does their story check out? Is the perp a juvenile and have the parents been called? The sergeant is the first line of checks and balances between the arresting officer and the rest of the criminal justice system. You don't have a ton of authority in that position, but the authority you do have is important.

I was on the four-to-twelve shift, same as in the one-fourteen. We had suspects coming in tuned up. Black eyes, busted noses, split lips. And it was always the same excuse: resisting arrest. As a patrolman, the only thing I could do was refuse to participate. As a sergeant, I had control over my squad. Anytime I got to the scene of an arrest and the suspect was bruised and bloodied, I would take him aside and—

in front of the arresting officers—I would ask him, "Did these officers do this to you? Did they beat you up? Tell me what happened."

My guys would look at me like I was crazy, but I didn't care. I asked every single time. Of course, sometimes the cop was right: The suspect did resist and there was a scuffle. It's also true that perps will lie through their teeth to get out of an arrest. But most of the time they're pretty bad liars, making up stuff that no cop would ever do. I'd have to use my discretion to decide whether I believed the cop or the perp. But my reason for asking wasn't about getting to the truth on any one arrest. The fact that my guys knew I was asking those questions changed how they behaved on patrol. They knew: Sergeant Pegues ain't playing. They knew they were being watched.

I didn't wait for my squad to cause problems. At roll call I'd say, "Guys, let's go out there and have a safe tour. And remember, if you do something you're not supposed to do, I'm calling IAB. I'll give them your name, your shield, everything. So you won't ever have to sit around and play no guessing game about who called IAB on you. You're looking at him." I would put that out there every day. I only had authority over eight officers out of thirty thousand, but I was doing what I could.

The place where sergeants have the most authority is in the role of desk sergeant. All the sergeants rotate through that position. You sit at that big desk in the front of the precinct and you're the administrator for the shift. The arrests and complaints that come in, you enter them into the logbook and have the final approval over what goes through. When you sign off on an arrest, one of the things you have to do is make sure the crime being charged is the crime that happened. Crime classification is a big deal, and under Compstat it's become even more important, because everyone is trying to make the numbers. Late one night I was on the desk, and an officer from Anti-Crime came in with this twenty-something black guy in handcuffs. Anti-Crime cops are tasked with getting illegal guns and making major felony arrests. They actually can't make misdemeanor arrests.

That's part of their mandate. So this cop came in with the perp and I said, "Yo, what you got?"

"Robbery. From a Rite-Aid on Broadway."

"What happened?"

"Theft of property," he said. Then he put a tube of toothpaste up on the desk.

I said, "A tube of toothpaste? That's the felony you're bringing in here?"

"Yup."

I said, "Let me guess: guy shoplifted the toothpaste, security guard tried to stop him, guy pushed the security guard away and ran out the store. That it?"

"Yup. That's exactly what happened."

And here's where the classification of crime becomes important. Larceny is the taking of someone else's property. In New York, theft of property worth less than $250, like shoplifting, is petty larceny. Robbery is theft involving the use of force or the threat of force against the victim's physical person. Petty larceny is a misdemeanor. Robbery is a felony.

This cop wanted to charge a guy with a felony, and the only reason he wanted to do that was because he was under pressure to produce felony arrests. What that cop was doing to that guy was what's called "flaking," giving people charges that don't exist. My guess is either it was the end of the month and he needed to make his quota, or, worse, it was the first of the month and he wanted to get a felony arrest out of the way so he could coast for a while. The only problem was: This wasn't a robbery. Robbery is when somebody puts a gun in your face and says, "Gimme your wallet." That's robbery. A guy shoplifting toothpaste is not robbery. I don't care who he pushed on his way out of the store.

First of all, it wasn't like the guy was stealing cigarettes. He was stealing toothpaste. That doesn't mean it's not a crime, but if a grown man is stealing toothpaste, it's because he needs toothpaste. Have a little compassion. Second, the district attorney was never going to take it anyway. No DA on Earth is going to take a tube of toothpaste to trial for a felony conviction. It was going to get dropped down to petty larceny no matter what. But the way it works is this: If an officer makes a felony arrest, and the DA later pleads it out as a misdemeanor, the officer still gets to keep it as a felony arrest for his monthly stats. The change doesn't come back to the NYPD records. So the cop doesn't care what happens to the guy after the arrest. He just wants the arrest.

I wasn't having it, and as the desk sergeant I had the authority to stop it. I told this cop, "No way. That's not going to fly. He stole property under two hundred fifty dollars. That's petty larceny. It's a misdemeanor. Write him a desk appearance ticket and send him home."

The officer said, "No way. This was a fucking robbery. Put it through as a robbery."

I said, "That's not going to happen."

We got in a huge argument. The perp was sitting right there in cuffs, watching us go back and forth. Finally the cop walked off and came back with his sergeant, the one who'd signed off on the arrest at the scene. Sergeant was all pissed. He said, "Corey, what the fuck is going on? My guy says you're saying this ain't a robbery. It's a fuckin' robbery."

Now things got heated. Me and the sergeant went at it. I held up the toothpaste and said, "Sarge, you approved this shit? *This* is a robbery? This ain't no fuckin' robbery. No way this is going through my desk as a robbery."

"It was the forcible theft of property. It's a felony."

"Really? In the 81st Precinct, where people are getting shot and murdered? That shit might work in Park Slope, but it don't work in Bed-Stuy. In Bed-Stuy, this is a petty larceny. That's the only way it's going through my desk. It's a misdemeanor. Write the guy a citation and cut him loose."

"This is bullshit."

"Look, it's not happening."

"You want me to call the lieutenant?"

"Call the lieutenant? Fuck that, I'll call the captain. I'm pretty sure the captain doesn't want to go to Compstat next month and explain to the chief of department and the chief of patrol why his Anti-Crime squad is wasting its time bringing in guys for shoplifting fucking toothpaste. So, yeah, if you want, we can call him right now."

We had a bureaucratic deadlock. Me and this other sergeant were both the same rank, and it was his arrest, but since I was the desk sergeant I had the final say over what went through. It was getting near the end of my shift, but I had to stay on duty until I made sure the arrest wouldn't go through.

We ended up calling the district attorney, who said exactly what I knew he would: His office wouldn't take it as a felony. It got knocked down, the guy took his citation and went home. But if I hadn't been there to stop it, that guy would have gone into the system, been sent down to Brooklyn criminal court to see the judge, and from there, if he couldn't make bail, he'd have gone to Rikers Island with a felony arrest on his record—all over of a tube of toothpaste.

That was the problem with Compstat. When it started, everybody embraced it. The immediate results were phenomenal. But in short order it turned policing into a numbers game.

On the one hand, there has to be accountability for police. We can't go back to the pre-Bratton days when cops sat around the precinct all day reading the newspaper before hitting the bar at three in the afternoon. If I work at McDonald's, I can't flip two burgers in a month and keep my job. I have to perform. There has to be an incentive to perform, and there has to be a way to measure that performance. The difference is, at McDonald's, once I've made enough burgers to feed the customers, the manager can see the orders have been filled and I can ease back and go on break. But the way politicians handle policing and crime, it's never enough. You can always get tougher. The politicians are leaning on the chiefs, who are leaning on the captains, and the pressure is coming down. I felt it myself.

The way Compstat works, if you have a sudden increase of crime in an area, they designate it an Impact Zone, flood it with officers, and expect those officers to deliver results. They might deploy a squad of eight officers and expect to see ten summonses each, so eighty summonses over a given period of time. One time they did it and my squad was out in the designated zone, but it was the middle of January and there was a cold snap. It was twenty degrees out, and nobody was on the street. No shots being fired, no cars getting broken into. It was too damn cold. My guys weren't coming back with anything. I went out and patrolled myself to see why the numbers were low. I saw maybe two people in two hours. Still, I got chewed out. "Where are the arrests? Why aren't you writing summonses?"

I said, "There's nobody there. There's no crime. I was over there myself. Nothing's happening."

They didn't want to hear it. They wanted me to find people. In that scenario, every pedestrian becomes a suspect. If firemen spend a whole month sitting in the station house not putting out fires, that's a good thing—it means there were no fires. But with cops it was: Give me the numbers. Give me the numbers. Give me the numbers. We went from a system of chronic under-policing to a system of relentless over-policing. Warnings turned into misdemeanors. Misdemeanors turned into felonies. And when armed police are out there in these minority communities, hunting and hunting and trying to hit quotas for felonies that don't exist, that's when things go horribly wrong.

———

Under Giuliani and Safir, nobody on the force was under more pressure than the Street Crime Unit. In the two years since the unit tripled in size, it had only become more aggressive in its efforts to get illegal guns off the streets. Late at night on February 4, 1999, four Street Crime officers were patrolling on Wheeler Avenue in the Bronx when they saw a black man standing in the vestibule of an apartment building. He was sticking his head in and out the door, waiting for someone. The officers stopped and approached the man to question him.

What happened next, the cops claimed, was that the man turned away and reached into his pocket. One of them yelled, "He's got a gun!" and they started firing. All four cops pulled their weapons and shot. Forty-one shots were fired. Nineteen hit the victim. He died on the spot. The man they shot was Amadou Diallo, a twenty-three-year old immigrant from Guinea in West Africa. He was completely unarmed. He was likely going in his pocket to grab his wallet to show ID—assuming it's true that he reached in his pocket at all.

People were outraged. The media went crazy with the story. Even the *New York Post*, probably the most pro-cop newspaper in the country, ran headlines like IN COLD BLOOD and JUSTICE MUST BE DONE. The NYPD made up all these justifications for the shooting. They said Diallo fit the description of a rapist wanted in the area. They said he was making "furtive gestures," like he was a lookout for a burglary team, but no burglaries had been reported in that neighborhood that night. They said Diallo was acting strange because he was an illegal immigrant, but it turned out he was here legally.

Every justification they floated fell apart. To me, the real reason for the shooting was obvious: The rapid expansion of the Street Crime Unit under Giuliani and Safir had put undue pressure on officers to meet unrealistic quotas. The four officers were indicted, but the trial was moved to Albany in a deliberate attempt to avoid facing a jury in the Bronx. There were no eyewitnesses to the shooting besides the cops themselves. They all walked.

The only political casualty of the shooting was the Street Crime Unit. Safir knocked them back down from plainclothes to uniformed patrol, and in 2002 the unit was formally disbanded. But Street Crime was only the most visible part of a problem that ran department wide. Cops have always harassed young black people in the streets, tossing us up against the wall, cussing us out. It's a power thing, their way of reminding us who was boss. But when I was growing up, it was random, here and there. A cop saw you and didn't like you, he was going to give you a hard time. It didn't happen all day every day.

The law that allowed them to do this came from a 1968 Supreme Court case, *Terry v. Ohio.* It says a cop has a right to stop and question someone if there is a "reasonable suspicion" that criminal activity is taking place. Not every stop results in a frisk. Frisking is technically only allowed for the officer's safety. If I'm afraid you're going to pull a gun on me, I need to protect myself. If I frisk you and feel a weapon, only then am I allowed to go into your pockets and see what it is. Every time a cop executes a stop, they fill out a report called a UF-250, explaining the details of the stop and the reason for it.

That's how it's supposed to work. The purpose of Stop, Question, and Frisk is to get information—it was never meant to be a tool to search for contraband or illegal guns. But under the zero-tolerance policy of Bratton's Broken Windows policing, that's what it became. The pressure to make quotas—even if we don't call them quotas—kept creeping up and up and up, especially in the high-crime, low-income, heavily black and Hispanic neighborhoods.

After Diallo, Attorney General Eliot Spitzer threatened to subpoena the Street Crime Unit's UF-250 records from the past two years. Giuliani reluctantly agreed to turn them over. Once the data was analyzed, it showed what everyone already knew to be true: Blacks and Hispanics were being stopped at wildly disproportional rates: 62.7 percent of all people stopped by the unit were black. For every stop that resulted in an arrest, the cops stopped 16.3 blacks, 14.5 Hispanics, and 7.9 whites. And those were just the official numbers. Everyone knew that Street Crime wasn't filing a report on every stop; they were rolling up, tossing guys, and moving on.

Shutting down the Street Crime Unit was the right thing to do, but the heavy-handed use of Stop, Question, and Frisk had already seeped into the culture of the whole department. It was how things were done now. Which meant the tension between blacks and cops was only going to get worse. There was bound to be another Amadou Diallo eventually. It was only a matter of where and when.

27

Theft of Service

Howard Safir resigned as police commissioner in August of 2000. I was so happy when he did. Between Louima and Diallo, Safir's tenure had been toxic for race relations in New York. He was never popular with the rank-and-file white officers, either. He was seen as a fireman, never one of us. But if we thought we couldn't do worse than Safir, we were wrong.

At that point Joseph Dunne was the chief of department, and clearly, obviously, next in line for commissioner. Dunne was well liked, a cop's cop; he would have been ideal for the job. But Giuliani passed him over for Bernard Kerik. It was the biggest joke the department had ever seen. Kerik had never held a rank in the NYPD higher than detective. His only qualification, like Safir, was that he was Giuliani's boy; Kerik had been his bodyguard and chauffeur during the 1993 mayoral campaign. From there Giuliani made him commissioner of corrections. But corrections has only two thousand officers. The NYPD is the largest police force in the world.

Joe Dunne stayed and took the position of first deputy commissioner. Joe Esposito was appointed chief of department. I'd interviewed with Esposito the year before, when he was commanding officer of Brooklyn Borough North; I'd applied for a transfer to training sergeant under his command. Esposito was old school. Italian guy, born and raised in Bensonhurst, joined the force in 1971, walked the beat in Crown Heights and Bushwick. Cops had a lot of respect for him. He was like a regular guy who'd worked his way up through the ranks. Unlike a lot of the older generation, he'd adapted to the Compstat era well, was a smart commander. Sitting across from him in my cornrows, I wasn't sure how he was going to take me. But he was very friendly, amiable. We had a good rapport, and I felt like he gave me a fair shot. I didn't end up getting the job, but it was a good opportunity to get my name and résumé in front of an important guy. I stayed in touch with Esposito after that, keeping him up-to-date on what was happening with me. It was a great relationship for me to have in my pocket.

Dunne and Esposito ran the NYPD. Those were the men that we took our orders from. Kerik was this buffoon in the corner office. Among the rank and file, everyone I knew thought he was a clown. Giuliani lost all our respect with that appointment. Despite what people thought at the city hall rally in 1992 or when they elected him in 1993, Giuliani wasn't really pro-cop. He just wanted to wrap himself up in the NYPD the same way presidents wrap themselves up in the American flag; he wanted to bask in our reputation and exploit it for his own gain. That was all he'd ever done. After 9/11 it was all he'd ever do again.

When the first plane hit on September 11, 2001, I was on my way to pick up my daughter from school in Forest Hills to take her to an appointment. By the time I got to her school the second plane had hit and it was chaos, all the parents trying to find their kids and make sure they were safe. I rushed my daughter home and flew back to the precinct. I wasn't on duty that day, but I knew everyone would need to be there.

In the days after, nearly every cop in the city was down at Ground Zero, searching for bodies, helping out. Somebody had to stay behind, and since I was a training sergeant and not on patrol at the time, I got assigned to man the desk back at the precinct. Which was fine with me. I went down a couple times, but I got a bad feeling being down there. I didn't believe what Giuliani and the EPA administrator,

Christine Todd Whitman, were saying about the air being safe to breathe. At Ground Zero, cops and firemen were down there digging in the rubble with no masks on. They were breathing in pulverized glass and cement, insulation, asbestos, toxic chemicals. We've buried too many people in the past few years because of the air at Ground Zero. I've lost friends, and I'm still losing them.

That January, thankfully, Giuliani's term limit was up. Michael Bloomberg won the election that year over the Democrat, Mark Green. All the black cops I knew supported Green, but after Bloomberg got in we were happy with his choice for police commissioner: Ray Kelly, who'd held the job as interim commissioner during the Dinkins administration. After a fireman and a clown, it was good to have a real cop back in the job. Kelly had held every rank in the department, from PO up to commissioner. He understood the job.

Kelly also had strong ties to the black community, having done so much outreach to black churches and leaders under Dinkins. He understood the tensions between minority groups and law enforcement. A couple of years before, he'd given a speech denouncing the heavy-handed policing that went on under Safir and Giuliani and the harm it had done. "A large reservoir of goodwill was under construction when I left the Police Department in 1994," he said. "But it was quickly abandoned for tough-sounding rhetoric and dubious stop-and-frisk tactics that sowed new seeds of community mistrust." I said to myself, "Finally, here's a commissioner who's going to be good for the department, good for black cops, and good for the black community." That's honestly what I believed at the time.

———

As Kelly was being sworn in, I was coming up on the list for promotion to lieutenant. A few days before I sat down to interview with the promotion board, I got a call from a friend. He had a message for me from the chief of personnel: If I wanted the promotion, the cornrows had to go. It would have been illegal for the department to tell me that officially; it's blatant discrimination. But they were letting me know, off the record, that that was how it was going to be.

I never wanted to compromise who I was for the sake of the job. But at the same time, you pick your battles. I wasn't going to blow up my career over a hairstyle. The cornrows came out, I passed the interview, and I got the job. I was moving up the ranks now, and it gets whiter and whiter the higher you go. At my promotion ceremony, there were only two blacks out of the fifty-plus lieutenants promoted that day.

For my assignment, I wanted to stay in Brooklyn. I didn't want to go to the Upper East Side and sit on my thumbs. I knew it was unlikely, because Ray Kelly liked to move cops around to different boroughs. I reached out to Chief Esposito. I'd been keeping my relationship up with him, and now that he was chief of department he had the leverage to help me out. When I called him, he said he couldn't send me to a precinct in Brooklyn, but he could send me to transit in Brooklyn.

New York's three police forces—transit, housing, and city—had merged under Giuliani in 1995. The Department of Education's School Safety Unit merged with the NYPD in 1998. Each force became its own unit within the larger department. Esposito wanted to send me to Transit District 30, stationed at Hoyt/Schemerhorn, which covers fifteen different subway lines in over thirty different stations around downtown Brooklyn: Borough Hall, Atlantic Terminal, from Fort Hamilton down in Windsor Terrace up to Nassau Avenue in Greenpoint. There's no action in transit. None. But I'd asked Esposito for the favor, and you don't say no to any promotion in the NYPD. You kiss the ring and wait for the next opportunity. That's how it goes.

I reported for my first day at transit on February 11, 2002. It was as dull as I predicted. In the eight-one, we were averaging fifty felonies a week. In transit it was maybe four, and that's across all fifteen lines we covered. Mostly I supervised the various squads that gave out citations for littering, urination, riding between the cars.

The main job for my platoon, same as it had been under Bratton, was going after turnstile jumpers. "Theft of service" is the official charge: TOS. I'd go out with a team of men and women in plainclothes. We'd hang around the turnstiles, wait for the turnstile jumpers to come through, and nab them on the platform. Guys were always surprised when I'd show up in my doo-rag and my sweat suit and flash the badge.

"*You're* a cop?"

"I'm the lieutenant."

It was easy work. Three days after I started, an officer, PO Brown, brought in this sixteen-year-old black kid for theft of service. Brown was black, a big fat slob, lazy, totally unprofessional in every way. It was only my first week on the job and I already couldn't stand him. Brown came in, I logged the arrest and left for a while, thinking the kid would be on his way. Theft of service is like shoplifting. It's a misdemeanor. If you qualify, you get a desk appearance ticket and you're sent home. But when I got back the kid was still there. I asked Brown why. He said he was putting the kid through the system because he didn't have any ID.

It's not a crime to not have ID, but it is a catch-22. You haven't committed a felony, but since we can't establish your identity, we have to arrest you, fingerprint you, and put you through the system to determine you are who you say you are. So even though there's no crime, there's an arrest on your record. The next time cops pull you over, they see you've been arrested before, and it colors how they treat you, which could lead to an incident. You get that knock when you're sixteen, and it follows you.

Turnstile jumpers are likely to be teenagers, and they're likely to be black or Hispanic. Since city kids don't drive, it's perfectly normal for them not to have government-issued ID. I told Brown, "No way. That kid's not going through the system. Get on the phone. Find his mother. Find a relative. Get somebody down here who can ID him, give him a citation, and send him home."

I could tell Brown wanted to argue with me, but he couldn't. Eventually we got the kid's mother to come down and vouch for him and take him home. She took me aside and thanked me over and over again for keeping her son out of the system. I told her to make sure he always had subway fare on him and to get him an ID. Once she and her son left, I had to call Brooklyn central booking. They'd already received the paperwork, and I had to tell them that this kid wouldn't be coming down. I spoke to a young black female officer there, told her what had happened, and she thanked me for not sending him down. Talking to her was when I discovered the problem: This was happening all the time, kids being sent through the system for having no ID. It had become standard practice in transit. This officer down at central booking said she saw it every day. She thought it was terrible, and she'd been waiting for someone to step in and put a stop to it.

Jumping a turnstile should be treated like a traffic ticket; that's basically what it is. It's like rolling a stop sign. It shouldn't get you sent to central booking. But dozens of young black and Hispanic kids were being fed into the system every week for that reason. It wasn't right. The next morning at roll call I announced a new policy for the platoon: No perps, especially minors, were to be sent to central booking for not having ID without first making an exhaustive effort to find a relative or a guardian to come in and ID them. There were a few black officers in the room nodding along; they recognized the problem and were glad I was fixing it. But for the most part there was a lot of grumbling.

Two weeks later I found out why. I had a friend, Janice, another black cop, who worked in transit in another district. I got a call from her. She said I should watch out, that my name was all over transit—people didn't like me because of the changes I was making. Anytime you have to stop and put someone through the system, you're going to book a couple hours of overtime, which meant there was a strong financial incentive for cops to process the no-ID arrests. Janice said,

"Corey, you're messin' with cops' paychecks, and they're pissed. Theft of service was our bread and butter when I was there. We *always* put people through the system. That's how we made our overtime."

I said, "Are you out of your mind? Janice, you're black. And you're down with putting black kids through the system so you can see a bump in your paycheck every two weeks? Seriously?" I told her, "Don't call me with this anymore. Whatever talk you hear about me, I don't care." And I hung up the phone. I didn't talk to her for months after that.

Her telling me that pissed me off more than anything else I'd ever experienced on the job. It's one thing to see white cops treat young black people like they don't matter. It's worse to see black cops do it. At transit, we collared white kids all the time for vandalism and petty teenage crap. I guarantee you no white cops were sending middle-class white kids from Park Slope to central booking for not having ID. But black cops would do it to black kids without even thinking. My friend Janice was black. PO Brown was black. But they had that house-slave mentality. "Yo, I'm in the big house. I'm eating well. I couldn't care less what happens to the negroes out in the field." Everyone says we need more black cops for the system to be fair, but being black isn't enough. If you're black but you're not willing to challenge things or stand up to the culture of the department, you're actually making things worse, because you're putting a black face on a corrupt system, which helps excuse it and perpetuate it.

I spent five of the most boring months of my life in transit. The only upside was that I had plenty of time to study for the captain's exam, which I took that June. Same as the two tests before, I walked out certain that I'd passed. Then, days after taking the test, I got a call from my old mentor at the one-fourteen: Clarence Drummond. He'd been promoted to deputy inspector, and was finally being given his own command: the 28th Precinct in Harlem. He was calling to ask me to be his administrative lieutenant, his chief of staff. It wasn't just a huge step up from transit. It was a chance to work with an incredible mentor I admired. On top of that, Mike Williams, my old friend from the one-fourteen, was already working at the two-eight as a sergeant. I'd be reunited with him as well.

The two-eight covers the heart of Harlem. Central Park North to 127th. Fifth Avenue to Morningside Park. It's the Apollo Theater, Sylvia's Restaurant, Malcolm X Boulevard. I was *pumped*. I couldn't have been more excited. Me and Williams and Drummond—three brothers running the show in the single greatest black neighborhood in America.

It was, hands down, the worst experience of my entire career.

Executive

Executive

28

Across 110th Street

The worst rank you can hold in the NYPD is lieutenant. As a captain or an inspector or a chief, you have real executive authority. As a patrol officer or a sergeant or a detective, while you don't have much authority, you're out in the streets doing real police work. But a lieutenant is the dictionary definition of middle management. You run a platoon, and you get to wear the nice white shirt and you get the stripes on your uniform, but you have almost no decision-making power of your own. All you do is pass orders down from above and report back on developments from below. That's it.

The only thing worse than being a lieutenant is being a lieutenant who's passed the captain's exam. I made the captain's list in February of 2003, seven months after transferring up to Harlem. Once you pass the test, you're waiting for the promotion, and there aren't a whole lot of openings for captain and they don't come up that often. Depending on where you land on the list, you might wait three or four years for the call to come through. And while you're waiting, you can't go anywhere. If you request a transfer, no one will take you. Because they know if they take you, you don't really want to be there; you're going to get promoted out and leave them hanging. Wherever you are the day you pass the captain's test, you're going to be stuck there for a while—and the two-eight was hell.

As the commanding officer, the CO, Drummond had three right-hand guys, his executive officer, who ran patrol; the special operations lieutenant, who handled the narcotics unit, the Anti-Crime Unit, and other dedicated details; and the administrative lieutenant, my new job, which was exactly what it sounds like. You oversee the running of the precinct: payroll, staffing, training. It's mundane, but it's useful experience if you're trying to make captain, because you'll need to be familiar with those aspects of the job.

Being an administrative lieutenant has nothing to do with fighting crime, but there wasn't that much crime in the two-eight anyway. Between gentrification and the economy doing better, things were pretty calm above 110th Street. Harlem wasn't like the Harlem people imagined anymore. I was responsible for briefing the new rookies and getting them settled in. We had this one white kid who showed up right after I got there. He was young, skinny, red hair, with pimples on his face. After the first briefing he came up to me and Drummond and said, "Um, is it possible you could get me a transfer? To Queens maybe?"

I could look at his face and see: He was terrified. He'd been watching *Shaft* and *New Jack City* and had this idea of what it was going to be like being up here with all these black people, like this wasn't what he signed up for. Drummond and I chuckled to ourselves. I couldn't have transferred him if I'd wanted to. In the NYPD, wherever officers are assigned, that's where they work. I was like, "Sorry, guy. You're stuck. But don't worry, these black people, they're not animals. They're not going to kill you."

It was funny, but also worrying, because that's exactly the kind of kid who would go out all nervous and jittery and shoot somebody because he's scared of black people from what he's seen on TV. I made an effort to bring the kid into my office and talk to him. I said, "Look, this ain't the concrete jungle. Forget *New Jack City*. The Carter? That building Nino Brown takes over in the movie? It's going co-op now. It's real nice. You and me, we couldn't afford to live there." The kid worked out fine. Harlem was fine, too, as far as crime went. In the two-eight, the drama was inside the precinct.

At the one-fourteen, Clarence Drummond had been my savior and my protector, my mentor and my idol. I had that man on a pedestal so high nothing could touch him. But that was before. I first realized I was going to have problems with him as a commander because of this civilian employee, a woman named Rhonda, who worked in the complaint room. Her job was to process and record the grievances of people who came into the precinct. It's a public-facing, customer-service type of job, a position where you want to put someone with good people skills, and she was an incredibly rude and disrespectful person. She might have been the nastiest person I've ever met in my life. She would sit at the complaint desk listening to her Walkman with headphones on. In a police station. Where her job was to greet the public. I had to tell her all the time to take the headphones off.

I mentioned to Drummond several times that I felt she should be transferred to a different job. He would say he'd handle it and then nothing would happen. One day I asked Rhonda to type something up for me, and she flat out told me no. The NYPD is a paramilitary organization. I was a lieutenant, she was a civilian. You don't get to say no. But she was real snide with me and told me flat out, "I ain't your assistant. You have to get someone else to do it."

I went to Drummond and said, "I've had enough with her. I'm writing her up for being insubordinate."

He said, "No, no. Let me talk to her. Don't do that."

Don't do it? What do you mean, don't do it? I've got the whole precinct out there looking at me. I've got cops, sergeants, detectives, and they see me being disrespected and not doing anything? That can't happen. But he didn't back me. He didn't do anything. He left her there.

That's how it was with everything. I was constantly being undermined. Drummond's executive officer was a white captain, James Green. Drummond had the higher rank, but Green had more time at the two-eight, so when Drummond first came in he relied on Green's knowledge about the precinct. Which is normal, for a month or two, until you get the lay of the land. But even after a year, Drummond was constantly deferring to the lower rank.

Green and I didn't get along. It was typical office politics. Whoever has the commander's ear wants to keep it that way. He knew I was the CO's boy, so from the day I arrived he had his eye on me, trying to size me up. He'd say things to me like, "You're not a captain yet." Because he knew I'd passed the test, but he wanted to remind me who was in charge.

Everything I did or tried to do, Green was looking to put me in my place. I'd go to Drummond and say, "I'm moving these guys to the day tour." He'd say okay. Then a day later Green would come in and reverse the decision, and Drummond would sign off on it. I'd give someone a negative performance review, and Green would go behind me and change it. Drummond wouldn't say anything. It was minor stuff—staffing decisions, budget decisions—but it added up. I'd sit in meetings and watch Drummond defer to Green on almost every single decision. It was the strangest, most disappointing thing to witness. To me Drummond was Malcolm X, this incredible, imposing black figure, finally given the big chair, *in Harlem*, but the white captain was pretty much running things.

I felt that Drummond couldn't make a decision to save his life. I knew he wasn't protecting me or promoting my interests the way he had at the one-fourteen. The little bit of responsibility I had as a lieutenant, even that was taken away from me. I was a guy in an office pushing paper around. I spoke to him about it several times. I was vocal; I don't hold back. I told him, "Boss, you're supposed to be my guy. You're the one who inspired me to be where I am. All the motivational talks, all the hours you let me study on the job, and I come here and I get treated like shit." He'd apologize and, still, nothing would change.

Like most jobs, what moves your career in the NYPD is having the higher-ups notice you and take an interest. But if you're never given a chance to shine, you've got no opportunities to impress anyone. Your career stalls out. I'd been on the move since I was a thirteen-year-old kid in St. Albans, hungry for something to eat, hungry for a better life. I'd been hustling nonstop. I hustled in the streets, in the army, on patrol, passing my exams. I'd been moving, moving, moving. Then I hit the two-eight and it was like my whole world came to a dead stop—and the man responsible for that was the father figure I loved and respected as the father I never had. It crushed me.

———

Pretty soon after my arrival at the two-eight I learned who was the hothead in the precinct. Lieutenant Ken Ford. Ford was black, and a real nasty piece of work. Just disgruntled, unpleasant. He'd cuss out his subordinates. He was real heavy-handed in the streets, too. And this was a guy Drummond had brought with him to the two-eight. Which was amazing to me. I couldn't believe that an upstanding guy like Drummond would want anything to do with him.

From the day I met Ford I had the feeling that he was a ticking time bomb. I didn't have a hard time envisioning an Abner Louima situation going down with him. It didn't matter that Ford was black; black cops can be as nasty and brutal as white cops. I'd been telling Drummond for months, "This guy is rogue. He has to go. You have to do something." As usual, Drummond didn't do anything.

One night Ford brought in a perp, had him at the desk in the front for the desk sergeant to log the arrest. The perp was cuffed, but he was yelling and cursing. "Yo, you take off these cuffs, I'll fuck you up!" Ford lost it and choked the guy out for mouthing off. A handcuffed prisoner. Ford grabbed his throat and choked him down to the ground and left him gasping for air. Right in front of everybody.

My man Mike Williams was there that night and he saw what happened. Witnessed the whole thing. Mike don't play. He's the straightest guy I know. He called IAB and reported the whole thing. A couple days later, Ford and Williams got called into Drummond's office to sort it out. Ford lost it again. He jumped up out of his chair and got in Mike's face and was threatening him—in front of Drummond. Still nothing happened to the guy. Ford wasn't disciplined at all, to my knowledge. Drummond didn't take a stand, didn't do anything. He wanted to calm everyone down and talk it out and move on.

I was convinced that Ford was disturbed, a real nutcase. He and I never got along, and I tiptoed around him for months, waiting for Drummond to step in, but he never would. Finally the whole uneasy situation came to a head that spring. It was May 8, 2003, my last day before taking my family to Disney World for a week's vacation. My daughter Kenyetta was taking debutante classes in Harlem at the time. She'd take the train in from Queens after school, go to her class, and then wait in my office for me to drive us home at the end of the day. This one particular afternoon she was sitting in my office while I was off handling something. Ford walked by, saw her, and went in and got real gruff and confrontational with her: "Who are you? What are you doing in this office? You can't be in here."

Everybody in the precinct knew Kenyetta was my daughter. She'd been in my office twice a week for a year. She explained to Ford who she was, and finally he left her alone. When I came back, she told me what had happened. I was pissed. Ford had no business telling anyone in my office what to do or not to do, and I didn't like the idea of that violent creep being anywhere near my kid. I found him in the hallway and laid into him. I said, "Look, Ken, you don't ever say anything to my daughter again. You crazy? Don't ever speak to her. And if someone's in my office, that means I put them there. You don't question them."

We exchanged a few words. I could see he was getting hot. I walked off and went downstairs with Kenyetta to leave. Ford followed us. While I was at the front desk signing out, he stood there a few feet away, punching the desk with his fist. I ignored him, took Kenyetta, and went out to my car. Ford followed us again. I was pulling out of the lot when Ford came over and got in the window and started yelling. "You want some of this? You want some of this?" His eyes were bugging out. I knew that look. He wanted to go. He wanted to fight.

Kenyetta was in the car, crying. I'd had enough. I stopped the car, got out, and told him to back off. He got right up in my face. My foot went back in this defensive stance. I was either ready to take a punch or throw a punch. Ford started taking off his gun belt, like he was getting ready to do it, and he turned around and walked over to put the gun belt down. That's when I said to myself, "No. I'm tired of this." I wasn't some sixteen-year-old gangster anymore. I didn't wait for Ford to come back. I got in my car, a detective came over and got in between us, and the whole thing was over.

Drummond came down to find out what was going on. I told him, "I can't do this anymore. I'm not working with that nut job. When I come back, either he's is gone or I'm gone." Drummond said to go enjoy my vacation. He'd take care of it. That was on a Thursday afternoon. I came back the next Tuesday . . . and Ford was still there. He was walking around the hallways, puffing his chest out and yelling, "This is *my* motherfuckin' house!" Dude was *disturbed*. I didn't even dress out in my uniform. I wasn't going to set foot in the locker room with that nut job walking around. Drummond tried to tell me that he'd inquired about a transfer for Ford and was waiting to hear back. I think he was trying to smooth things over, same as he always did. Apparently he hadn't understood what I said before I left: I wasn't coming back as long as Ford was there.

The next morning I didn't report for duty. I went straight to see Chief Dellatore, the XO for Manhattan North. I waited two and a half hours and finally got in to see him. I wasn't wasting any more time dealing with Ford; I escalated the situation to the highest possible level. I said, "Chief, I'm in fear for my life and cannot return to work." I told him I wanted to file a UF-61, an official complaint; I wanted a full IAB investigation opened immediately; and I wanted a radio to carry off duty for my own and my family's protection.

Dellatore had heard what happened, and he knew I was dead serious. He said that if that's what I wanted, he would do it, but that I should think twice about making this such a big deal. Anytime there's an officer confrontation, Internal Affairs has to be notified right away. Drummond should have opened an IAB investigation the day it happened, but he hadn't. If I escalated things now, it would reflect poorly on my boss, and Dellatorre knew Drummond and I were close. I said, "Y'all can fire Drummond, I don't care. You do what you have to do." Ford was transferred that night.

I couldn't believe it. A man had threatened me in front of my own child, and Drummond hadn't even opened an official complaint. I had to go over his head to get anything done. Mike Williams and I had both looked up to Drummond at the one-fourteen, and we were dumbfounded by it. We used to sit around and talk about how bad it was. It took me months to come to terms with it, but I finally became convinced that Drummond simply wasn't CO material. As a rookie in the one-fourteen, when he was my lieutenant, I'd idolized him as this powerful Malcolm X figure. But now that I was a lieutenant, I knew that the position doesn't give you any actual power. Being a precinct commander is a true executive position. You have to act fast, make decisions, carry them out. In the end, that wasn't Drummond. He wasn't a leader. He wasn't the man I thought he was.

Part of the problem was that Drummond was older. The job had passed him by; he leaned on Green out of necessity. Drummond had come up in the pre-Compstat era. He was used to working with the old, drunk Irish commanders. But those days were gone. Drummond didn't know anything about gathering data, analyzing information, deploying personnel. Every time he went to Compstat, he'd get totally embarrassed at the podium. He'd be up there flustered, forgetting answers to questions. I'd get phone calls the day after: "Yo, your boss is a fucking horror show."

The other part of the problem was that Drummond had been set up to fail. The NYPD wanted a black face in Harlem. It didn't matter if the person they appointed was qualified or not. And because of decades of terrible recruiting and hiring of black officers, there weren't many black faces in the pipeline. So they dusted off this old black guy from the 1970s and put him in the big chair.

The real problem wasn't Drummond. It was the culture of the department. If you were a black cop in the seventies and eighties, the only way to get ahead was to do nothing. Don't make waves, keep your head down, do the work, play the game—and when they need a black face somewhere, you'll get the nod. If you were outspoken or difficult, they'd wear you down. You'd get blackballed, pushed out. But leaders are outspoken. Leaders don't keep their heads down. Leadership is something you have to learn, and black men and women weren't being groomed to be leaders. I'd watch Drummond in meetings with Green. Green's default position was to defend the status quo. "Well, this is the way we've been doing it." And Drummond would go along. He didn't like to ruffle anybody's feathers. But you can't be Malcolm X if you don't like to ruffle people's feathers.

That headline the *New York Post* ran about David Dinkins at the height of the crime epidemic, DAVE, DO SOMETHING, that's how I felt every single day: Drummond, do something. Do anything. Change something. Change anything. Drummond was like Dinkins. They were cut from the same cloth. They both wanted to smooth everything over, be above the fray. And it wasn't only Drummond. There weren't many blacks in the upper ranks, but I felt like almost all of them fit the same mold: Be patient. Just wait a little longer. It'll work itself out. But that isn't the solution to everything. Sometimes you have to be willing to stand up and fight.

There was a generation gap in the department. There was a wave of black cops who'd come in under affirmative action in the early 1970s, and then there was a whole bunch of us who came in under the Safe Streets program in the early 1990s, and the two groups didn't always see eye to eye. As a sergeant, I'd started to get active in the black police community. You had groups like the Guardians and NOBLE, the National Organization of Black Law Enforcement Executives. Both of them were dedicated to improving conditions for black cops on the force and improving relationships between cops and black communities, but both of those organizations were older and reflected that older generation's tendency toward slow, incremental change.

The loudest, most outspoken group was 100 Blacks in Law Enforcement Who Care. 100 Blacks was cofounded by Eric Adams in 1995, specifically in response to Giuliani's election, and it had been a thorn in the mayor's side all through the Louima and Diallo scandals. Eric and I were close friends. We studied for the captain's exam together. He was a city kid, like me, had grown up in Bushwick and South Jamaica. He had graduated from the police academy with the highest grades in his class, and after making captain he went on to become a state senator and Brooklyn's first African-American borough president.

Eric was one of the leaders of the younger generation. You also had guys like Phil Banks, who was a few years ahead of me. He'd already been promoted to deputy inspector and would go on to serve as executive officer of Brooklyn South, commanding officer of Manhattan North, chief of Community Affairs, and would eventually be named chief of department in 2013, replacing Esposito when he retired and becoming the highest ranking black officer in the NYPD.

Eric Adams and Phil Banks and I were all fighting the same fight. Coming up behind us, you had guys like Mike Williams, ex-military, on his way to two master's degrees. Before Mike became a sergeant, he'd taken the shortcut to become a detective in narcotics. Then he saw me and these other guys moving up the ladder, proving that it could be done. He always tells me that's what motivated him to start studying and take the exam himself. More and more young guys were going that route.

We were the new generation. We were young, hungry, ready to shake things up. For the guys who'd come before us, it was a victory just to get on the force and keep your job. I think they'd been beat up so bad that by the time we were coming up, they were willing to go along to get along. I was sick of that. I'd expected racist white cops to stand in the way of my career; I'd never imagined that complacent black cops would do the same. We had this one meeting of 100 Blacks in Law Enforcement, and I was tired of everyone sitting around and talking about what needed to be done and not doing it. I stood up and said, "Yo, these black officers at captain and above? They ain't worth shit. They ain't doing nothin' to help us." And those guys were in the room. They all heard me. I didn't care.

As a young black person, you're taught to have so much reverence for the older generation, the heroes who came before you and fought for your freedom, the preachers and civil rights icons and Jackie Robinsons. You put them up on a pedestal, but the day comes—and it's a painful day—when you recognize their limitations. They were legends of their time, but they were also prisoners of their time. What was bold then isn't bold anymore. In Harlem, I realized that if black cops of my generation were going to see any real change, it wasn't going to come from the black captains and chiefs ahead of us. We were going to have to do it ourselves.

29

Thug Life

Brendale and I were out celebrating in the West Village one night. It was around two in the morning, and we'd had a lot to drink. We weren't married yet, but I'd been joking with her all night that I loved her so much I was going to get a tattoo of her name. I was completely wasted, just messing around. I didn't want a tattoo—she loved the idea.

There was a shoe store down there that was open late, and Brendale wanted to stop in and look at shoes. The girl who was helping us had this big tattoo right on her neck. Brendale was like, "Ooh, let me see that. I like that. Where did you get it?" The girl pointed to this tattoo parlor right across the street. Brendale looked at me, and I was like, "Yo, let's do it!"

I only said it because I knew I didn't have any cash on me. I'd spent my last $5 at the bar. I thought I wouldn't have to get the tattoo because I knew we couldn't pay for it. So we went over, told the lady at the tattoo parlor what we wanted, and asked how much. She said it was $110. I said, "Oops, too bad. Can't do it. Don't have the cash."

Brendale said, "Do you take credit cards?"

"Yes, we do."

Bam. She whipped out the plastic and slapped it on the counter. "Do it quick before he changes his mind."

So I did it. I got her name written in cursive on my neck. It was a fun, impulsive, drunken night that's stayed with me forever. One year later, we proved the tattoo wasn't a mistake when we got married. On March 8, 2003, we chartered a yacht, one of those big party boats you take out on the Hudson River, and had two hundred friends for a huge ceremony and party. We still had that photo of me walking her down the aisle at our sixth-grade graduation. We blew that up into a poster and had it at the ceremony, like this wedding was always meant to be. We moved out to Hempstead, Long Island, and settled into a quiet suburban life with the kids.

My tattoo took on a life of its own. Somewhere the rumor started that it said "Thug Life." Like Tupac's. It became one of those urban legends. Guys would be in the locker room saying, "Dude's tattoo says 'Thug Life.' I *swear*. I was standing right next to him. I saw it myself." The other rumor was that I only got my wife's name tattooed on my neck to cover up my old "Thug Life" tattoo. But you can't write over writing and have it be legible. Try it. It don't work.

The whole thing was ridiculous. The truth was that I was a family man working hard to take care of four kids. But this legend started to spread that I was some kind of gangsta cop. Corey "Thug Life" Pegues. Like I was Denzel Washington in *Training Day* or something. There are still people who believe it to this day.

———

The NYPD has a medical division. There are these mobile medical vans that come and visit the precincts to give you a physical, take your blood pressure, do EKGs. In February of 2004, they made their annual visit to the two-eight and we all got checked out. Drummond went down for his EKG, and they found an abnormality. He was taken to the hospital and had to have a stent put in his heart. For a while we weren't sure if he was going to be okay. I was devastated. My relationship with him was so complicated. I loved him like a father, but there were days when I hated him.

Drummond ended up staying out a few months. In the interim they appointed Captain Ken Thompson to serve as acting CO. Even after Drummond came back, Thompson stayed on as an additional executive officer, because Drummond wasn't physically up to the demands of the job anymore. From that point on, Thompson basically ran the precinct, but life under him wasn't any better than it had been under Drummond. Thompson was in his fifties, another one of these older black cops who played the game. Thompson and Green were buddies, and Green still didn't like me, so my situation didn't improve at all. I was a black lieutenant working under a black captain and a black precinct commander in the blackest neighborhood in America. My career should have been on fire. Instead it was stagnant. I'd been there two years, and I felt like I hadn't moved forward an inch. I was suffocating.

All the joy and romance of being in Harlem was ruined for me. The only good thing was that I could go out on my lunch break and walk down 125th Street, and the community showed me a lot of love. I'd have the white shirt on. People would see that and know I was a lieutenant. They didn't get to see too many black guys in the white shirt. They would smile and clap and give me the nod and say, "Wassup, Lieutenant?! Lookin' sharp." That would make my day. Then once I went back through the precinct doors it was hell.

My man Mike Williams was the only one keeping me sane. In October of 2004 he was called up to serve in Iraq. We gave him a big send-off, and once he left I was on my own. I wanted out. I scoured the department job postings. I applied for anything and everything, but of course no one would take me because I'd passed the captain's exam and would be leaving at the first opportunity. I applied for a transfer to narcotics. Didn't get it. I even applied to join the APD, the Applicant Processing Division. It's one of the most boring jobs in the NYPD. All you do is process applications for the police academy. It's 100 percent paperwork. I didn't get that, either.

I heard about an opening for an investigator in the vice department. It would have been a great move for my career. I applied for it. Vice handles gambling and prostitution. It's part of the OCCB, the

Organized Crime Control Bureau. The OCCB was run by Douglas Zeigler, a three-star chief who at the time was the highest-ranking black
officer in the department. I thought, Here's a black officer with real
leverage, a three-star chief. If I apply for this, maybe he'll help me out.

My interview was with Captain Warren, CO of the OCCB Investigation Unit. It was a tough interview. He grilled me, asking why he
should take me over guys with more experience. I told him that I was
young, but I was motivated and eager to learn. I told him I was uncor-
ruptible, which can be a big plus in vice. I also told him that I was still
probably two years away from promotion to captain, so I wouldn't be
leaving him in the lurch. By the end of the interview he said he was
impressed and that I'd be hearing from him soon. The next day Warren's lieutenant called and said the same thing. He said, "You aced
it. You're good." A week went by and I didn't hear anything. I called
the lieutenant, and he told me that I didn't get the job. I'd impressed
the captain, but Zeigler had finally made up his mind and weighed in
against me.

The white captain wanted me. The black chief said no.

It was the same with Thompson up in Harlem. He wasn't promoting my career or giving me opportunities to shine. It was so much
better back at the eight-one or the one-fourteen, dealing with racist cops like O'Rourke and Greeley. Racism I could handle. But these
older black officers, they were so insecure in their positions. I think
they felt like my "Thug Life" reputation was going to rub off on them
if they vouched for me. They played it safe and respectable. They'd
carved out their little forty acres in the department, and they held on
to it for dear life.

I loved being a cop. After growing up in the streets, I liked being
one of the good guys. But I was never a part of cop culture. These
old Irish and Italian guys, third- and fourth-generation cops, the
job was everything to them. They lived and breathed it. That wasn't
me. I didn't have a lot of cop friends. I didn't drink in cop bars. I went
home to Long Island and spent time with my family, or I went back

to Queens to hang out with old friends. I never left my community when I became a cop. The rule in the NYPD is that you can't associate with anyone who's a convicted felon. That's hard on black cops, because there's so much crime in our communities. A lot of us have convicted felons in our families.

Smooth didn't have a record, plus he was a corrections officer, so we could hang whenever we wanted. The other guys, I couldn't call them or reach out to them in any way, but I couldn't help it if we ran into each other at a bar every now and then. Mark was still in the game, still hustling. I didn't see him much. Dre got out of prison and was working as a maintenance man in an apartment complex. A lot of the guys from the Supreme Team went into hip-hop, managing or doing security. Malik was working with LL Cool J. Big Dave was working with Ja Rule at Murder Inc.

Those were my people. They were good people who'd made mistakes and changed their lives. I didn't stop being friends with them because I became a cop, and I didn't think I was better than them because I was a cop. I was going to succeed by being true to myself and my community, or I wasn't going to succeed at all. But it cost me. The way I dressed, the people I hung around with, it made my career much more difficult than it had to be.

———

There's this impression from the movies and TV that the Internal Affairs Bureau is this useless organization that doesn't do anything to catch bad cops. That's not exactly true. Bad cops do get away with abuse, and the blue wall of silence does protect them, but the NYPD is still a government bureaucracy. When you're a cop, IAB is all over you. Everything that happens gets documented. Any complaint that's filed, no matter how minor, there's an investigation. The bank lost a paycheck of mine once, and I had to file to get the check re-cut. Even that triggered an investigation, because they had to make sure I wasn't running a payroll scam.

It's good that IAB is vigilant, but the downside is that if there are cops who don't like you, the disciplinary system can be used against you, and it will grind your career to a halt. I was hassled constantly, given write-ups where other cops got warnings. I was investigated where other cops never would have been questioned. The same way black kids in the street are stopped and frisked for doing nothing, that's how the internal rules of the NYPD were applied to me. I was made a suspect for being myself.

As administrative lieutenant, one of your jobs is to arrange police details for special events. We had celebrities and politicians doing appearances on 125th Street all the time, book signings at the Hue-Man Bookstore, record signings at different music stores. I'd help coordinate the police presence with the retailers, and I'd usually show up on-site to make sure everything was going smoothly. I met a lot of celebrities that way: Bill and Hillary Clinton, Jay Z and Beyoncé, Kareem Abdul-Jabbar, Snoop Dog, Nelly, Bow Wow, Ja Rule. With the rappers and R&B artists, especially, because of my connections with LL Cool J and Queens hip-hop, I usually knew somebody who knew somebody in the entourage and I was able to go up and meet them and say hi.

One of my first events was a store opening for the beauty care company Carol's Daughter. Mary J. Blige was an investor, and she was there for the day. They were giving away promotional CDs. She signed one for me and we took a picture together. The photo ended up running in the *New York Daily News* the next day. I was all proud of the picture. I cut it out of the paper and put it in an album. Green wrote me up for it. He issued me a command discipline, a CD. The charge was having a personal cell phone displayed; you could see my phone in the picture.

This was when cell phones were new. As a cop, you were allowed to carry a personal cell phone, but you couldn't have it displayed, like on a belt clip. It was one of those rules that nobody followed and no one enforced. Of course the CD wasn't about the phone. It was Green trying to keep me in my place.

I was like, Okay, you want to write me up for this? Fine. Let's go. For the rest of the afternoon, every single cop who walked into the precinct with a cell phone, I wrote them up. Black, white, Chinese, didn't matter. "Hey, is that a cell phone? Gotta write you up." I wrote up something like twenty-six people in less than two hours. Cops were furious. Green's office was flooded with calls, guys complaining. He called me up and said, "What the hell are you doing?"

I said, "What? This is the new policy, right? We're enforcing the cell phone rule now, right?"

Green got flustered, because he knew I had him. I said, "Either you can get rid of mine, or I can keep doing this all day." He rescinded the CD. But it didn't end there. That November I was informed by the two-eight's PBA delegate that at least ten officers in the precinct had been called to testify in an IAB investigation into me. The charge was accepting unlawful gratuities—the album Mary J. Blige had signed for me. But it was a promotional disc. It was free to everyone in the store. It can't be unlawful to accept something that's free.

It wasn't just Mary J. Blige. IAB was asking questions about Nelly, Jay Z, Ja Rule. Because it was my job to manage these special events, I'd gotten autographed CDs from those guys, had my photos taken with them, and now all that was being investigated as being "improper." How many white cops do you think have been investigated for getting baseballs signed by Joe Torre, or getting their photo taken with Bruce Willis at a movie premiere? I guarantee you it's zero. It's never happened. But I was associating with rappers, and someone at the precinct had decided to report it as reflecting badly on the force.

When people couldn't use something like the Mary J. Blige photo to trump up charges against me, they made things up. In April of 2004, somebody sent an anonymous letter to Commissioner Ray Kelly. It said that I "talk to everyone like a thug" and that "he stands at Roll Call sometimes with his doo rag/hat backwards pants falling off his person (thug outfit)." It said I was "a menace" to the precinct; that I was having sex with women behind locked doors; that I was drinking and driving home from work; that I was so drunk at the Christmas party that I pulled my pants down, took my dick out, and pissed out a window. It was complete fiction. It was to smear my name. But the complaint was made, and so an IAB investigation had to be opened.

It was exhausting. By the summer of 2005, I'd been in the two-eight for three years, two and a half of them on the captain's list, waiting and waiting to be promoted, and my number was finally getting close. I didn't need any entanglements slowing me down. Then, on August 2, I got called down for another investigation. Three guys had been picked up in Los Angeles on a gun charge. Two of them were executives with the rap label Murder Inc, Dexter Ottley and Tanik Williams. The third guy was a rapper with the label, Taheem Crocker, "Cadillac Tah."

Crocker had my business card on him. That was it. That's what triggered the whole investigation. I couldn't believe it. Anybody who's ever seen a cop show on TV, what do the cops do with every single person they meet? "Here's my card. Call me if you see anything." That's what cops do. We give out business cards. Cops give out business cards *to criminals* all the time, because criminals are useful contacts for solving crimes. But somebody had found my business card in a rapper's car, and that was enough for somebody to open an investigation and call my character into question.

I didn't know Crocker. I had no relationship with him. Rappers did shows at the Apollo and album release parties all the time in Harlem. I'd probably given my business card to every rapper and hip-hop executive who'd come through while I was at the two-eight. And from that somebody suspected that I was associating with felons in a criminal enterprise. It was all I could do not to laugh in the IAB investigator's face. I said, "Do you have any idea how many business cards I give out every month? It's got to be hundreds. I'm responsible for where they all end up?"

I was exonerated of the charges, every time: the unlawful gratuities, the lies about the Christmas party, the business card crap. If any of it had been true, I'd never have made deputy inspector. I was the cleanest cop on the beat, because I knew what people thought of me. I knew they looked at me like a thug, so I walked a straight line.

Still it was a major hassle, and it was becoming a drag on my advancement. Just because you pass the captain's exam and your number comes up, that doesn't mean you get the promotion. If you've got open investigations, the department can hold up your promotion, make you wait. Or they can send you out to be a captain in the 123rd Precinct out in the middle of nowhere at the far end of Staten Island. And these investigations, once they're open, they can take forever to resolve. You have no control over how fast they move. A higher-ranking officer can help you out. They can call IAB and move things along, but the black captains and chiefs, they weren't doing that for me.

To succeed in any job you have to have a rabbi, someone who counsels you and looks out for you. Fortunately I didn't just have a rabbi. I had the ayatollah: Chief of Department Esposito. We weren't drinking buddies or anything like that, but we'd become friendly. I'd drop him a line here and there, stay in touch. Now he was the top uniformed officer in the NYPD, on his way to being the only four-star chief in the department. I never played the game the way a lot of other black cops played it, by trying to make friends with white cops I knew would never respect me anyway. But I knew I needed relationships with the right people, and when you're one of the few black faces in an organization like the NYPD, you develop a sense for finding the people who'll give you a fair shot. You grab those people and you hold on to them. Esposito was one of those guys. As my number got closer and closer and I had all this IAB crap hanging over me, I reached out to his office. He said he'd make a call. I don't know what he said to people, but it probably went something like "Hey, you got an open case on Corey? Is it something big? No? Okay, close it out, because we're looking to promote him." Once he did that, my problems went away.

That's how the game works. Esposito vouched for me in ways that Zeigler and Thompson and even Drummond never did. Black officers worried about all that thug nonsense rubbing off on them. Esposito was white and powerful; he didn't care. When I first interviewed with him, I had the cornrows and everything. For whatever reason, he looked at me and he didn't see a thug. He saw a young cop with potential. But if I don't know Esposito and he doesn't make that call, the process moves slow and my whole career slows down—and a lot of black and brown cops don't have anyone to make that call.

30

Black Friday

The whole spring and summer of 2005 I was marking time, trying to keep my head above water, waiting on my promotion.
That April, Drummond was transferred out, sent to head up the
school safety division for Queens South. School safety is what's
called a black-track job. Same with community affairs. You're black
and you've got the rank and the seniority, but you're never going to
get one of the big, heavy-hitter jobs, like chief of department or head
of counterintelligence. So they promote you to a peripheral department like school safety or community affairs where you'll stay until
retirement.

In May I completed my master's degree in criminal justice leadership from St. John's University in Queens, and with that I applied
for a teaching position at Monroe College. I started teaching Intro
to Criminal Justice two days a week. I felt like I was filling out my résumé, showing initiative. In retrospect, none of that mattered. Once
you hit captain and above, it's who you know and who you blow.

Finally, after the longest three and a half years of my life, on December 28, I got the call promoting me to captain. The promotion
came with a $25,000 bump in salary. Needed that. Was happy to get it.
I called my wife and told her. Called my friends and family. A couple
weeks later I got a call from Assistant Chief Joseph Cuneen, borough
commander for Brooklyn North. He congratulated me and asked me
which precinct I'd prefer. I said, "I'd love to go to the seven-five."

He said, "Good. Because that's where we're sending you."

He told me they were making me executive officer at the 75th Precinct in East New York. When he told me that, I was floored. I suspected Esposito's fingerprints were all over it; he was giving me my shot. The seven-five is not a black-track job. It's not a dead-end promotion. You only get a posting like that when the higher-ups think you've got a big future ahead of you.

The seven-five is an unusual precinct. It's the largest in New York, so big it's divided into three different zones. Each zone has its own executive officer, and within that zone the executive officer functions like the commander of his own mini-precinct. You have your own anti-crime team, your own narcotics team, etc. The seven-five is also, without question, one of the most violent parts of New York. The 75th, the 73rd, and the 67th, covering East New York, Brownsville, and East Flatbush, respectively—those are three adjoining precincts in the heart of Brooklyn. They form the most violent corridor in the entire city. Every year they're the top three precincts for murder, rape, robbery, theft, you name it. In the NYPD, if you want to get ahead, you have to go where it's hot, and the seven-five was on fire.

On January 20, I reported to 2000 Sutter Avenue in East New York to meet with the other two executive officers, Captain Foster and Captain Marshall, and with the precinct commander, Inspector David Barerre.

I liked Barrere right away. Guy was sharp as a tack. He was a real rising star in the department. He was young, too. Only a few years older than me and he'd already made full inspector. Like me, he was also first-generation NYPD, new blood. He didn't seem to have the same mentality as the third- and fourth-generation guys who'd grown up deep in the culture. I could tell that for him it wasn't about protecting the old ways of doing things. It was about doing the job and doing it well.

We chatted a bit. I could tell he'd heard a few things about me, but he seemed like a guy who was going to hold off judgment and make up his own mind. He was frank with me about my promotion. East New York is mostly black, with a few Hispanic pockets here and there. The community leaders had been asking for a black executive officer for a while, to foster better relationships with the community. That was part of the reason I was there, which meant I was going to have responsibilities beyond the other XOs.

He told me, "Listen, for me to run this precinct well, I need you to know everything I know. Any meeting I have, you can come with me." He told me to dress the part, come in looking sharp, suit and tie every day—and get ready to work. Other bosses at other precincts had always tried to keep me in my place. But with Barerre, from that first meeting he was telling me to reach higher, do more. I walked out of his office feeling like I was finally being given a chance to prove myself.

A couple of days later I reported for my first full day of work. I let my wife take the car and I took the train in from Long Island. A patrol officer picked me up at the East New York Station to drive me to the precinct. In the forties and fifties East New York was mostly Italian and Jewish, but even then it wasn't a nice neighborhood. It had lots of problems with crime. In the sixties and seventies the whites fled. Blacks and Puerto Ricans moved in. Slumlords exploited the poor residents and ran the housing stock into the ground. Several public housing projects had been built in the area. They were meant to be middle-class housing for the veterans coming back from World War II, but they were mismanaged and underfunded and segregated and they turned into slums.

By the height of the crack-cocaine era, East New York and Browns-ville were like a war zone, whole blocks of vacant lots and abandoned buildings, places burnt-out and boarded-up, squatters, gangs. In the late eighties, a cop from the seven-five walked to a bodega across the street from the precinct to get a soda—and got shot. Right across from the precinct. That's how messed up East New York was.

By the time I arrived in 2006, crime in the seven-five had come down significantly along with the rest of the city, but it was still a violent place, a poor neighborhood. There were no major businesses serving the area. You'd drive around and there'd be a 99-cent store and a liquor store every other block. Pawnshops and pay-day lenders. Nail salons and beauty shops. Fried chicken joints and Caribbean fish joints and Chinese takeout. That was it. At the north end of the precinct was Highland Park, which had some nice, million-dollar homes, but that's a small slice of the precinct. Below that it was a lot of single-family homes, mostly Hispanic. In the center was where you found most of the housing projects: the Cypress Hills Houses, the Linden Houses, Fiorentino Plaza, the Boulevard Houses, the Pink Houses—the Stinky Pinks.

To the south of that was what we called the Flatlands. That was the industrial zone—warehouses, shipping centers. At night it was deserted, and that's where prostitutes would be out, up and down Stanley Avenue, whistling and flashing their tits at passing cars. From there it ran down to the Jamaica Bay, where you had the wetlands around Fresh Creek Park and Spring Creek Park. With all the killing that went on in the seven-five, it was a popular place to dump bodies. We'd pull them out of there all the time.

When starting a shift as a commander, the first thing on your agenda is to check in with the dispatcher. They're going to tell you how many jobs you've got. That's how many calls from 911 are open and need to be resolved. It's your job to look at the manpower you've got and decide what to prioritize and who to send where. In Bed-Stuy or Harlem, you'd come in and the dispatcher might say, "You're hauling eight jobs." Maybe eleven if it's a busy Saturday night. In the seven-five, I'd walk in and the dispatcher would say, "Captain, you're hauling fifty jobs." And that was on a regular Tuesday. That's fifty people who've called 911 and who are still waiting for officers to arrive. It's a stabbing, three shootings, ten domestics, five robberies, and so on. You don't have enough cops to cover all of them. You don't even have time to sit down. You're watching the jobs come up on the screen, and you're on the radio to your patrol cars: "Adam, what are you doing? You're on a domestic? No. Leave that. We've got a stabbing over on Pitkin. I need you there." It's like being an emergency room doctor in the middle of a natural disaster. You're trying to stop the bleeding.

East New York was out of control. From day one it was like being thrown to the wolves. In the one-fourteen or the two-eight, there was crime, but the truly violent crimes were rare. The seven-five was so violent that the violence became normal. It all blurred together. I only remember certain cases because I put them down in my diary: A female college student's body, pulled out of Betts Creek, bound, gagged, and raped. Four people, including a child, gunned down in a mass shooting at Long Island Baptist Housing. A three-year-old girl found beaten to death at nine in the morning. A black stripper pulled out of the Fresh Creek basin, stab wounds in her neck and chest and burns all over her body. A sixteen-year-old killed by her stepfather, who butchered her with a kitchen knife and then hung himself in a closet. An eighty-two-year-old woman and her sixty-year-old mentally retarded son found dead in the summer heat because they had no air-conditioning.

It went on like that. My first six months in the seven-five we had thirteen murders, the most of any precinct in the city. For that year the seven-five had twenty-nine murders, fifty-eight rapes, eight hundred robberies, nearly five hundred stolen cars, and over seven hundred felony assaults. That's more than double the numbers coming in at the two-eight in Harlem or at the eight-one in Bed-Stuy.

Every Monday we had crime strategy meetings. It was Barerre and the three captains. He'd bring in narcotics, anti-crime, the warrant squad. He had maps up on the wall, spreadsheets on the projector, everybody communicating and sharing information and analyzing it. "Narcotics, where you at? We got four people shot on the east end of the precinct. What's your activity over there? Any stash houses?" We'd have a cluster of auto thefts and we'd be pulling five years' worth of data on who'd been stealing cars, which ones were just out of prison, where they lived, where they worked. Every day in the seven-five was lunch at your desk, poring over crime statistics, studying the data, looking for patterns.

Barerre was a true Compstat-era guy. Super-sharp. He could reel statistics and numbers off the top of his head and analyze information on the fly. It was like he had a map of the entire precinct in his mind and could see what was happening when and where. I knew about crime from the street level, from being a patrolman and, formerly, a gangster. Barerre taught me how to think about crime from the top down, how to look at a neighborhood from ten thousand feet and see how everything worked together. At these crime strategy meetings, he'd pull out a map with a cluster of robberies and say, "Corey, why is this happening here? What do you see when you see this? What should we do?" We'd break everything down and talk through the strategy.

Every few weeks, Barerre had to go and take the podium for Compstat meetings, and as XO I would go with him. He said, "I'm going to show you how to do this, because you'll need to know." The guy was an ace at those meetings, cool under fire. He rarely had to check the book; he knew everything from memory. I watched how he studied, how he prepared, how he handled tough questions. Even though I was rarely called on to speak, every time the seven-five was up for Compstat, I stayed up all night studying the data from my zone as if I was going to be grilled myself.

As teacher and student, Barerre and I clicked. When you're a captain, you're given a performance review at six and ten months. You're rated from one to five on a number of metrics: communication skills, managerial skills, community relations, and so on. A three means you've met department standards, a four means you're above average, and a five means you've exceeded all expectations. In both of my evaluations as captain, Barerre gave me straight fives across the board. Drummond never gave me those kinds of ratings.

The other two XOs in the seven-five, Marshall and Foster, were both good cops, and they both had seniority over me. But soon after I arrived, Barerre was delegating responsibilities to me that should have been theirs. If he couldn't make a meeting, he didn't think twice about sending me to speak for him and represent the department. The first time he did that I'd only been at the precinct six weeks. Congressman Ed Towns, East New York's representative in DC, was holding a town meeting to discuss community issues and problems. It was with a group of three hundred people. Barerre was supposed to go and address local crime concerns, but he couldn't make it and asked me to go instead. I'd never done a meeting like that in my life. I said, "Sir, I'm not sure. You want me to handle this?"

He said, "Corey, you'll be fine."

I went. The place was packed with community officials. It was Ed Towns; his son Darryl Towns, the state assemblyman for the district; Charles Barron, the city councilman for the district; several leading pastors; and community activists. Everyone there knew I was the new guy. Plus these people hadn't seen a black captain in a long time, so they were anxious to see what I was all about. They grilled me about everything that was going on with the police and the community, but I handled myself well. After the meeting, Ed Towns was like, "Captain Pegues, you did a great job. Welcome aboard."

From that point on, Barerre kept me in a public-facing role with the community and the community leaders. Once you make captain, you're like a local politician. Your promotions from there on are discretionary. If the community doesn't like you or organizes against you, it can hurt your career. Charles Barron was especially hard on the NYPD when it came to abuse and brutality in the black community. By giving me face time with these people, Barerre was giving me the opportunity to build the relationships I'd need to continue to move up.

In Harlem, Drummond and Thompson taught me nothing. Literally nothing. They never let me shadow them at Compstat. They never took me aside and said, "Hey, you're about to make captain. You need to know this, that, or the other." That never happened. Barerre was doing for me what the NYPD had failed to do with black executives for the past forty years: He was grooming me to be a leader. He wasn't trying to keep me in my place, he was showing me how to move up and take his place. He taught me the right way and the wrong way to do things. He let me make mistakes and learn from them. He gave me the room to run and stretch my legs and do the best that I could.

I knew part of the reason I was getting these opportunities was because the department needed a black face in East New York, but I wasn't being treated like a token. Barerre was delegating real, substantial responsibilities to me, over and above what he needed to. It felt so good to have someone believe in me like that. I felt empowered. It was the same way I felt when I climbed in that army recruiter's car and sped off down the Belt Parkway, leaving my life in the streets behind. When I got in that recruiter's car and went off to join the army, that was the first time I felt like I was in control of my life. *I* was in charge. *I* was making the decisions. When you're young and black and poor, you feel like you don't have any power, any control over your own life. Kids join gangs and sell drugs because at least it gives them the feeling that they're doing *something*; they're making money, asserting themselves. In the Supreme Team, when someone like Prince or Malik promotes you to run a corner or handle a package, you feel good because it's probably the first time someone's given you respect and responsibility. It's a trap, because it's a dead-end that leaves you in jail or in the morgue, but kids keep doing it because no one is offering them anything better. The situation in Harlem was depressing because I'd worked so hard to lift myself up only to find myself powerless again. I couldn't make things happen for myself. Now, at the seven-five, I had this commander telling me, "Corey, take the ball and run with it." I did, and it was amazing.

The seven-five was the best-run precinct I'd ever worked. Not only was the administration efficient, but we regularly interfaced with the people we were sworn to protect. There's always friction between cops and minority communities, even when times are good. We had civilian complaints. We had testy meetings with community leaders, but we managed it well. The year I made captain was the year stop-and-frisk started to become a flashpoint with the public. In 2002, New Yorkers were stopped by the cops 97,296 times. In 2006, they were stopped 506,491 times. Citizen complaints about stop-and-frisk had more than doubled and now made up 33 percent of all complaints filed citywide. In the seven-five, civilian complaints about stop-and-frisk were definitely on the rise, but complaints about abuse and brutality were surprisingly low, or at least it felt that way to me.

Perps getting tuned up, guys coming in with the turban on—back in the one-fourteen that was a regular Saturday night. In the seven-five I rarely saw it, and the seven-five was *way* more violent than those other precincts. If anything, there easily could have been more abuse, more brutality, more cops going off out of fear and frustration. But there wasn't. I give Barerre a lot of credit for that. In a paramilitary organization, it's up to the commander to show leadership and set the tone, and Barerre did. When he addressed the troops, he would remind them, "Treat these people with respect. This is their community. We're here to serve them and protect them."

When we had problem cops, those with too many civilian complaints, Barerre would be on it. He'd punish them, put them on a desk, transfer them out. PBA delegates were up in Barerre's office all the time, bitching and moaning about their guys having to actually follow the rules, and Barerre would tell them, "I'm the commander of this precinct and this is the way we're going to do it and that's that." And when it came to the real hotheads, the ticking time bombs, Barerre didn't play. He wasn't going to have an Abner Louima on his watch. He would say that at roll call: "If you do anything to embarrass this command, I will crush you." That's how he would talk.

I was only at the seven-five for a brief time, eleven months. If my career had been on a normal trajectory, I probably would have been in that post for two or three years and I might have seen more. But it turned out my career wasn't on a normal trajectory at all. Early on the morning of November 26, I was at home asleep when I got the call: fifty shots fired outside the Club Kalua right by the Jamaica train station, one man dead, two others injured. The dead man's name was Sean Bell. I didn't have to ask to know that he was black. Club Kalua was a strip club right in the middle of my old stomping grounds in southeast Queens. Bell was out with friends celebrating for his bachelor party. Undercover cops watching the club said there was an argument outside on the sidewalk; they claimed they heard somebody say something about getting a gun, so they followed this group of guys back to their car, weapons drawn. When Bell saw men in plainclothes coming after him with a gun, he panicked and tried to pull away. His bumper clipped one of the cops and they panicked, too, and emptied fifty rounds into the car. Bell was killed just after 4 a.m. on the day he was supposed to get married.

When I heard, my first thought was, Oh, man. Here we go. Another one. There'd been other high-profile killings of unarmed black people by police since Diallo, all on Commissioner Kelly's watch. In Harlem in 2003, a fifty-seven-year-old woman named Alberta Spruill died of a heart attack when police broke down her door and threw a concussion grenade into her apartment, thinking it was the apartment of a drug dealer. That same year, an African immigrant named Ousmane Zongo was shot four times, twice in the back, in a warehouse in Chelsea. It was a raid on a CD/DVD counterfeiting operation, but Zongo wasn't a part of the operation. He was a guy who happened to be in the building at the wrong time. In 2004, a nineteen-year-old kid named Timothy Stansbury was shot on the roof of the Louis Armstrong Houses in Bed-Stuy. A cop panicked at the sight of him and shot, never identifying himself as a police officer. All the kid had on him were CDs he was taking to a party.

And those are just the stories that made the biggest headlines.

In the cases of Spruill and Stansbury, the officers involved were never indicted; both incidents were ruled accidents. In the case of Zongo, the officer was convicted of criminally negligent homicide but didn't serve any jail time. In all three cases, there was no change in department policy, no damage to Kelly's reputation.

Sean Bell was different. Fifty bullets fired at one unarmed man. It was on the level of Louima and Diallo. Kelly didn't have any political cover—he didn't have any black faces to hide behind. Serving under Dinkins, Kelly had had a fantastic reputation with the black community. Under Bloomberg, it was different, especially in the upper ranks of the department. Kelly didn't have any black officers in his top circle of advisors. At the time of Bell's shooting, there wasn't a single black borough commander, and Kelly hadn't appointed any in his term. There were only four black chiefs in the whole department: James Secreto, Elton Mohommed, Gerald Nelson, and Douglas Zeigler. None of them held key positions. Secreto was the executive officer at Brooklyn Borough South. Mohammed was head of the Applicant Processing Division, a black-track job. Nelson was head of School Safety, another black-track job. Zeigler, the only three-star black chief, had been head of the Organized Crime Control Bureau when I applied to go to vice in 2004. But earlier in 2006 Kelly had moved Zeigler to Community Affairs—also a black-track job, a far less important one, and a huge demotion. For the top spot at OCCB, Kelly replaced his only three-star black chief with a two-star white chief, Anthony Izzo.

On December 19, Deputy Chief Cuneen was retiring from Brooklyn North, and they were having a walkout for him. When a high-ranking executive retires and walks out of the precinct for the last time, everybody lines up outside to congratulate him and applaud his service; that's what's called a walkout. I was there, and Deputy Chief Marino, XO for Brooklyn North, pulled me aside and said, "Look, Esposito called me and asked if you're ready for your own command. I told him you are. You better not let me down." I went numb. I stood there dead in my tracks. I couldn't believe it. I wasn't expecting my own command or any kind of promotion at all.

Three days later, on Friday, December 22, Gerald Nelson was promoted to commanding officer of Brooklyn Borough North, replacing Cuneen. Phil Banks was promoted to deputy chief and assigned as the executive officer of Brooklyn Borough South, replacing James Secreto. Secreto was promoted to take Nelson's old spot as the head of School Safety. Eddie Caban, who's Hispanic, was assigned as the commanding officer of the 25th Precinct in Manhattan. And I got the call from Chief Marino telling me I was being named commander of Police Service Area #2, which covered housing projects in North Brooklyn.

I called it Black Friday. Five minority executives getting moved up to precinct or borough commands in one day? That was unprecedented. I don't know if it's happened since, but it had definitely never happened before. It wasn't how I wanted my first command to come: getting promoted because the department needed political cover after another unarmed black man got shot. But you don't have any control over how these things happen. All I could do was make the most of the opportunity. This was the moment Barerre had been grooming me for, and I knew that Esposito and Marino wouldn't have given the go ahead unless they thought I was ready.

I knew I was ready, too.

31

Everybody Is Looking for You to Fail

The day before I took over PSA #2 I got a call from Chief Zeigler's secretary. He wanted to meet with me to congratulate me. I'd never felt particularly close to him, ever since he passed me over for the investigator position with vice, but I was happy to take the meeting. I told her, "Okay, I'll come down to his office."

She said, "No, he'll come to you."

Zeigler drove out to my office and sat with me for four and a half hours. I'll never forget it. He sat there the whole morning and gave me a man-to-man talk. He said, "Look, you're here, and all eyes are on you. Everybody is looking for you to fail, which is why you have to succeed—and I'm here for you if you need me."

I'd never felt any love from the black chiefs. I felt like they were distancing themselves from me because of the "Thug Life" rumors and all that. But Zeigler said he'd been watching me work and he was impressed. He'd come around and now had a lot of respect for me. It felt good to finally have his approval, and I know Ray Kelly hadn't given me a command without getting a sign-off from the black chiefs. I know he called them up and said, "What do you think about Corey?" And they had to have said, "Give the kid a shot." I know that for a fact. That's how it works for black cops.

I won't lie: I loved being in charge. It's so rare that black men are given real authority in America, real opportunities to flex our muscles and show our full potential. I grabbed that authority with both hands and ran with it. I saw commanders come in wearing a button-down shirt and jeans, and they'd call that dress code. I'd come to work in a suit and tie every day, rain, sleet, or snow. I had a hookup, a friend who worked in fashion. He'd get me high-end suits at a deep discount. Most cops dress like they bought everything at JCPenney. I was wearing Calvin Klein and Ermenegildo Zegna, Gucci shoes and Ferragamo loafers. Nobody in the projects had ever seen anything like it. I'd walk through the houses in designer suits, with a neck tattoo and a ditty-bop in my step. Other cops would be running up and saluting me and saying, "Yes, sir," and the kids would see that and they'd be like, "Yo, that's the fuckin' *boss* right there."

If you walked into the headquarters for PSA #2, you wouldn't think it was much of a command. It's nothing like a precinct. Precincts are big. PSA #2 is a squat, dingy building on Sutter Avenue just inside the seven-five. The gym and locker room in the basement were always flooding because the sewer would back up and the toilets would overflow. The city needed a new pump that cost something like $100,000 and there was never any money for it. Cops would be down there trying to get dressed and there would be shit lying on the floor.

That may make it sound like I'd been given a terrible posting, but the NYPD doesn't work like most employers. The best jobs are in the worst places. PSA #2 was the most violent housing precinct in the city. It was all the projects of East New York, plus Brownsville—where you've got the Tilden Houses and the Van Dyke Houses, which are even more violent than the ones in East New York—and Crown Heights on top of that.

There's a saying in the NYPD: "Housing's not available." Anytime there's a radio call for housing, the dispatcher will come back, "Housing's not available." As a precinct commander, you've got about four hundred people working under you. In housing, I had a hundred and fifty cops to patrol forty separate housing projects. That's it. Despite being merged with the city police, housing and transit were still the stepchildren of the department. The only reason housing and transit continued to function as separate divisions was because the city still got federal dollars to operate them that way. We're talking millions of dollars a year. Operationally, there's no real reason for housing to exist. Housing cops respond to radio calls and complaints, but there's no detective unit, no narcotics unit. Anytime there's a shooting or a major crime in the projects, housing cops take the call, but the investigation and follow-up goes back to the precinct level. So there's this weird jurisdictional overlap, and housing is always an afterthought.

I didn't know housing when I started. I had to learn it on the fly. It's completely different from any other type of policing. It's the opposite of transit. In transit you have millions of people on your watch, but they're passing through, total strangers. Even in a precinct, you're usually moving around too much to get to know people well. Housing is intimate. You're dealing with people where they live. You get to know everybody, and it's the same people, month after month, year after year. Some of these families are third and fourth generation, stuck in the same place.

Outsiders don't come into the projects. You'll never meet anyone and hear them say, "Hey, let's go hang out at the Pink Houses." You don't live in the Pinks, you ain't goin' to the Stinks. It's not happening. The only people in a project are the people who live there. Crime in the projects is different, too. You don't get a lot of property crime. Very few stolen cars, not much breaking and entering; people don't have much worth stealing. What you do have is pockets of drug crime that usually become violent. Drug-related shootings are common. So is gang activity. The Crips and the Bloods, and every project has its own gang, too. It's territorial.

With shootings, it's usually project against project. The Tilden Houses and the Van Dyke Houses are literally across the street from each other. People from Tilden won't go into Van Dyke. People from Van Dyke won't go into Tilden. If they do, guys start beefing over turf and they're all armed to the teeth and things get violent. That kind of crime is hard to deter, because it's crime of passion, driven by revenge. I've had cops on patrol and gangsters would roll up and shoot someone with the cop right there. They don't care about the cops.

My first year at PSA #2 I had 12 murders, 12 rapes, 72 shootings, and 255 felony assaults. Low-income areas are always going to have a higher index of crime. You can't take thousands of poor people and ex-convicts, warehouse them in one place, give them no opportunities, and not have drama. It don't work. People are desperate. Addicts can't get treatment. People living on the margins of the system, people who don't trust the cops or the courts, are more likely to settle things with a gun than go hire a lawyer they can't afford in the first place. More than likely they'll seek out safety in numbers, which is why you have gangs.

Gangs have existed for decades. Not just black and Latino gangs, but Irish, Italian, Jewish—everybody. Gangs serve as families and institutions in neighborhoods that have no institutional support, where families are torn apart by having so many men in prison or out of work. The difference is that, back in the day, a gang member might be carrying a switchblade or a set of brass knuckles, maybe a .38 revolver. Gang fights usually ended with a trip to the hospital, not the morgue.

With gangs, that territorial, street-tough machismo hasn't changed. What's changed is the access to firearms. The streets are flooded with illegal handguns, shotguns, automatic and semiautomatic rifles. The thing about illegal guns is that they're easy to get and easy to conceal, which makes it almost impossible to get them out of circulation before a crime is committed. So far, police departments have come up with only one effective tactic for getting illegal guns off the street: Stop, Question, and Frisk.

The abuse of Stop, Question, and Frisk by the Street Crime Unit

under Giuliani and Safir—rolling up on the corners, randomly tossing everyone in sight—those tactics were flagrantly unconstitutional. They were racially targeted and antagonized black and Latino
communities. But those tactics did get a lot of guns off the street, so
city hall demanded more, more, more. Then Ray Kelly came back
and—even though he'd denounced the abuse of the practice while
out of office—as commissioner he doubled down on it. He made it
the signature, the hallmark, of his administration. In 2002, New Yorkers were stopped by police 97,296 times. The next year people were
stopped by police 160,851 times. In 87 percent of the stops the person was totally innocent and never charged, 54 percent of the stops
were of blacks, and 31 percent of them of Latinos. In 2006, the year
before I assumed my command, the number of stops had exploded:
to 506,491.

The NYPD isn't entirely to blame for the abuse of Stop, Question,
and Frisk. Much of the blame lies with politicians. Politicians are so
beholden to the gun lobby that they won't pass gun control legis-
lation at the state and federal level. So the streets get flooded with
guns. Which means there are more shootings and killings. Then those
same politicians start breathing down cops' necks, saying "Catch the
perps. Get the guns." So the pressure to meet quotas goes up and up
and up. But short of unconstitutional stops and illegal searches, it's
almost impossible to get the guns once they're in the streets.

Another reason Stop, Question, and Frisk exploded, in my opinion, was because of one of the measures that tried to fix it. Under
Giuliani and Safir, the UF-250 reporting form had a blank space for
officers to write in the reason for the stop, and half the time, whatever cops were writing on the form came out illegible. Opponents of
Stop, Question, and Frisk wanted better reporting data on why the
stops were happening, so in 2001 the blank space was replaced with
a series of boxes to check. The boxes gave you reasons you could tick
off, like "suspicious bulge" or "time of day."

The boxes made things worse. Before, when you had to write it out, you at least had to be able to articulate a reason in your own mind. You had to describe a narrative that bore some passable resemblance to reality. But with the boxes, you didn't even have to make up a pretext to stop someone. The pretext was already made up and spelled out for you on the form. With that, you could stop anybody at any time for no legitimate reason. Add that to the political pressure coming down from city hall, and the number of stops exploded.

————

Public housing was ground zero for Stop, Question, and Frisk. When I got to PSA #2, it was out of control. I started going to community meetings with the tenant association presidents, and they'd chew my ear off about young men getting hassled. At the time the total population of the projects in PSA #2 was 47,250 people. The year before I arrived, in 2006, there were 18,667 stops—a 44 percent increase from 12,944 stops the year before. And that's just the number of times they got stopped by PSA#2 cops; that doesn't include any stops by precinct cops.

People in the projects have nowhere to go. The streets and the sidewalks are their front yard. The drunks are out there on the benches, getting wasted; that's their summer vacation. Down at the sidewalk you've got young guys on the scaffolding—there's always construction scaffolding on the projects—they're down there doing pull-ups on the bars. That's their gym. They're home from prison and there are no jobs for them, nothing else to do. In the projects, private spaces are public spaces, and public spaces get patrolled by cops. The things people do in their backyards and get away with—getting drunk, getting into fights, and getting loud—people in the projects get hassled over it.

Technically, the cops have a right to stop and search anyone who enters a housing project without a key; that person has to prove that he or she lives there. But the locks on most of the front doors in the projects have been busted for years, and there's no money to fix them. So nobody uses keys, which means everybody can be stopped. Imagine if you had a cop in the foyer of your house, waiting to search you every time you came home. You might start to resent it, too.

The cops have these quotas to meet, but because there are no outsiders coming into the projects, you've got the same small pool of young black and Latino men getting stopped and searched over and over and over again. They're getting searched four and five times a week, and it's four or five different cops doing the searches because no one's sharing information. How many times are you going to stop and search the same innocent person?

Stop, Question, and Frisk is necessary. It is useful. If you see a guy in a trench coat in the middle of July and he's walking down the street with a limp, that's a guy you might want to stop. Odds are he's got a shotgun. But if you see a group of guys on a corner and one of them actually does have a bulge in his waistband, you don't go and toss the whole corner. You wait until that guy peels off and you stop him alone around the corner. That's police work.

Indiscriminately searching people is not police work. It's a response to political pressure. It's not something that most cops *want* to do. Most cops actually aren't thrilled about searching people. Most cops don't want to start drama that's going to escalate. They want to work their shift, avoid problems, and go home alive. If you give a cop permission to *not* do something, he's usually more than happy to not do it.

At that time, in almost every precinct in the city, the pressure was on cops to show they were making stops. So when I got to PSA #2, I reversed the pressure. I called my cops out if their numbers were too high. The only thing I looked at was the ratio of quality stops. If you came to me with a hundred UF-250s and you had only one gun, I knew that the majority of your stops were bogus. If you came in with twenty UF-250s and you had three guns, okay, I'd take it. If 40 percent of the guys you stopped had priors, fine. I knew you were looking at gangsters and not hassling high school kids. You were doing police work.

The year after I got to PSA #2, UF-250s were down nearly every week. Usually 30 to 40 percent, sometimes 50 percent. Because of that, it was my turn to get reamed out at Compstat. I always killed it at Compstat. After all those years of studying twice as hard to pass my promotion exams, poring over books at the dinner table, my brain was a machine for memorizing data and crunching numbers. I'd usually go in there on a few hours' sleep. I'd stay up the night before in my office, poring over the stats. I could get up at that podium and fire off answers like it was nothing. They would try to rattle you, intimidate you, but I never let them get to me. I'd have a dozen shootings and four bodies in the streets, and I could give you the whole rundown on every single one without even checking the book.

I'd get grilled about the UF-250s. "Why aren't you stopping people? You've got two shootings in the Pink Houses and only five stops. Where are the stops? Why didn't you blanket the area?"

I'd stand my ground. "Chief, I was there. Those were the only five people we felt could have committed the crime. The rest we didn't have a reasonable suspicion to stop." The thing that saved me was I could point to the quality of my stops. We were still getting a decent number of gun arrests. We had a quality hit rate of stopping felons instead of innocent pedestrians. And nobody could argue with the results: At the end of my first year in PSA #2, despite the rash of shootings, overall major felony crime was down 9.4 percent. I had two more homicides than the previous year, but in every other major index—rape, robbery, felony assault, burglary, grand larceny, and grand larceny auto—crime was down. I'd proved that I could do the job.

I'd been at PSA #2 for eighteen months when I got the call. It was late on May 29, 2008. I was sitting in my office and the phone rang. It was Janet Fitzpatrick, Ray Kelly's secretary. I picked up, and she said, "Captain Pegues, how're you doing?"

"I'm doing fine."

"Good. I'm just calling to let you know that Deputy Commissioner Wuensch wants to speak with you."

Joe Wuensch was Kelly's chief of staff, his right-hand man. He came on the line and said, "How are you, Captain?"

"Everything's good, sir."

He said, "Listen, I wanted to be the one to call you with the news. The commissioner is fond of the work that you've been doing and he would like to promote you tomorrow to the rank of deputy inspector. How do you feel about that?"

I said, "Sir, I feel fantastic about that."

And I did. I was floored. I said, "Please tell the commissioner I said thank you. Tell him I won't let him down. I'm grateful for this opportunity, and I appreciate being recognized for the hard work that I've done." I was taken completely by surprise. I'd been a captain for less than eighteen months. To move from captain to deputy inspector that fast is unheard of, but at that point my career was moving at warp speed. I was on a rocket.

That night I barely slept. I was too pumped. I went home and made sure my uniform was tight, pressed up, shoes polished. I made about a thousand phone calls, trying to get my family together to come to the event on short notice. I set up a big lunch at Red Lobster the next day to celebrate. I called up my man Smooth. We had a good laugh talking about the old days, looking back on who we were and how far we'd come. I'd gone to his promotion ceremony when he made captain as a corrections officer, and I definitely wanted him there for my big day, too.

The ceremony was held in the auditorium at One Police Plaza at 11 a.m. When I walked in, I showed my ID. They took it from me and gave me a new one that said "Deputy Inspector." Then they handed me my new shield. I ducked into the bathroom to check the mirror one last time, make sure everything was in place. Then I took my seat in the auditorium with the rest of the officers receiving promotions.

It was a nice ceremony. Ray Kelly said a few words. I watched the others walk across the stage, shake hands with the commissioner, and get their picture taken. When they said, "Now introducing Deputy Inspector Corey Pegues," I walked up onstage, and I got the loudest, biggest ovation in the place. I'd invited more friends and family than anyone, and they were going crazy clapping and cheering and calling my name.

Getting that promotion was a big deal. At deputy inspector and above, promotions are discretionary. They're political. To get that nod means the commissioner has recognized you. He's put his eye on you. You've been handpicked. Out of over thirty-four thousand uniformed police officers in the NYPD, there are about eighty deputy inspectors. Only a handful of them are black. The executive ranks of the NYPD are an old boys' club. It's like the mafia. Somebody has to vouch for you; that's the only way you get in. It's closed off, secretive, very old, and very white—Irish, really. I was the opposite of that. But I'd made it. I was in. I was thirty-nine years old, less than sixteen years on the job, and I'd just become the thirteenth-highest-ranking African-American officer in the entire New York Police Department.

Within a few weeks after my promotion to deputy inspector I was already hearing rumors that I was going to another post, a bigger command. Esposito had mentioned to me a few months earlier that something was in the works. "We got plans for you," he'd said. I didn't know what he meant, but I was anxious to find out.

Early one morning in late June, around 6 a.m., I got a call from Chief Nelson. He said, "Corey, what's that thing on your neck?"

I said, "It's my wife's name."

"It's not 'Thug Life'?"

"It's not 'Thug Life.'"

"You *sure* it's not 'Thug Life'?"

"Chief, I swear to you. It's not 'Thug Life.' Why?"

"Because the boss wants to know."

Ray Kelly was asking about my tattoo. He was vetting me for

something big. That whole week I was getting calls from Nelson and from Chief Mohammed telling me that something was happening, I was in the running for a major precinct, and I wasn't to say anything to anyone. Around noon on June 25, I got a call from Phil Banks. He'd recently been made chief and was now the XO at Brooklyn South. I was in the middle of an important meeting with the PSA commanders and the chief of housing. I didn't care. I took the call anyway because I knew as soon as I answered it I wasn't going to be working for those people anymore. As soon as I picked up, Phil said, "Son, you got the six-seven."

I said, "Don't you play with me."

He said, "I'm telling you. You're the new commander of the 67th Precinct."

I don't remember what happened the rest of that meeting. I was so geeked. Never in my wildest dreams did I think I was getting a command like that. The 67th Precinct is the same as the seven-five out in East New York. It's a violent, high-crime area, the kind of place you go when there's no doubt you're on track to make chief. When it came to places like the six-seven or the seven-five, black cops used to say, "That's for their boys." That spot's reserved. That's where the white commissioners put their own people to make sure they got groomed to move up. And until that day that's what the six-seven was. There had never been a black commander in the history of the precinct. I was the first.

32

Broken Windows

After six weeks at the six-seven I thought my career was already over. On Thursday, August 7, 2008, three cops from the borough's auto larceny unit were chasing a stolen Mustang GT down Remsen Avenue around 8 p.m. They cornered the car, and the officers got out to apprehend the suspect. When they did, the driver, a twenty-five-year-old black man named Ortanzso Bovell, gunned the engine and tried to run one of the cops over to escape. As he dove out of the way, the cop, Lieutenant John Chell, who is white, pulled his gun and fired one shot into the car, killing Bovell.

I raced to the scene as fast as I could. It was bad. I had a white cop and an unarmed black man, dead as a doornail in the middle of Remsen Avenue in the August heat, with night starting to fall. An angry crowd was gathering around the police tape. *"You fucking killed him! Fucking Sean Bell, motherfuckers!"* All I could think was, This is how riots start. My phone was blowing up. Charles Barron, the city councilman, was the local watchdog on police abuse and brutality. He was all over me trying to get answers.

I couldn't believe it. I'd spent fifteen years working my way up, trying to make things better between blacks and police, and now I was going to be the one hung out to dry because of another controversial shooting. But the incident was caught on a nearby surveillance camera. NYPD guidelines say you can't shoot at a vehicle unless that vehicle is being used as a weapon against you or someone else. When you looked at the tape, it clearly showed Borvell in the stolen car trying to run the lieutenant down, and the cop firing his gun as he was being knocked to the ground. Borvell also had a rap sheet a mile long, more than a dozen arrests for robbery, assault, and weapons possession.

I hate the phrase "good shooting." To me there's no such thing as a good shooting. Anytime a cop has to use his gun it's a regrettable incident. Could the cop have jumped out of the way without firing? Maybe. But in the messed-up jargon that cops use, this was a good shooting. It was legally justified. When Charles Barron saw the video, even he admitted as much.

There weren't any protests, and nobody called for my replacement, but it was a reminder of the difficult position I was in. The relationship between cops and the black community is rarely good. After Sean Bell and the explosion of Stop, Question, and Frisk, it was getting worse, and the six-seven was one of the spots where things could easily explode.

———

The 67th Precinct covers the neighborhood of East Flatbush. It sits east of Prospect Park and south of Eastern Parkway, from Bedford Avenue out to East 98th Street, bounded by Clarkson Avenue on the north side and Ditmas Avenue to the south. It's over 90 percent black, almost all Caribbean, mostly Jamaicans. On the south side, around Newkirk Avenue, you've got the second-largest Haitian community in the United States; the largest is in Miami. The rest is a mix, but you've got everybody in there: Trinidadians, St. Lucians, folks from St. Vincent, from St. Croix, everybody. The census said there were 166,000 people living there at the time, but it was easily double that, if not more. Folks were packed in: families bringing over cousins and aunts and uncles, people over on short-term work visas, people there illegally.

It was a great place to work. All the things people go to the Caribbean for, we had them right there in East Flatbush. We had the food,

the music—everything but the beach. Over on Avenue A and Remsen there was a jerk chicken guy I loved. He wasn't a restaurant, just a
guy with a barbecue pit parked on the sidewalk outside a corner deli,
making the best damn jerk chicken you've ever had in your life. I'd go
over there and get lunch from him at least a couple times a week. I'd
pick up an order for me, one for my driver, and I'd say, "Make it hot.
Make it hot."

The Caribbean community is tight knit. Good people. Festive
people. Food, drinks, music. That's what they do. A lot of nightclubs,
a lot of block parties. In East Flatbush, people don't need much of
an excuse to throw a party. Somebody needs to paint his house, it's
"Hey, we're having a paint party," and they'll have twenty-five people
out there. They'll fire up a grill and barbecue and everybody grabs a
brush and helps out. Every year the whole neighborhood explodes
for J'Ouvert (pronounced Joo-vay), which is their Mardi Gras. It's
hundreds of thousands of people in the streets for four days straight.
Music blaring, costumes, parades. There's nothing like it.

Linden Boulevard runs from the heart of East New York through
Brownsville down to East Flatbush—the seven-five to the seven-
three to the six-seven. That's the most violent corridor in New York
City. But East Flatbush is a different environment from the other two.
Out in East New York and Brownsville there are so many housing
projects and abandoned lots that it would be hard to make it nice
even if you tried. But East Flatbush is more like Harlem. It was built
for white people. Italians, mostly. They left when the blacks moved
in. The housing stock is good. Single-family homes. Big, pre-war
apartment buildings with courtyards. There are no housing projects
anywhere in the six-seven. There's one massive apartment complex,
Flatbush Gardens, a sprawling development that looks like a housing project but it's not. Flatbush Gardens had its own security team,
mostly ex-cops, and they kept things pretty quiet.

East New York is almost all African-American, people who came
north during the Great Migration and wound up stuck in the ghetto.

What you've got out there, especially in the projects, are families trapped in third- and fourth-generation poverty. There are high unemployment and low civic engagement. It's people who've been pushed to the margins of society. East Flatbush is the opposite. Island people are not disaffected and disengaged. They work two and three jobs. They open small businesses. They came here to hustle. They came here to get a piece of the American Dream.

You walk around parts of East Flatbush in the middle of the afternoon, and it feels like a solid, stable working-class neighborhood. You'd never know it was one of the most dangerous places in the city, but it is. Gang culture runs deep in Caribbean communities. Caribbean people love guns. They love to smoke weed and they love to carry guns. I got in trouble for saying that at a community meeting once; the council president took offense. But I was just telling it straight. In 2007, the year before I took over, the six-seven had 242 gun arrests, the highest rate in the entire city by a wide margin, and we were on track to be number one again for 2008. I'd never seen kids packing like I did in East Flatbush.

Most of my shootings were gang-related. We had the old-school gangs like the Crips and the Bloods, but we had this proliferation of younger, smaller gangs, too: the Blood Stains and the Outlaws, the Rockstars and the Young Assassins, GS9, the Very Crispy Gangsters, the BMWs (Brooklyn's Most Wanted). The Crips and the Bloods were bad, but they weren't the real problem; they were older and at least had some sense to them. It was the young gangsters with something to prove. I can still remember their names: Joshua Byrd, aka Gangbino. Jermaine Douglas, aka Bomb Bomb. Sheakwan Grey. He's dead. Earl Facey. He's dead, too. A lot of them are.

I had a bulletin board up in my office with what I called my Top 17, the worst violent offenders in the six-seven. These kids were eighteen, nineteen, twenty. They were killing each other. It was over turf, drugs, old beefs. I can remember one week when I had seven shootings in seven days. I had a guy shot dead while walking his two-year-old home from day care; the boy was found sitting alone on someone's front steps, covered in his father's blood. I had one afternoon where three guys shot each other dead in broad daylight. It was a straight-up Mexican standoff, like a gunfight out of the Old West. This was on the same block as my jerk chicken guy, right in front of his spot. I showed up and I had three bodies lying in the street.

There were a dozen people standing there watching that day, and nobody saw anything. That was the biggest obstacle to policing in the six-seven. Nobody talked. You think there's mistrust between American blacks and the cops, but it's nothing like it is with Caribbean blacks. In those island nations, the cops are the last holdover from the colonial occupation, and they're all corrupt. Island people do not trust the police, period. They do not go to the police, period. More than once I'd have shooting victims come in and we'd go to talk to them and they would lawyer up. You know it's bad when the *victims* lawyer up.

The six-seven routinely tops the list of most open homicide cases in the city. Nearly three-quarters of the shootings and murders go unsolved. The detectives have nothing to go on. It wasn't unusual to have fourteen shootings on the board with a zero clearance rate. Gangs were bringing guys over from the islands to do the hits. They'd fly over, do the dirty work, and leave. Sometimes we solved them, usually we didn't.

But if the people of East Flatbush didn't trust the cops, the cops weren't doing anything to earn that trust back. East Flatbush was a place where you could see the failure of Broken Windows policing plain as day. I had a guy Mark who came to me a month after I arrived. He owned a mom-and-pop auto repair place over on Utica Avenue, and he had his guys working on cars in this tiny un-air-conditioned garage in the middle of August. It had to be a hundred degrees in there, and at the end of the shift they liked to have a couple of beers. The patrol officers were going by and, because the garage door was open to the sidewalk, they were writing the guys up for open container violations.

That's not police work. That's harassment. Those guys weren't criminals. They were mechanics. But that's what you get after fifteen years of this relentless push to make cops meet quotas and put up the numbers. I was getting complaints like that from all over the community. I had Mark's open-container citations thrown out.

Broken Windows policing was based on the idea that having a zero-tolerance policy for small crimes creates a sense of order that acts as a deterrent to people committing larger crimes. And when Bratton introduced the concept in the mid-nineties, crime fell dramatically, so people came away with the conclusion that it worked. But the reason Broken Windows "worked" was because the city had been so under-policed for so long. In 1994, if you rolled up on the stoops and the corners in the ghetto and started handing out citations for open containers, chances were you'd sweep up a dozen guys with outstanding warrants for assault or burglary or whatever. But there are only so many bad guys. You hit a point of diminishing returns pretty quickly. By 1999, when you rolled up on those same stoops and corners, you might get one arrest out of every twenty stops. The rest of it, you were just hassling guys trying to unwind with a beer at the end of a long week. And it would be one thing if zero tolerance actually meant zero tolerance, but it doesn't. When the symphony plays in Central Park, the yuppies are out there with their bottles of wine and it's given a pass. If an open container is a crime, it should be a crime everywhere. But we don't treat it that way.

Broken Windows and zero tolerance may have been a necessary corrective to decades of lazy policing, but once we'd cleaned up the mess left over from the seventies and eighties, we should've pumped the brakes. We didn't. As crime went down across the city, the pressure to make quotas actually went up. Policing became a numbers game more than anything else, and the mentality in the department hadn't changed since Richard Perry and I were on patrol in the one-fourteen: When you're under pressure to make arrests, where do you go? You go to the hood.

The fatal flaw of Broken Windows is that, in policing, zero tolerance isn't nearly as important as good judgment, discretion. In poor
communities and immigrant communities, you're going to find good
people who color outside the lines, people who go have a beer on the
stoop because it's the only cool place they have to sit, people who let
their car inspection slide because they can't afford to get it done. Technically they're breaking the law, but they're also just trying to get by.

My jerk chicken guy is the perfect example. He didn't have a per-
mit to do what he was doing. He was out there smoking up the sidewalk. His whole operation was one big health-code violation. If I'd
taken a zero-tolerance approach, I would have closed him down. But
that guy's working. That's his hustle. What good comes from closing
him down?

You think back on the poor Italian and Jewish neighborhoods
in New York, all the little things people had to do to get ahead. How
would they have fared under zero-tolerance policing? Not well. But
those communities were allowed to breathe. For black and brown
neighborhoods, that's never been the case. Fortunately, once I
started going to my jerk chicken guy, the cops in the precinct knew to
leave him alone. Nobody's busting the place where the commander
goes for lunch.

In the six-seven, twelve years of Broken Windows policing had
shattered, maybe beyond repair, the relationships between the police and community leaders, and you cannot police a community
where there's no trust between cops and citizens. If I wanted to have
any chance of stopping the violence and solving the murders, re-
building those relationships and fostering that trust would have to
be my number one priority.

33

Daybreak

The six-seven was not in good shape when I arrived. The commander who preceded me was no David Barerre, let's put it that
way; he wasn't running a tight ship. Mike Williams saved me. After
leaving me at the two-eight to go and serve in Iraq, he was back from
his tour and had made lieutenant. The way Drummond brought me
to the two-eight, I brought Mike in to be my administrative lieutenant. He found these old cops pulling ridiculous amounts of overtime
for doing nothing. People weren't conforming to the dress code. He
found this one girl in the summons office who had something like
ten thousand summonses stashed away in a closet that she'd never
processed because she was too lazy to bother. Mike helped me clean
all that up.

I had a target on my back and I knew it. I was the first black person
to sit in that chair. If a white CO had walked into that office, his authority wouldn't have been questioned, but I knew I had to establish
my authority, demonstrate it. If I didn't, I'd lose control of the whole
precinct. Then the next time they wanted to put a black cop in a spot
like this people would say, "Remember? We tried it with Pegues and
look what happened."

The six-seven is part of Brooklyn Borough South, whose commander at the time was Chief Joseph Fox. I had problems with him
from the jump. I'd made powerful friends downtown. I had my rabbi,
Chief of Department Esposito. I'd also developed a strong relation-

ship with Chief of Patrol Robert Gianelli (chief of department is in charge of all uniformed divisions; chief of patrol is in charge of the precincts and reports to the chief of department). Gianelli and Ray Kelly were close. Ray Kelly was Gianelli's kid's godfather, and Gianelli was Ray Kelly's kid's godfather. Gianelli took an interest in me because Chief Nelson and Chief Zeigler were pushing for me.

Those were the guys pulling strings for me with the commissioner, and Kelly had put me in over Fox's objections. That caused a lot of friction. Phil Banks was Fox's executive officer, and he pulled me aside my first day at the precinct and told me, "You weren't handpicked by Fox. You're not his guy. He's going to try to put somebody else in. Don't trust him."

Gianelli also hated Fox with a passion. He told me as much when I started. The protocol for communication in the department was that Gianelli should have contacted Fox and then Fox would call me. But Gianelli would communicate with me directly. "Hey, Corey, what's going on with this shooting?" He'd cut Fox out of the loop, and that pissed Fox off even more.

As an executive, Fox was the exact opposite of Barerre. Barerre mentored me, groomed me. Fox would micromanage and undermine and do everything he could to keep me in my place. One time I put in to transfer a half-dozen cops to a different shift. Fox called me up in the middle of the night to tell me I had to move them back. Borough commanders don't get involved with personnel decisions at the precinct level. It's not done. They've got bigger things to worry about. But Fox would ride me every chance he got.

My biggest problem was the executive officer I inherited from the previous command, Captain Dave Clark. Clark was Fox's boy; they'd been together in the seven-one. He was Fox's eyes and ears inside my office. Clark didn't like me. He'd been the XO in the six-seven for years, and I'm sure he felt like the top spot should have been his. I didn't fault him for feeling that way, but I had my program of changes I wanted to make and he wasn't going along. He had a whole crew of people inside the precinct who were loyal to him, and they would listen to him instead of me. It was a problem.

I recognized what was happening with Clark right away because I'd seen it before: with Drummond and Green in the two-eight. Clark thought I was going to be another black figurehead sitting at the end of the table while he'd be the white XO who quietly ran things behind the scenes. It was the same dynamic. Once I realized that, I knew I had to get rid of him as soon as possible.

My opportunity to do that came when I got a call from a friend of mine at One Police Plaza downtown. A piece of paper had come across her desk, a request for a department transfer, and it had my signature on it. She was curious why I'd authorized it. She called me and said, "Corey, did you sign off on this?"

"No."

"Well, it has your signature on it."

I asked her to send it to me. She faxed it over. Somebody had signed my name. I took it and showed it to Clark. I said, "Dave, you know anything about this? Who did this?"

He was stuttering and stammering. "I-I-I don't know."

I knew he had something to do with it. I called a supervisors' meeting and I laid down the law. I told everyone that I knew my signature had been forged on the transfer, and I said, "Listen, there's only one CO in this precinct. Ray Kelly put me here. Until he puts someone else in this spot, there's no paperwork that leaves this precinct without my signature. I don't care if I'm in the Bahamas drinking a martini. You call me before anything goes out. And until I find out who did this, there are no days off for anyone in this room. No vacation. No leaving early. You tell your wife she's got to leave *her* job to pick up the kids, and then you can listen to her yell at you when you get home."

Over the next couple of days my special ops lieutenant started acting funny around me. He wouldn't look me in the eye, wasn't talking straight. I pulled him into my office and said, "Is there something you want to tell me?"

He said, "I signed the transfer."

I said, "I know you didn't do something like that on your own. Did Captain Clark tell you it was okay?"

"Yes, sir."

He thought I was going to give him the axe right there. But I said, "Look, I'm going to give you a chance because you were honest with me. You just need to know I'm the boss, and nothing like that can ever happen again." After that he became one of my closest confidants. He turned out to be one of the best cops I had. I even gave him a special assignment that got him bumped up to captain's pay.

Now I had the leverage I needed to get rid of Clark. I started making his life hell. Every morning I'd make his schedule for him. I'd have him in meetings eight hours a day. I didn't let him do anything. After I figured he'd had enough, I called up Fox and I said, "Look, you can keep him here, but I'm not happy with the guy and I'm just going to keep making his life miserable. I think maybe you should find him a new home." With that, Clark was gone. If Fox didn't have it in for me before, he definitely did from there on out. But as long as I could keep him off my back I was able to run my precinct my own way, and I did.

———

That October I had my first meeting with the leaders of Community Board 17, which represented the neighborhood. The board members were fed up with the constant harassment from the police—too many quality-of-life summonses, the abuse of Stop, Question, and Frisk. I told them straight up, "You're not going to have Sean Bell cops or Louima cops in the Sixty-Seventh Precinct, not under my watch." I told them about my own life, growing up in southeast Queens, getting hassled by the cops, getting tossed up against the wall and frisked and pushed around. I told them I would tackle the gang violence head-on, but I would treat the people and the community with respect.

Most of my shootings came in the northeast part of the precinct, in the pocket around the East Nineties near Remsen Avenue. Based on the high frequency of shootings there, that October the department designated the area an Impact Zone. I had an additional 111 officers from the police academy walking the beat in that neighborhood, a cop on every block.

The strong police presence would curb the frequency of the shootings, but I knew they weren't going to stop, and with every shooting there was the potential for the streets to erupt, either with protests or with more gunfire in retaliation. So much of the frustration that builds up around shootings, especially ones that involve cops, is because there's no transparency with cops. People want to know what's happening, and they can't get answers. The NYPD always tries to withhold information in order to control the narrative. I did the opposite. What I did—and what no one else had done before me—was I made a list of every single community leader, elected representative, and church pastor in the 67th Precinct. I told my community affairs rep, "Anytime there's a shooting, anytime a gun goes off anywhere in this precinct, we are going to call every single name on that list and give them every piece of information we have."

He said, "Commander, we don't do that."

I said, "We do now."

I would make the important calls myself, to Borough President Marty Markowitz, Congresswoman Yvette Clark. I'd call Congresswoman Clark on her cell phone, and she'd step out of meetings on Capitol Hill to take the call. I'd say, "Congresswoman, I know you're busy. I just want you to know we had a shooting on Church and Forty-Fifth, a black male shot another black male. We have recovered a pistol. I'll keep your office abreast."

She'd say, "Thank you so much. No one has ever done this before."

I worked so closely with the pastors on my list that we eventually created something called the 67th Precinct Clergy Council, at the time the only one of its kind in the city. Whenever there was a shooting, they'd get a call, an email, or a text message. They'd show up in yellow jackets with the council's name. Sometimes they were the first ones on the scene. They'd pray with the crowds, try to get witnesses to cooperate, act as liaisons between cops and bystanders. People started calling them the God Squad.

When I learned that most of the homicide victims couldn't afford funerals, I started asking the Clergy Council to help raise money for services and burials. Marlon Hinds, aka Tommy Kid, one of my Top 17, had already racked up ten arrests for assault, robbery, and grand larceny by age eighteen. Marlon was with the Outlaws. A rival gang shot him dead on the sidewalk right outside his mother's apartment. I called up Reverend Gilford Monrose from Mount Zion Baptist over on 37th, and he went over to do the service. Even the hardest of hardcore gangsters is somebody's brother, somebody's son. I made sure the victims were treated with respect so their families and community could mourn properly.

I tackled the quality-of-life harassment head-on. Caribbean people, as I said, are a festive people, a lot of nightclubs, a lot of block parties and barbecues. We had problems with violence at the nightclubs. About a quarter of the precinct's shootings were in or near the clubs. Pat's Palm Tree, Rose Garden Catering, Club D'Joumbala. The problem in those places was the patrons, not the owners, but the cops treated the owners like they were the ones responsible. Anywhere black people are getting loud, cops treat it like a thing that needs to be eliminated, not an opportunity to help the community function better.

The owners and the cops should have been working together to end the violence. Instead the cops were killing the owners' businesses. If a club was a problem spot, the cops would do everything they could to shut it down. That was the default strategy. The owner would get papered with inspection violations, patrons would get harassed going in and out, radio cars would park out front, lights flashing.

One of the biggest clubs in East Flatbush was the Caribbean Performing Arts Center, C-PAC. The owner, George, had a million-dollar lawsuit against the 67th Precinct when I arrived. Cops were going in and shutting down his business all the time. They were running his patrons off. C-PAC did have legal issues. It was this big building down in the industrial warehouses off Farragut Avenue. Rick Ross and other major hip-hop acts played there. They would have "cooler parties," where everybody came and brought their own coolers of food and liquor. They'd have thousands of people in there, and they'd pour out, totally wasted at four in the morning, leaving empty bottles in the streets, disturbing the neighbors.

I needed a compromise. My first month I held a summit, a sit-down with my supervisors and the club owners. I told the owners I was going to work with them instead of harassing them. I told them the security measures they needed to have: extra security, clean-up crews, ID scanners at the door, no guns. I said, "You do this for me, you won't see my cops at your place." George worked with me, and after that his club was the least violent club I had. Other clubs fell in line, too.

Bringing the cops around on not harassing the local businesses and their patrons was relatively easy. My biggest challenge was J'Ouvert. J'Ouvert is a contraction of the French phrase *jour ouvert*, meaning dawn or daybreak. It originated in Trinidad as a celebration to mark the end of slavery—the dawn of emancipation. It's like Mardi Gras.

In the weeks leading up to Labor Day weekend, these places called mas camps pop up all over East Flatbush. They're in empty lots, in different storefronts. People gather and spend days making these elaborate costumes. There's a steel drum band, somebody's usually barbecuing. When Labor Day weekend comes, for four days straight there are at least seven, eight hundred thousand people out in the streets, partying nonstop. The heart of it is along Church Avenue. From Flatbush to Kings Highway there's a sea of people, walking up and down the street. We kept floodlights up at the major intersections, and the party went all night. People didn't sleep.

After three days the festival climaxed with the West Indian Day Parade. That part was the easiest for me because the parade ran down Eastern Parkway, which is over in the seven-one. The parties in my precinct would stop and people got dressed in their costumes and marched over to be in the parade. We got a break of about fifteen hours while everybody watched the parade. Then everyone flooded back to Church Avenue to party all night.

The logistics for policing J'Ouvert were crazy. I called it the Super Bowl, because it was that big. I had over nine hundred cops coming in from all over the city. I had thousands of metal barriers we'd have to deploy in the streets to control the crowds. For a week straight I wouldn't go home. I'd catch four or five hours of sleep on my office couch, shower downstairs, and head back out.

My first Superbowl came two months after I arrived, and since I had no experience with it, I listened to the officers who'd been there for years. I followed their playbook, thinking they'd have a coherent plan for handling the event. That was a mistake. It was worse than the clubs. I showed up to work the first day of the festival and there were two tractor trailers parked behind the precinct. I said, "What's that for?"

"That's for the DJ equipment," I was told.

These cops were going around and anytime a mas camp or a party got out of control, they'd shut it down and take the DJ's system. They were randomly closing down any party or club or barbecue whenever they felt like it. People were pissed. The whole festival my phone was blowing up with people calling and complaining. "Your cops were just here, pushing people around, confiscating gear." I got complaints that my cops were randomly tossing people for guns. I got complaints that my cops were going around with black tape over their shield numbers, the license plates on their patrol cars bent up, so they couldn't be identified in any complaints. I had to address it directly at roll call. I said, "If I catch anybody with their license plate bent up or tape over their shields, we're gonna have a major problem. You're gonna have to deal with me."

Anytime black people are out in the street in large numbers, white cops automatically treat it like it's going to be a problem, like those people don't have a right to be out there. There is violence at J'Ouvert. Every year there are at least four or five shootings. But you're talking about an event with over seven hundred thousand people. You can't treat seven hundred thousand people like criminals because a couple of them are getting drunk and popping off guns. But my guys were out there like cowboys. People were trying to celebrate, and instead of keeping them safe so they could have a good time, the cops were hell-bent on shutting everything down. This is a festival to celebrate the end of slavery, and these cops were going around acting like an occupying army trying to put down a rebellion.

The next year I threw out the playbook and I told everybody, "We're doing this differently from here on." I got rid of the tractor trailers. I said, "We're not taking anyone's equipment anymore." When the parties and mas camps threatened to get out of control, if the drinking spilled out into the street and fights were breaking out, I'd go to the DJ and the people throwing the party and I'd give them a chance to rein it in. I'd say, "Look, I want you to have a good time. But these people drinking outside and urinating in the street, I'm going to give you thirty minutes to get them back inside. If you can't do that, I've got no choice but to shut you down."

I let people police themselves; for the most part they did. If I had to crack down and break up a party, all I did was confiscate the DJ's mixer for a few hours. I never understood why the cops were lugging these huge speakers back to the precinct anyway; take the mixer and the guy can't make any more sound come out. Other than that, I kept the crowds under control and I let people party. There wasn't any more or less violence at the festival than before, but there was a lot less friction between the cops and the community.

I saw it as my job to change the culture in the department, to mend fences, reduce tension. With J'Ouvert, I led by example. I'd been going to parties and barbecues in East Flatbush for years, long before I worked there, and I went to the parties as a commander, too. I was working eighteen-hour days; I needed to relax and unwind a bit. I'd go around from party to party checking things out, but mostly I was there to get to know people, make sure they were enjoying themselves. I remember one year I stopped by this party and while I was there a team of my cops showed up to shut it down. They came in and I was in the back dancing with girls and eating barbecue. I said, "Guys, this one's good. You can go to the next one."

34

Leadership

On February 10, 2009, I had another officer-involved shooting. At around two-thirty in the afternoon, PO Jovaniel Cordova was patrolling the Impact Zone on a three-wheeled scooter when he stopped an eighteen-year-old kid on the corner of East 93rd and Winthrop. He asked the kid to put his hands on the scooter to conduct a search, and the kid ran. Cordova took off after him. The kid was running south on Ninety-Fourth Street when a gun popped out of his waistband, a .357 Magnum. He reached back to try to grab it. Cordova pulled his weapon and yelled for him to drop it, but the kid reached anyway and Cordova fired off one round. He shot the kid in the face. The bullet grazed his chin and he was taken to Brookdale Hospital, where he was listed in stable condition. The gun wasn't legal, and the kid was charged with criminal possession of a weapon and resisting arrest.

Within hours of the shooting, my community affairs team was on the phone, making their calls to the pastors and local officials. Cordova was new. He was maybe two weeks out of the academy. It could have been an explosive situation, a rookie cop and a teenager shot in the face in broad daylight. I went over the evidence and scrutinized the testimony backward and forward to make sure everything stood up. It did. This wasn't Sean Bell. We took an illegal gun off the street before it was used to kill someone. That's police work. Cordova's supervisor nominated him for Cop of the Month, and I approved it.

In my three years at the six-seven I had twelve officer-involved shootings that resulted in at least five or six fatalities. That's a lot for one precinct. The gangs were out of control. Out on Church Avenue and over in the East Nineties it was like the OK Corral. But with those twelve shootings, I never had a single protest. Not one. They were all justified shootings, but more important than that was the fact that the community believed me when I said they were justified shootings. I'd been transparent with them. I'd been building bridges of trust and communication with people. They knew that I wasn't going to have my cops indiscriminately shooting people.

Sometimes Councilman Barron would come into my office with a complaint, a black kid getting tossed, a cop being disrespectful. I'd hear him out, investigate the claim, and I'd punish whoever needed to be punished. Other times Barron would come in with a complaint, I'd follow up, and I'd say, "I'm sorry, Councilman. I have to back my guys on this one." Even when we disagreed, we stayed on good terms because we knew we both shared the same long-term goal of helping East Flatbush. Not many precinct commanders in the city had that kind of relationship with the black community leaders.

One Sunday a month I'd go to services at one of the churches in the precinct. The pastor would invite me up to speak, and I'd share my story. I'd talk about growing up on welfare, eating mayonnaise sandwiches, cereal with water. I'd talk about being in the streets. I wouldn't share too many details. I'd say I grew up in a rough neighborhood, started running with the wrong crowd, and did some bad things before I straightened myself out. I wanted the mothers and fathers in the pews to know that I was one of them.

A couple of times a week I'd go out with my officers on patrol. I'd stop by the barbecues people were having in their yards. I'd call out to the chef, "Yo, you got a turkey burger? Throw a turkey burger on there for me! And let me get some of that macaroni and cheese. With hot sauce!" I'd sit and break bread with them. I'd usually have a couple of white cops patrolling with me. I'd say, "You guys want anything?" They'd never join in, never sit down. They'd stand off to the side. They didn't feel comfortable—and that's the whole problem right there. You can't work with people if you don't reach out to them and try to relate to them.

Word started to spread. "Yo, we got this young black commander. He's from the streets like us. He's not here to hurt us. We can trust him. We need to reach out to him." We'd have shootings, and no one would talk to the detectives. But I would get calls on my cell phone, people reaching out to me through the pastors or the community groups. They'd say, "Don't tell anyone where you heard this, but you need to be looking at such and such building on Nostrand Avenue, Apartment 7A. You need to be looking at this guy Joey who lives there."

I'd pass that information along to the detectives. They'd say, "Where'd you get this from?"

I'd say, "Never mind where I got it from. This is where you need to start your investigation."

People did that all the time. They wouldn't snitch, but they'd snitch to me. I got illegal guns turned in to me, too, hand-delivered. People didn't trust bringing them in to anyone else, but they'd bring them to me. I worked hard for that trust. I earned it with the way I did my job.

———

I hear people talk about the different solutions for this friction we have between cops and minority communities. People want body cameras, independent prosecutors to investigate misconduct. Those are important steps, but real change can only come when you change the culture of the department, and in a paramilitary organization, changing the culture comes down to one thing: leadership.

When Bill Bratton walked into the Dirty Thirty in 1994, marched the corrupt cops out the door, and threw their badges in a trash can, he set a tone: This won't be tolerated. Police corruption went way

down. Not because of IAB investigations or fear of independent prosecutors, but because Bratton changed the culture. Being a dirty cop
became a mark of shame in the eyes of your fellow officers. It's the
same when it comes to fixing attitudes toward young blacks and minority communities. There are deeply ingrained patterns of behavior
and ways of thinking that have to be broken down and built back up
again.

Changing the culture starts with something as simple as changing the way people speak. We had these third- and fourth-generation
white cops on the force. They'd grown up listening to their brothers
and uncles talking about the spics and the coloreds and how you've
got to knock them around to show who's boss—the racism gets
passed down. Guys come in looking at black people like animals, and
their language reflects it. I'd be at events around the city and cops
would say to me, "Wow, the six-seven? You work in that shit hole?"

These were fellow captains and commanders talking to me like
this. That's the way black neighborhoods were referred to; nobody
challenged it. I would. I'd say, "Shit hole? I grew up in a community
like that. Those are good people. I don't think it's a shit hole. Why
would you call it that?" I wouldn't get angry. I'd just ask the question,
and they'd usually get flustered because they had no idea what to say
next.

David Barerre was a good CO when it came to setting the tone.
He'd say, "Be respectful of these people. This is their community." I'd
take it a step further. I'd say, "Be respectful of these people. This is *my*
community." My cops knew I was going to show up at roll call at least
once a day and say, "If I catch anybody doing something wrong in my
community, you're going to have problems." I made it personal. My
cops knew I took ownership.

I did everything I could to challenge perceptions, to change the
mentality of treating every black and brown person as a suspect. I
did things that were totally unorthodox in the NYPD. It's customary
to have neighborhood people come and talk to the cops at roll call, a

way of getting to know the community. It's usually the local pastor or a prominent businessperson. I never saw the point of that. My cops aren't going be having run-ins with the pastor on Church Avenue at two in the morning.

I'd bring in guys off the street, ex-cons. I'd meet them through the church or walking the neighborhood, and I'd invite them in to speak. I'd introduce them at roll call and say, "Look, this guy's an ex-felon. He did two years when he was seventeen. Now he's thirty-five. He's got the sleeve tattoo, the saggy jeans, the hat to the back—and he works for ConEd, making ninety thousand dollars a year. He's making more than you, but you stopped and frisked him six times in the last year, and not one of them was a good stop. I want you to listen to what he has to say." Then I'd have the guy tell the platoon about his experience. A lot of cops hated when I did that, but I knew I was reaching some of them.

I had a zero-tolerance policy for abuse. The way I used to handle my squad as a sergeant, asking every suspect if the cops had mistreated them—now I had the authority to enforce that across the entire precinct. I would head into work an hour early, get a cup of coffee, drive around, park down the street from my guys on patrol, and keep an eye on them, watch how they interacted with the people, with the business owners. I tried to do that for an hour or so a few times a week.

Every single one of my cops knew: If you bring in a perp tuned up, the commander is going to be all over you. But if you come in with a clean arrest, your stock will go up. When I had cops with issues, I'd pull them aside and talk to them. I had this one guy, a white kid from Long Island. He had a pile of civilian complaints from before I arrived. He'd been heavy-handed in the streets, was always tossing kids, roughing them up. He had an uncle who was a chief downtown, so his problems were always allowed to slide. Phil Banks flagged the kid's file for me when I came in. I pulled the kid aside and talked to him. He was straight with me. He said, "Boss, when I first got here I didn't understand these people. I didn't trust them, and I was fucking them up because I didn't know how else to handle things."

I appreciated his honesty. I said, "Look, I understand you came in here and there was a lot you didn't know. But I'm here now. You understand these people now, right? Everything's good? I'm going to give you a clean slate, and let's see how you do." I started monitoring him and watching him. I encouraged him and gave him positive reinforcement every time he made a clean arrest. He turned out to be a good cop. Cops are regular people. They want to be satisfied in their jobs and rewarded for doing good work. But that has to come from the top or it doesn't happen. That's why leadership is the only thing that works.

———

For the life of me I wish I could remember the name of the cop who reached out to me at Andrew Jackson High School. That cop saved my life. When he looked at me, he didn't see a thug. He saw a confused kid who needed help. When I looked around at the kids on the corners in Brownsville and East Flatbush and East New York, I didn't see a bunch of hoodlums. I saw myself.

The cycle of violence in black communities has to stop, and because cops are on the front lines there's so much we can do to help. We're in these kids' lives for better or for worse, so we should strive to make things better. Programs like Scared Straight are worthless. We bring kids in and yell and scream and read them the riot act. Then after we scare the hell out of them, what do we do? We put them right back on the same corners where we picked them up. You can't just scare them with the negatives. You have to show them the positives, and the positives have to be real.

When I arrived at PSA #2, a new program had just been started, and it fell to me to implement it. It was a pilot program being tested for the rest of the city, called the Juvenile Robbery Intervention Program (JRIP). The kids selected for the program had to be from the projects, under the age of seventeen, and have at least one arrest for robbery on their record. JRIP was an example of the data from Compstat being put to good use. Every time a kid's name was entered into the system, we'd get a notification. If he was absent from school, we were notified. Anytime he was stopped and frisked or arrested, we were notified. That allowed us to intervene quickly and get them back on track.

I had a whole team of people responsible for keeping an eye on these kids. We would make home visits, talk to their parents, talk to their probation officers, connect them with social services. If they had a court date, we'd show up to talk to the judge. If they needed work, we'd hook them up with summer job programs and other opportunities. We did everything we could to make a positive impact in their lives. The results were incredible. We had 230 kids in the program. Prior to the monitoring program, they were responsible for 278 robberies. After the monitoring that number fell to 40.

Give young people support and opportunities and a real sense of hope and they won't commit crimes—this isn't rocket science. I didn't have the funding to bring the whole program with me to the six-seven, so when I got there I started my own scaled-down version of it. I called it the Juvenile Recidivist Reduction Unit. It wasn't department-sanctioned; it was something I did on my own. Whenever juvenile offenders were picked up and brought into the precinct, I'd pull them into my office and talk to them. "Why are you doing this? What do you think you'll get out of this?"

Some kids you can't reach. They're hardheaded, don't want to listen. But a lot of these kids are like I was growing up. They're in the streets because they're confused. They need guidance. The kids I thought we could help, I had my guys start keeping tabs on them the same way we did with the JRIP program. We connected them with local businesses to get jobs. We had sixty-eight kids in the unit to start. It worked.

I started an annual essay contest. Every year I'd send my cops into the elementary and junior high schools to host the competition with the teachers, and every year it was the same question: "As the commanding officer of the 67th Precinct, what would you do to combat gang and gun violence in your community?" Some of the answers would break your heart: "When I was six years old I witnessed my father's death right in front of my eyes. When I turned nine I was shot while walking with my mother. Now I am eleven years old and got over my father's death and myself getting shot." Stories like that were all too common.

As far as what the kids wanted to do about the problem, their solutions were dead-on. They wanted better jobs and better education to give people an alternative to crime. They knew that the single biggest deterrent to gang violence was giving children a sense of self-worth and self-esteem, breaking the cycle of anger and negativity that fuels the violence in the first place. They all wanted more cops, too. That was the amazing thing. The younger kids, they weren't angry yet. They hadn't been stopped and frisked and harassed a dozen times. They still believed that cops were there to help them, not hurt them. They still believed in Officer Friendly walking the beat. I didn't want them to lose that. I wanted the kids to see my cops as role models and protectors—and I wanted my cops to see the kids as kids.

In my second year, along with the essay contest, I started an annual Cops and Kids Sports Day. It was one of my biggest successes as a commander. For a whole day the precinct took over Paerdegat Park. People from the neighborhood donated coolers of drinks for the kids. We raised money to grill burgers and hot dogs. We had a band play music. Cops brought their spouses and their own children. Kids from the neighborhood came with their parents. And we had games for everyone to play. We had baseball games, basketball games, double dutch, cricket, soccer.

All of our elected officials came out: Congresswoman Yvette Clarke was there. I even had Commissioner Kelly out there. I submitted a request to his office and he came out for the day and played cricket—the commissioner of the NYPD running and laughing and having a great time with a bunch of West Indian kids in East Flatbush on a sunny autumn afternoon. I still have the cricket bat Kelly used; he autographed it for me. I still look back on those sports days, and to me, they represent everything the relationship between cops and black kids should be.

———

The gang war in the six-seven raged on no matter what we did. I did my best to contain the violence, protect the people who were outside of it, keep young kids from getting into it. But the guys who were already in it were hell-bent on destroying each other. In 2009, my first full year as commander, we had eighteen murders, the same as the year before. But shootings went up nearly 10 percent, from sixty-two to sixty-eight, averaging one every five days. But even with the jump in gun violence, overall crime in the precinct went down. At the end of 2008, major felonies in the six-seven were down 3.5 percent. At the end of 2009, felony crime was down another 9.1 percent. Add in PSA #2, and in my first three years as commander, crime was down three years in a row.

The fact that Ray Kelly would come out to my sports day was proof of how well I was doing. The commissioner definitely had his eye on me. Earlier that year he'd nominated me for Columbia University's Police Management Institute, an executive leadership school for police officers, one of the most prestigious programs of its kind in the country. You go up to West Point in the Hudson Valley and take courses and seminars one weekend a month for nine months. From then on you're in this fraternity of select officers who've been through the program. I was doing that once a month in addition to my work as commander.

Kelly handpicked me for another prestigious assignment, too. The New York City Police Foundation is a nonprofit organization that supports the NYPD. They donate millions every year for new programs and equipment that the city can't or won't pay for. The foundation has a program called Commanding Officer for an Evening, where corporate honchos and political VIPs are given the opportunity to ride along with a CO, go to roll call, meet with staff; it's the department's chance to put its best foot forward and keep the donations coming in. Ray Kelly only chooses twelve commanders out of the entire city to serve as escorts. If he picks you, that's it: You're in. You're one of his boys. That year he picked me. I was chosen to take out a top executive from KeySpan Energy, a big corporate donor. I was also asked to take out Bishop Lester Williams—Sean Bell's pastor. Anything to do with the Sean Bell shooting was a major political responsibility, and the commissioner trusted me to handle it.

I was having an incredible year. There were days my feet were barely touching the ground. All the signs pointed toward a promotion to full inspector and, eventually, chief. I could look around me and see that my hard work was paying off. My ideas and plans to fix policing in the black community, those were paying off, too. Crime was down. My youth programs were taking off. Community relationships in the precinct were at an all-time high. I had the commissioner, the chief of patrol, and the chief of department in my corner. I was rolling. Then I took this beautiful, wonderful career I had built and I got behind the wheel and I drove it full speed into a wall, and after that it was never the same.

35

The Blue Wall of Silence

I had five people shot on Winthrop. The call came at four in the morning. It was the dead of winter, freezing cold out. I got up and got dressed and raced into the city. Six people had been partying at the Rose Garden on Church Avenue, five guys and a girl. They left the club in a Chevy Yukon, and when they stopped at the light on Winthrop and Remsen this other car pulled up alongside them and sprayed the SUV with bullets. *Boom! Boom! Boom! Boom! Boom!* There was a line of holes you could trace down the driver's side of the car. The girl wasn't hurt, but all five guys took at least a bullet each, including the driver, who managed to speed off and drive to Brookdale Hospital, a couple of blocks away.

Ron Williams, one of my Top 17, was in the car. He was just out of prison; it could have been a hit on him. I didn't know if the shooters were going to try to get him again. I didn't know if the whole neighborhood was about to blow up. I needed cops on the streets to lock everything down.

I was already short on manpower. I'd sent a sergeant and five officers to the seven-one because a Hasidic person's tire had been slashed. That's how it works in Brooklyn. Anytime anything happens to anyone in the Hasidic community, it's a bias incident. A Hasidic woman gets her purse snatched, it's a bias incident. A Hasidic family's car gets stolen, it's a bias incident. Everything is a hate crime, and every other precinct has to send two or three cops over to the seven-one to help out. That's how much pull the Hasidic lobby has with city hall.

The same isn't true for black folks. I had five people shot, and now I was the one who needed extra manpower. I called Fox and woke him up and I told him, "Chief, I'm stressing out. I need help. Everybody counts. I need everything."

Fox sounded like he didn't want to be bothered with this in the middle of the night. He said, "Look, nobody downtown cares about five people getting shot in East Flatbush."

That's word for word how I remember it. Even with all the callous, racist bullshit I'd heard in twenty years on the job, that still stands out as the most shocking thing anyone has ever said to me. I told him, "Chief, I understand if downtown they don't care about five people getting shot, but you're the borough commander. I would think that you'd care just a little bit."

I slammed down the phone. I couldn't deal with the guy anymore.

It's hard, in today's world, to prove somebody is a racist. Back in the day, sergeants would walk around calling me "that nigger Pegues" out in the open. That doesn't happen anymore. But people aren't exactly subtle about it, either. It's in the way they talk to you, how they treat you compared to everyone else. It's a bunch of things that all add up.

In my personal opinion, Joseph Fox was racist. He'd talk down to me. He was rude, dismissive. He went against department protocol time and again to meddle with how I ran my precinct. I was the only black precinct commander in Brooklyn South, and I was the only one being treated that way. Ray Kelly thought enough of my performance that he nominated me for Columbia's Police Management Institute. Fox treated me like I was something stuck to the bottom of his shoe.

Phil Banks was the XO at Brooklyn South when I got there, and he told me straight-up on the first day that he thought Fox was no good. When Banks got promoted to CO of Manhattan North, Chief Stephen Bonano replaced him. Bonano would come into my office and tell me the things Fox was saying. "Fox *hates* you," he'd say. "He's after you. Watch your back."

As a black police officer, racial bias and double standards are a part of the job. You have to pick your battles. Phil Banks took the Colin Powell route. He was a solider. He kept his head down and did the work and eventually rose to succeed Esposito as chief of department, becoming the number three man in the NYPD, a powerful position for a black officer to have. Banks used his power to do the right thing and stood by his principles, but he didn't rock the boat. When it came to speaking out he was like a church mouse.

At the other extreme you have officers like Eric Adams. Eric was a thorn in the department's side, speaking out on the killing of Amadou Diallo and the abuse of Stop, Question, and Frisk. Eric never compromised, but his career was never going to make it past captain. He was never going to get a discretionary promotion. That was okay for him, because his plan was to get out and become a politician anyway, but you can't be Eric Adams if you want to be Phil Banks.

I believe we need people taking both of those routes. We need strong men and women on the inside, amassing power and flexing as much muscle as possible. We also need outspoken critics, speaking out and holding the department accountable at every turn. I have a ton of respect for both Phil and Eric, and both of them are good friends. I was coming up a few years behind them, and I tried to split the difference in following their examples on how to deal with racism in the department. With the people below me, I was always outspoken. Whether I was a sergeant with an eight-man squad or a commander with a four-hundred-person precinct, I would call out any racist or abusive behavior that I saw, and I never apologized for who I was. But I never kicked up. I never broke rank and called out my superiors. If I had, I never would have made commander. I also never spoke publicly on issues of race and policing. That would have been career suicide.

After eighteen years of enduring things like that phone call with

Fox, I was ready to start speaking up. Once I made commander at PSA #2, I had the profile and I had the podium. If I hadn't used them to do the right thing, I wouldn't have been able to sleep at night. At the same time, though, part of me still wanted that Phil Banks spot; the changes I was making in the six-seven, I wanted the authority to implement those ideas across the whole borough, the whole city.

I found what I thought was a good compromise. My sister-in-law Sheila Wimberly was a detective in Nassau County on Long Island. With a lot of black families moving to the suburbs, racial profiling and harassment were serious issues out there, and there weren't any major organizations lobbying for changes in the way they policed out in the county. Because I lived in Hempstead, Sheila came to me and asked me to start a NOBLE chapter for Long Island. It seemed like the ideal solution. My kids were walking around and driving on the streets of Long Island. I wanted to make sure they and their friends were growing up in a safe environment. So I founded the chapter and became the president of the National Organization for Black Law Enforcement Executives, Long Island. Out in Nassau and Suffolk counties I could be fighting for the cause, and inside the NYPD I would make positive change with the people under my own command.

One of the first actions I took as president thrust me abruptly into the national spotlight. The town of Hempstead, where I live, is majority white but has large pockets of black and Hispanic residents in the twenty-two separate incorporated villages inside it. It's a segregated area, and there's a good deal of racial tension. The Hempstead Police Department at the time was about 50 percent white, 50 percent officers of color. On September 29, 2007, a noose was found hanging in the locker room of the Hempstead police station. This came a few months after the Jena Six case in Louisiana, where a noose had been hung from a tree in a school courtyard, so there was a lot of interest in the story. I called Eric Adams and we called a press conference.

Everybody was there, all the local news affiliates, FOX News, MSNBC. I was getting calls to be on CNN and NPR. Because of the public pressure we were able to generate, in May of 2008 New York Governor David Paterson signed a law making the display of a noose a felony punishable by four years in prison, putting it in the same category under state law as a swastika or a burning cross. That was one of my proudest moments as a cop, to take a stand on something and see it result in real, tangible change, and I didn't get any blowback from One Police Plaza for speaking out. I thought I'd be able to keep my activism separate from my service in the NYPD. I was wrong.

In March of 2010, I got a call from a young black NYPD officer. Kenneth Kissiedu was a sergeant with sixteen years on the job. He lived in Yonkers and worked midnights at the four-one in the Bronx. On February 3, a month before he reached out to me, he'd been on his way to work when he stopped at an ATM in Yonkers to get cash. A woman had reported her purse stolen at that same ATM earlier in the evening. As Kissiedu walked to his car, two uniformed Yonkers cops, Thomas Cleary and Jared Singer, both white, were driving by in their patrol vehicle. They saw him and yelled out "Yo!" several times from the street. Kissiedu didn't answer to "Yo!" He kept walking. At that point the officers got out and confronted him. Things got heated, and Cleary punched Kissiedu in the face. He would later say he thought Kissiedu was reaching for a gun. The cops wrestled him to the pavement and cuffed him. Only then did they open his jacket to see his gun and his badge.

The officers arrested Kissiedu and put the blame on him. They claimed they'd stopped him because he "fit the description" of the purse snatcher, and he'd responded by being belligerent and uncooperative. The only charge against Kissiedu was obstruction of governmental administration—resisting arrest. Anytime someone is picked up and the only charge is resisting arrest, that right there tells you something. What was the underlying crime he was being arrested for that led him to resist? If there wasn't one, why were they attempting to arrest him? You can't be walking down the street and get a charge for resisting arrest. It don't work.

Once the media got ahold of the story, the head of the Yonkers police union came out and put it on Kissiedu for not identifying himself as a police officer sooner. But what did that mean? If he'd been a civilian, they'd have been justified in mistreating him? Then, even after learning that Kissiedu was a cop and a terrible mistake had been made, the Yonkers DA insisted on going ahead with the prosecution on the obstruction charge. They could have said, "Hey, our bad. You're free to go." But if the city admitted to being in the wrong, they'd expose themselves to a legal claim from Kissiedu for the officers' behavior. At the time, the Yonkers Police Department was already under investigation by the Department of Justice for alleged civil rights violations.

Kissiedu was set to be arraigned in early March. That's when he reached out to me and the NAACP and several other organizations for help. He needed to shine a light on what was happening, and he wasn't getting any help from downtown. The NYPD wasn't even backing its own guy; Kissiedu had been suspended for thirty days without pay while the Yonkers officers stayed on active duty and weren't disciplined at all. I was furious. I went up there and I got right in the cameras. I told ABC News, "The onus is on the uniformed officers to step back, give clear commands of what you're looking for, not just grab people, beat them up, and find out that they are officers and lock them up."

I knew it was a risk, speaking out like that. But I did it because I knew I couldn't live with myself if I'd let it go. I also thought that as long as I stayed outside the five boroughs the top brass wouldn't get too upset. And besides: I was standing up for one of our own. But unbeknownst to me, the commissioner of the Yonkers Police Department was a guy named Edmund Hartnett. Hartnett was a retired NYPD chief, and he still had a lot of powerful friends in the city. One of those close friends was my boss, Brooklyn Borough South commander Joseph Fox. Another one of those close friends was my rabbi and mentor, Chief of Department Joseph Esposito.

Hartnett and Esposito and Fox had come up together. They were tight. Fox called me into his office the next day and chewed me out. "You know you gotta watch who you're talking about doing these press conferences. You gotta know who's who and what's what. We've got a good friend up there."

I said, "Chief, if he's your friend, why aren't you the one talking to him about two of his guys locking up a young black sergeant who works for the NYPD?"

Fox didn't want to hear it. A couple of days later, Esposito pulled me aside at a promotion ceremony at One Police Plaza, and he read me the riot act, too. "What are you doing? Why'd you do that to Hartnett?"

Fox told me I had to call Hartnett and sort it out. I called him. He was all chummy on the phone, like I was his pal, saying, "Hey, Corey. You didn't have to do all that on TV. You know you could have called me and we could have worked something out . . ." Sweep it under the rug, in other words. We didn't work anything out. He stood by his guys, and I told him I wasn't backing down on supporting Kissiedu.

I'd really stepped in it. The only thing that saved me was that Hartnett wasn't a Ray Kelly guy. Kelly didn't care. That's how the old boys' club works. It has nothing to do with right and wrong. It's who's buddies with who. That same week, I saw Kelly at a service funeral, and he told me not to worry about it.

Then I pissed Kelly off.

On March 22, Andrew Hardwick, the new mayor of Freeport, Long Island, called and asked me to make a statement at a town hall meeting. Freeport is one of these formerly all-white suburbs that have a lot of minority families moving in; it's about 43 percent white and 33 percent black. Hardwick was the first African-American mayor in the town's history, and his election had stoked a lot of racial tension. He was having problems between his black residents and white cops. He wanted to put in his own police chief, and he asked me to come and say a few words at this meeting in support of his move. Before the meeting, we were talking backstage and he mentioned to me what some of his residents had told him about cops in Freeport. Somebody had told him that in Freeport "the only difference between the criminal and the cop is that the cop has a legal gun."

The whole town hall meeting was a disgrace. These angry white residents were disrespecting the mayor at every turn, cutting him off and shouting him down. When I got up to make my statement, I repeated what the mayor had told me, about people believing the cops are no different than the criminals. I wasn't making an allegation; I was trying to convey what some of the black people in the town were feeling. But it was the worst thing I could have said in front of those people. The whole room erupted in boos.

At that moment I was fed up, with Yonkers, with the disrespect being heaped on this mayor. I kept my cool, but I also decided I was going to give these people a piece of my mind, remind them of who black people are in this country today. I said, "For the people that have problems with the first African-American mayor of this town, I just want to let you know: We're doctors, we're lawyers, we're town leaders . . . and we're also the president of the United States of America. Thank you for having me." The crowd lost it, booing and hissing. What I didn't know was that somebody was videotaping me. They put it on YouTube, and it went viral around the department.

Now everyone was mad at me, including the commissioner. Shortly after Freeport I was notified that Internal Affairs had opened a formal investigation into my activities as president of NOBLE. That's one of the ways they get you to shut up. But department rules aren't the thing that maintains the Blue Wall of Silence. It's your fellow officers who keep you in line.

The second week in May was my first appearance at Compstat since Yonkers and Freeport had blown up. The way Compstat works is you find out Monday morning if your borough is up that week. You have the rest of the day, Tuesday, and Wednesday to prepare. Thursday morning at 8 a.m. you're up, and you better be ready to defend yourself.

I took a lot of pride in being on my game at the podium, and I had plenty of cases to go over that week. The gang war in the six-seven was heating up. I'd started the year off with five murders in five weeks. I had fourteen shootings and not a single clearance on any of them. I spent that whole week going over my open murders and shootings, and I could speak to every facet of every case. I had it cold. I was ready.

Late Wednesday night, the head of my detective squad came into my office and said, "I've been told not to help you out tomorrow morning. It's a hit."

"What do you mean, 'It's a hit'?"

"They're coming after you. My boss told me I'm not supposed to help you answer any questions. It's all on you." The head of my auto crime unit came by and said the same thing. I was about to walk into a firing squad.

When you're the commander of a high-crime area like the six-seven, Compstat is about the bodies—the gangs and the shootings and the homicides. That's all the bosses want to know about, and that's what I prepared for. When I got up at the podium the next morning I was facing down Esposito; Deputy Commissioner of Operations Pat Timlin; Chief of Detectives Phillip Pulaski; and Chief of Patrol James Hall. They didn't ask me anything about the bodies. They went right into my stats for burglary and grand larceny auto. I'd barely looked at that information. I'd skimmed it. I typically delegated that to my executive staff so I could concentrate on violent crime, and they knew that. Which is why they'd told the head of my detective squad and my auto crime unit they weren't allowed to assist me. I was stranded up there.

For the next hour they kept me up at the podium, grilling me about the smallest, tiniest, most irrelevant things they could dig up. My squad had seven GLA arrests for the year. Esposito insisted on going through every single one: Who were the perps? Where did they live? What were their priors? What make and model did they steal? Who made the collar? How did we make the collar? For every single one. Going back five months. Then they went to burglaries. How many burglary parolees live in the precinct? Where do they live? What are their priors? How many times have they been visited in the last year? And on and on.

I had bodies in the streets, kids scared to walk home at night. I had real police work I needed to talk about. But Esposito wanted to play gotcha. How many times had my guys interviewed burglary parolees? Every single one? In the entire precinct? For the whole year? I had no idea. No commander has that information off the top of his head. Of course, the guys grilling me knew. Esposito and Timlin and Hall, they had my GLA and burglary information right in front of them, because they'd showed up prepared to do this to me.

It was a disaster. I prided myself on being the most thorough, the most organized commander at Compstat. But that day I was stumbling through my responses, flipping through my binders to look for information, getting numbers confused, apologizing for not knowing things. They talked to me like I was a third-grader who hadn't done his homework. "We're talking about nuts and bolts, meat and potatoes police work." "This isn't hard to do." "There's gotta be a little less talk and a little more action."

"Yessir, chief." "I'm sorry I don't have that today, chief." "I'll get that for you as soon as I can, chief." I looked like a clown. And that was the whole point: to embarrass me, make an example of me, and it wasn't just the people in the room who witnessed it. Compstat sessions are videotaped and they go out to every precinct in the city. Every executive in the NYPD saw me being shamed at that podium, and everybody knew exactly why it was happening. They got the message loud and clear: This is what happens when you speak up against the wrong people.

After Esposito's takedown, life changed. I wasn't a complete pariah, but people looked at me differently. People were less talkative around me. My phone calls weren't being picked up when I needed things. The most disappointing part of it was seeing my fellow black cops distance themselves from me. I had a lot of white colleagues who still had my back; they didn't have anything to lose. But there were black cops writing letters to Kelly condemning my actions, saying I didn't speak for them and this and that.

One night that summer I got a call from Chief Zeigler. He asked me to meet him at a diner on Utica the next morning. I got there and it was four out of the five black chiefs: Zeigler, Banks, Secreto, and Nelson. Mohammed wasn't there. They gave me a talking to. I was causing trouble. I needed to calm down, be a good Negro. I remember Zeigler saying, "Corey, you're not the only black person that's been through this. I've been through everything you've been through."

They told me to think about how I was making things harder for other black cops on the force by making us all look like troublemakers. They told me to think about my family, how if I killed my chances for promotion, I'd be hurting them. I said, "Guys, I grew up eating mayonnaise sandwiches. I'm pulling six figures as a deputy inspector. My kids go to good schools. How much more do I need to get before I stand up and say something to help people like this kid in Yonkers?"

They knew I was right, but they still weren't backing me. The last straw for me was when they told me I needed to work on fixing my relationship with Fox. I said, "Why aren't you sitting down with Fox telling him he needs to fix his relationship with me? You all got me at this breakfast as if I did something wrong, but I haven't done anything wrong." I was furious when I walked out of there.

On June 23, I got a letter of reprimand from IAB regarding my NOBLE activities. Black cops get these letters all the time; I call them "down boy" letters. IAB determined that I'd "disseminated misinformation to the public" about the Freeport police. If I did it again, it could result in disciplinary action.

My career ground to a dead stop. My special favors from

downtown—escorting the department bigwigs, the nominations for special programs like Columbia—all that dried up. I was in, and then I was out. Fox was still doing everything in his power to get rid of me. I'd started taping my phone calls with him. I knew if he came after me, I'd need a paper trail to prove he was deliberately trying to sabotage my career.

The second week of November I was back up at Compstat. Esposito was grilling me about my shootings. I'd had three on Church Avenue and two in Flatbush Gardens in less than three weeks. While he was grilling me, he kept checking his phone. I looked over and there was Fox, tapping away on his phone.

After Compstat, Bonano took me aside and said he needed me to see something. He pulled out his phone and showed me texts between Fox and Esposito that he'd been copied on during the meeting. Fox was feeding Esposito information about how I'd failed to prevent the shootings at Flatbush Gardens and where to hit me on it. "He's after you about the stuff you're doing off duty," Bonano said. "That's what it's all about."

I was being set up to fail. My own commander was trying to make me look bad at the podium. Normally, your CO has your back at Compstat, because if your performance is bad, it reflects poorly on him. Fox didn't care. He just wanted to embarrass me even more. I was glad I at least had the texts as proof in case I ever needed it.

That following Sunday, November 14, I went to the Guardians' prayer breakfast, which they do every year. It was being held at El Caribe, a catering hall in Brooklyn. All the chiefs come out for it, and I knew I'd see Esposito there. My daughter Kenyetta was becoming a cop. Despite the difficulties I had on the job, I always talked it up to my kids as a good career, a place where black people need to go and make our presence felt in spite of the obstacles we face. She'd enrolled in the academy and was about to graduate and I brought her with me to the prayer breakfast that morning.

Walking into the hall, I could see the top brass seated up on the dais. I walked over and I went to the black chiefs one by one, shook their hands, said my hellos. I could see Esposito out of the corner of my eye, trying to get my attention. I walked right past him. My whole career I'd made a point of respecting the rank even if I didn't respect the person, but with Esposito I was angry. I was hurt. Here was a guy who'd believed in me, who'd always had my back, and he'd turned on me and embarrassed me simply for doing what was right.

At the end of the breakfast Esposito came over to me on the other side of the room and said, "Corey, can I speak to you for a second?" We stepped outside to the parking lot, and he started going on about the Compstat meeting, saying things like "Listen, you know I'm hard on you guys, but, you know, I need to have you ready for Compstat at all times . . ."

He was trying to apologize without apologizing. I could see that he felt bad, but I wasn't having it. You want to embarrass me in public, then try to make up for it in private with nobody watching? That pissed me off more than if he'd said nothing at all. I said, "Chief, this is bullshit. I'll take your excuse, but you and I both know what that was about. You embarrassed me because I did a press conference for the guy in Yonkers. It's not right what you did, but hey, you've got four stars. You've got all the power. It is what it is." And that's where I left it.

Sergeant Kenneth Kissiedu spent the next eighteen months on modified duty, riding a desk until his case could go to trial. In September of 2011 he was fully exonerated on the obstruction charge. It took the jury less than an hour to come back with the not guilty verdict. Even the claim that Kissiedu "fit the description" turned out to be bogus—the purse-snatching suspect had been identified as Hispanic, not black. In 2013, Kissiedu sued the city of Yonkers for violating his civil rights. After two years, the city settled the lawsuit for an undisclosed amount.

I was the only NYPD officer who spoke out publicly on Kissiedu's behalf. Nobody at One Police Plaza spoke out. Nobody from the four-one in the Bronx spoke out. None of the black chiefs spoke out, either.

Which was disgraceful. Everybody saw what Esposito did to me, and nobody said a word.

The NYPD stands by its cops no matter what, even when they've done the most heinous things imaginable. The Blue Wall of Silence protected the killers of Amadou Diallo. It protected the killers of Sean Bell. But a black sergeant is assaulted and he gets hung out to dry, all because the chief in Yonkers has powerful friends downtown. If the NAACP and I hadn't brought media attention to the case, Kissiedu might have been convicted and probably would have gotten fired. I put my career on the line and I did the right thing . . . and I got punished for it.

36

Insult to Injury

The six-seven is supposed to be where you go when Ray Kelly has you on the fast track. Both of my predecessors were promoted out of that command in a year's time. After Yonkers and Freeport, I'd been there over two years, with crime down in both of those years, and I was still waiting for the call. They wouldn't move me up, but they couldn't fire me, either. They didn't have cause. They knew if they fired me, they'd have Eric Adams and Al Sharpton all over them. So just keep Pegues in the six-seven, they decided. Let him die there.

To be honest, I didn't entirely mind. Once you get promoted above precinct commander, your role is mostly administrative. You have fewer opportunities to engage with the people in the streets. I liked working with the community. I felt I was having an impact, connecting with young kids. I wasn't in a hurry to change jobs.

I also knew the nod had to come eventually. When it came to promoting blacks at the executive level, Ray Kelly only had so many options. The black chiefs who were ahead of me, there wasn't much room for them to move up, and I had more experience and time on the job than the other black officers at my rank. I was first in line for the next time the department needed to put a black face somewhere—the next Black Friday. You hate to think of your career in those terms, but that's the reality of it.

My third year in the six-seven was pretty much the same as the first two. My crime stats for 2011 started to creep back up a bit, but I wasn't worried. I was playing the long game. I believed that the outreach and youth intervention I was implementing would improve things over time.

After another long, hot summer it was time to get ready for J'Ouvert. It was my fourth Superbowl, and this one was especially brutal. That Labor Day weekend was a bloodbath across all five boroughs. There were fifty-two shootings that wounded sixty-seven and left thirteen dead. Eight of the shootings were related to J'Ouvert. Over in Crown Heights, two guys got into a gunfight in the middle of the street. A fifty-six-year-old female bystander was killed, and two cops were shot. Both of them were taken to Brookdale Hospital.

Around two or three in the morning I had my driver take me over to the hospital. Mayor Bloomberg and Commissioner Kelly were visiting the cops and the other victims and holding a big press conference to address the shootings. When I spoke with Commissioner Kelly he could tell that I was wiped out. I'd been clocking eighteen-hour days four days straight. He gave me a pat on the back and said, "You're doing a good job. Keep it going." I'd been hearing rumors that a promotion might be coming down soon. I'd spent the last year on the outs, but maybe the chiefs were warming up to me again. I hoped so. After working four J'Ouverts in a row, I didn't know if I was down for a fifth.

My driver and I left the hospital around five in the morning. We were driving back to the precinct on Church Ave. I had a weeklong vacation planned to relax at home and do nothing. At the corner of Church and Albany we passed a Rite Aid on our left, and out in the empty parking lot this young guy was fighting with his girlfriend. He was beating the hell out of her. I told my driver to turn around.

He made a U-turn and we pulled into the parking lot and got out of the car to intervene. We separated the couple and went to put cuffs on the guy. He was out of control, kicking, taking swings. It took both of us to wrestle him to the ground. Struggling with him, I felt a sudden sharp pain in my back, like I'd pulled a muscle. By the time we finally got him in the car, my back was killing me. I was having shooting pains in my lower legs, and my walk was stiff. I honestly didn't think that much of it. It's a pulled muscle and it'll pass, I thought. I'll go on vacation and rest up and I'll be fine.

The next three days I lay in bed and it only got worse. On the fifth morning I got up to use the bathroom, and I couldn't pee. I had to go bad, but nothing was coming out. That's when I knew something was seriously wrong. My wife drove me to my doctor's office and I limped into the waiting room. I didn't even make it to the nurse's desk. I fell down in the middle of the hallway in excruciating pain. I was howling, crying, screaming for help. The ambulance came and took me to the emergency room. On the way the paramedics hit me with the morphine and I was finally able to take a breath and not feel anything.

They rushed me to North Shore Long Island Jewish Hospital. We got there, the doctor took a bunch of X-rays and scans. He came back pretty quickly and said, "We have to go into surgery right now. You have a ruptured disc and it's pressing on your spine; it has to come out immediately or you could be paralyzed."

I didn't want surgery. I said, "No no no. You can't cut me open. You can't do that to me."

I wanted a second opinion. The NYPD has the best doctors in the world on call. They volunteer through the police foundation. Cops who are shot or injured in the line of duty get the best medical care imaginable. I wanted to talk to those guys. I called the medical division and asked to speak with the commander and told him, "Look, we have to get a specialist on the line because they're talking about cutting my back open."

A specialist got on the phone with the doctor at Long Island Jewish and they spoke. Then the specialist got on the phone with me. He said, "You have to do this now." My wife and my kids were crying, holding my hand. They wheeled me into the operating room. I was in surgery for eight hours. From there I went to rehab. I was there for a week and I was still in a wheelchair, still not feeling any better. Now I was able to consult with the NYPD specialists, the best that money can buy. They took me to NYU, where I had more scans done. That's where they discovered that not all of the damaged disc had been removed. The doctor told me, "We have to go back in."

I was like, "You gotta be *kidding* me."

They brought in one of the top spinal surgeons in the country, Dr. Martin Camins. He's world-renowned. Dennis Byrd, the New York Jets player who was paralyzed on the field, Camins was the doctor who made him walk again. He did my second operation, removing the rest of the injured disc and fusing two of my vertebrae together. I was up and moving the next day. I had to use a walker, but I could get around.

As soon as I was out of the second surgery, I sat down with my driver to fill out the paperwork for the line-of-duty injury. I hadn't done it the night of the accident because I was too tired and ready to go home, and at the time I thought it was a pulled muscle. We sat down with these forms. I recounted what had happened. My driver filled out his witness statement, and we sent it to Mike Williams, my administrative lieutenant, who submitted it for approval.

The next day Mike called me. He said, "Inspector Tomlin doesn't want to sign it."

Tomlin was the adjutant at Brooklyn South, the guy who had to approve my claim. Mike said that he was casting doubt on my claim because the paperwork hadn't been filed the night of the incident— the department was questioning if it was a real line-of-duty injury. I called Roy Richter and Chris Moynihan, the president and vice president of the Superior Officers' Union. They told me the same thing: Tomlin was giving them pushback on approving my claim, but they said the union was standing behind me and they were going to force him to sign off.

I couldn't believe it. Approval of a line-of-duty injury is practically automatic. It's even done for injuries that aren't job-related. I knew one officer who got shot when he was mugged while on vacation in Miami. He wasn't stopping a crime—he was being robbed! But the department flew him home and approved it as a line-of-duty injury. There was also Inspector Michael Shortell. He died by electrocuting himself when he was using a sump pump to clear out a flood in his house after a storm. Ray Kelly posthumously promoted Shortell to deputy chief, so his pension was bumped to the next pay grade. But I gave the job a disc out of my back, with a witness statement on record to boot, and I had to fight to prove my claim was legitimate? It was insult to injury, literally. Twenty years of service to the department and I was still fighting double standards from a bed in the hospital.

After thirty days of in-patient therapy, I was able to go home. It was a slow road back. I was walking with a cane and going to physical therapy out on Long Island. The injury itself was a freak accident. It hadn't been that difficult for me and my driver to wrestle the guy to the ground; I'd been in worse fights on the job over the years. But I'd been up for four days working J'Ouvert, sleeping on a couch in my office. I was already tired and bent out of shape and this guy torqued my spine a hair in the wrong direction and: *Pop!*

The injury accomplished what three years in the army and twenty years on the force never could: I lost the ditty-bop in my step. Eventually I was able to stop using the cane, but to this day I'm stiffer, slower. I've got a medicine cabinet full of painkillers and muscle relaxers. I've probably got 25 percent of the range of motion I used to have. There's a numbness in my lower extremities that's never gone away. At times I get these shooting pains. I have to lie down and wait for them to pass. I can't run anymore.

When I came out of rehab, the medical division put me on restricted duty. Technically I was still commander of the 67th Precinct, but an acting CO was handling my job while I recovered. I knew I was never going back to full duty again. To be considered for full duty with the NYPD, even as an executive, you have to be able to do things like wrestle a perp to the ground in a Rite Aid parking lot. The doctors said if I ever tried anything like that again, it could leave me paralyzed. But that didn't necessarily mean I had to leave the department. Detective Stephen McDonald was shot on the job in 1988. He took three bullets that left him a quadriplegic on a ventilator in a wheelchair. He's still employed by the NYPD today, giving motivational talks to the precincts; I had him out to the six-seven at least once a year.

I felt like I could have done something like that, worked as a liaison doing outreach with black youth and the black community. I had all this experience and knowledge from twenty years on the force. I didn't want it to go to waste because of a freak accident. You'd think the department would have felt the same way. They didn't. Without telling me, the medical division initiated the paperwork to start the process of medically retiring me from the department. Nobody asked me if that's what I wanted; they just did it, and I found out after the fact.

I could have fought it, could have made my case for staying, but at that point I was tired of fighting. A disability pension is three-quarters of your full salary, but it's tax free, so it's actually more money. My older kids were grown, but I had my son Cordale at home, who I never got to see because of all the late nights on the job. Brendale was pregnant with our youngest, Cori. I'd been hustling, one way or another, since I was thirteen years old. It had been an uphill battle every step of the way: the endless IAB investigations, the racial slurs, the harassment, the black chiefs coming down on me, being called a thug even with the stripes on my sleeve to prove different. I took the forced retirement. I was too tired to do anything else.

At that point there was only one thing I wanted: I wanted to go out as a full inspector. I wanted my family to see me walk across that stage one last time. I felt I'd earned it. If not for the blowback over my speaking out on the Yonkers case, I'd have made inspector a year earlier. Everybody in the department knew it. I'd lost a disc out of my back saving a young woman, possibly from being killed. That's how a good cop is supposed to go out: protecting and serving.

In city government it takes forever for things to get processed. A year after the injury, while I was still waiting for the paperwork to go through, I called Commissioner Kelly's office to ask for a meeting. On October 5, 2012, I put on my full dress uniform and I went down to One Police Plaza. I didn't bring my cane. It was difficult for me to walk without it. My steps were short and I was still walking gingerly, but I wanted to walk into the commissioner's office on my own two feet. I waited for a few minutes outside his office. Then he was ready to see me and I went in.

I taped the meeting. I was still taping my conversations and phone calls with the department. After they'd tried to deny my line-of-duty injury, I was being extra careful to make sure everything was documented and my pension was protected. Kelly and I chatted for a bit. He asked how I was doing, how my recovery was coming. I didn't want to waste his time, so I got right to the point. I said, "Commissioner, I want to thank you. You gave my family and myself some opportunities. Every executive who gets promoted to captain would love the assignments that you gave me, and I really appreciate that. You sent me to PMI, gave me the command at PSA #2 and the six-seven. Some choice assignments.

"This is the first time I've ever requested a meeting with you. I would never complain. I'm a soldier. I don't know if you know, but I've only had two jobs in my life. Right after high school I went into the US Army, and eight months after that I came to the police department. I'm really indebted to this police department. I always wanted to be a cop. As you know, my daughter's on the job now, and my nephew just came on the job in the last class.

"But I spent a lot of time in that precinct, and I was actually the only person who wasn't rewarded by getting promoted out of that command. And I want to know: Was it something I did? I did a tremendous amount of work. I reduced crime two out of my three years there. I actually had the lowest index crimes of anybody in the history of the command."

He said, "You got injured. You did a good job there, absolutely. But your injury . . . I don't know. How long have you been on restricted duty?"

"I've been on restricted since May 15. I was injured September 5 last year."

"Yeah. So, you've been out for a long period of time. You were in the hospital. Then you were on restricted duty. Normally we wouldn't promote someone on restricted duty."

"Right. But I've seen people get promoted. You've promoted people who've been out sick."

"Yeah, if somebody got shot or something."

"Inspector Shortell. When he was electrocuted, he got promoted to chief by you."

"He was dead. You don't want to die to get promoted."

I laughed. "No, sir, I don't want to die to get promoted."

He kept telling me about department policy, but I already knew it wasn't department policy to promote people on restricted duty. I was there to ask for an exception. I was there to ask for an acknowledgment of my service—something that I shouldn't have had to ask for in the first place.

He asked if there was any medical hope of my returning to full duty. I told him the doctors had already done everything for me they could. He said, "If that's what the medical division is telling you, and that's their position, it would be pretty difficult to promote you. I think you definitely would have been promoted. No question about it. Unfortunately, it's bad luck to have this happen to you. But unless there are really extraordinary circumstances, I don't think we can do it. If you come back to full duty, it's a different story."

I offered to ask medical if I could come back to full duty for one week before retiring. That would give him a loophole. I was only half joking. He didn't go for it. I told him how much the job meant to me. I wanted him to see how important it was for me to have my kids see me walk across that stage one more time. I told him about the nights away from my family, laid out the numbers showing him the reduction in crime on my watch, reminded him of the programs I started for the community. "I did everything," I said. "I worked hard at that place."

He said, "I know you did. I think you did a terrific job. It's just difficult in this situation right now. Why don't we see what happens. Let me talk to the medical people about what your future is."

I knew what that meant. It meant he wasn't going to do anything, and he didn't. And I was okay with that. It was what it was. The promotion would have been a nice thing to have, but the main thing for me was to be able to go there and say my piece. Beyond that it was up to the commissioner to decide what he believed was the right thing to do, and he's the only one who knows why he made the decision that he did.

I could have done things differently. I could have kept my mouth shut and I'd have been a two-star chief by now, but I wouldn't be happy, because I wouldn't have been true to myself. I did things my way, and I did them the right way. I did right by the sergeant in Yonkers, and I did right by the community I served. That was enough for me.

Kelly and I chatted for a couple more minutes and then he had somewhere else to be. I pulled myself up slowly out of the chair. He walked around the desk and I shook his hand and I told him, "Like I said, sir. I'm very indebted. You've done a tremendous amount for my family, and we really appreciate it." I walked out of his office, said a few good-byes to his secretary and the staff, took the elevator down to the parking garage in the basement, and got in my car.

Then I went home.

198 and Murdock

October 15, 2014

One year ago, a few days after I signed the deal to write this book, I took a drive out to the old neighborhood. I had to pick up some pictures from my aunt Mary and uncle Gene. They still live in the same house right off 198 and Murdock.

I pulled up to the corner and of course there they were, three guys out hugging the block early in the morning, selling weed, a bit of crack. I recognized all three of them: Butch, Ty, and Eddie. St. Albans is still a small, tight-knit community. Everybody knows everybody. I pulled up alongside the curb, rolled the window down, and said, "Guys, wassup?"

They smiled and started yelling. *"Yo yo yo!"* *"My man!"* *"OG!"*

That's what they call me out here: OG. I left the game because I didn't want to be a street legend, but when you go from the corner to commanding officer of the 67th Precinct, you become a bit of a street legend anyway. I parked my car and got out to say hi. "You drinkin'?" they said. They had Styrofoam cups and half-gallon bottle of Hennessy wrapped up in a plastic bag from the liquor store. It was nine o'clock in the morning.

I said, "Nah, fellas. I'm good. I just stopped by to see what's up with you."

Butch, Ty, and Eddie ended up in the streets the same way I did: young, no good role models, no good choices, too shortsighted to see how much of a mistake you're making. Then the cops pick you up, and that's it. Once you get that felony charge, you're done. It follows you the rest of your life. There's no work for ex-felons. You get out of jail, you come out hungry, maybe there's a part-time construction job you can get, holding the go-slow sign for some road crew. But that's about it. Eventually that dries up and you drift back to the corner and the whole cycle repeats itself.

All three of these guys knew me back in the day; they were the shorties running around when me and Smooth ran the block. This kid Donte had been one of my soldiers on my crew. Donte took over the crew when I left, and Butch had come up under him. Ty was a neighborhood kid who played some serious ball in O'Connell Park, but he never made it anywhere with that, and he wound up on the corner. Both of them had spent the last twenty years in and out of prison. The guy I knew best out there was Eddie. Eddie's father, Tray, had been in the streets with me. Tray was murdered. Eddie's older brother was on the corner, and he'd been murdered, too. Now here Eddie was on the corner himself.

One month after I saw him on 198 and Murdock, Eddie got picked up. He'd moved in with a girl over in Jamaica, and he was there when the cops came with a warrant looking for a burner, an illegal gun. It wasn't even Eddie's apartment, but they hauled him in on the gun charge. Since he was already on probation for selling drugs, he was held at Rikers Island without bail to await trial. Eddie's got two kids, and odds are they'll grow up without a father the same way he grew up without a father.

And round and round we go.

My story is testimony to the fact that it's never too late to turn your life around. I smashed a 40-ounce across a crackhead's face. I put a gun to another kid's chest and I pulled the trigger. But the boy who did that at seventeen is not the man who came out of the army at twenty-two. And if someone had reached out to me and offered me real opportunities before I started selling drugs, I never would have set foot down that road in the first place. My whole life would have been different.

It would be wrong to say that nothing's changed since I was in the street. It's actually gotten worse. Back then you could make mistakes and still get out and turn your life around. Today, between the zero-tolerance practices of Broken Windows policing; the racially targeted abuse of policies like Stop, Question, and Frisk; draconian anti-drug laws; and mandatory minimum sentencing, young black kids don't stand a chance. They get swept up into the system, and they never get out. The guilty ones are marked as felons for the rest of their lives; the innocent ones become angry and embittered and live in fear of constant harassment.

The numbers speak for themselves: Historically, until the 1980s, America incarcerated about 100 out of every 100,000 people. Today we incarcerate 500 out of every 100,000. For black men, we incarcerate 4,749 per 100,000. Black men born in the 1970s have a 32 percent chance of going to prison. Black men without a high school diploma have a 68 percent chance of going to prison. One in nine black children are growing up with at least one parent incarcerated.

After I left the 67th Precinct, my successors took a different path. The youth sports day and the essay contests, they don't do it anymore. The juvenile intervention program I started, they don't do it anymore. The phone calls to community leaders in the wake of shootings, they don't do it anymore. On March 9, 2013, sixteen-year-old Kimani Grey was shot by two officers from the six-seven on East 52nd Street in East Flatbush. He was shot seven times, three times in the back. One of the officers, Cordova, had been involved in a shooting under my command, responsible for shooting an eighteen-year-old in the chin. Kimani Grey was different. There was no transparency, no attempt at accountability. The cops said Grey pulled a .38; witnesses said he was unarmed and the gun found at the scene was dropped there by police. The cops said Grey was a gangster; neighbors said he was a saint. Peaceful demonstrations broke out into violent protests, a drugstore looted, angry crowds marching on the precinct, hundreds of cops in riot gear, pepper-spraying everyone. Neither officer was indicted for the shooting, and the bitterness lingers. The trust I worked so hard to build between the police and the community, the discipline I fought to instill in my officers—without the right leadership, it's already coming apart.

In August of 2013, a federal judge ruled that the NYPD's abuse of Stop, Question, and Frisk was unconstitutional, that it unfairly targeted blacks and Hispanics. The number of stops fell from over sixteen thousand per week in January of 2012 to two thousand per week at the end of 2013. On January 1, 2014, after campaigning on a promise to fix the toxic relationship between minority communities and police, Democrat Bill de Blasio was sworn in as mayor of New York City. De Blasio brought Bill Bratton back to serve as his police commissioner. Bratton agreed to continue to curtail the use of Stop, Question, and Frisk, but insisted that the department would continue with the controversial and widely discredited tactics of Broken Windows.

The abuse of Stop, Question, and Frisk was only the most visible element of Broken Windows. The daily harassment is still there in countless other ways, and the results can too often be fatal. On July 17, 2014, Eric Garner was killed by Broken Windows policing, choked to death by Staten Island police who suspected him of no crime greater than selling loose cigarettes. Garner's death—preceded by the killing of Trayvon Martin in Florida and followed by the shooting of Michael Brown in Ferguson, Missouri—triggered the nationwide protest movement Black Lives Matter. Through sustained pressure and protest, its members have managed to shine a light on a problem that has persisted for far too long: Tamir Rice, killed by Cleveland police for playing with a toy gun; Freddie Gray, killed by spinal cord injury after a "rough ride" by Baltimore PD; Rekia Boyd, shot by an off-duty Chicago cop firing into a crowd; Walter Scott, shot in the back while trying to run away from a routine traffic stop; Sandra

Bland, found dead in her cell after being pulled over for failing to signal to change lanes; Sam Dubose, shot by University of Cincinnatti police over a missing license plate.

The list goes on. Through the constant vigilance of social media and cell phone cameras, we have found a way, however imperfect, to police the police. But nothing will change until the culture of policing changes. Nothing will change until zero tolerance is replaced by discretion and good judgment. Nothing will change until police departments make a real effort to hire not just black cops, but black cops who genuinely understand and relate to the struggles of the communities they patrol. And none of these changes can happen without leadership. In a paramilitary organization, change comes from the top or it doesn't come at all.

My own saga with the NYPD, sadly, continues to be one of discrimination and double standards. Since my retirement, and especially since the death of Eric Garner, I've been speaking out publicly and loudly on the issue of police brutality and abuse, tearing down the Blue Wall of Silence in any way I can. On August 13, 2014, while appearing on the Combat Jack podcast to discuss policing issues, I spoke openly about my past, about my years in the streets, about growing up with a convicted cop killer like David McClary. My purpose in doing so was the same as it always has been: to use my story as an example that you can turn your life around. The NYPD didn't take it that way.

On September 8, I made the cover of the *New York Post*. THUG COP, they called me, insinuating that I was somehow a criminal police officer. The *Post* has always served as a mouthpiece for the NYPD and the Patrolman's Benevolent Association. Without bothering to conduct basic fact-checking, the *Post*'s reporters repeated a number of lies fed to them by anonymous NYPD sources in an effort to slander me. The *Post* repeated the rumor that I had a "Thug Life" tattoo on my neck that I'd had removed, which is false. The paper also reported that "law enforcement sources" said my disability pension was due to "injuries related to falling off a chair while he was commander of the 67th Precinct," which is not only false but easily debunked with information available in public records.

The day after the *Post*'s article ran, at the NYPD's request, Hempstead police arrived at my house and confiscated the three department-issued firearms I still had in my possession, saying I was no longer fit to carry them. The next day the *Post* reported that an effort was under way to strip me of my pension; Commissioner Bratton confirmed to the paper he was looking into whether my pension and application should be reviewed. On December 6, Chief Joseph Resnick, deputy commisioner of Internal Affairs, mailed me a letter revoking my "good guy" status and demanding that I turn in my department ID showing that I was a retired officer in good standing. But I never lied on my application. I never committed, nor even tried to commit, any act of wrongdoing in my two decades on the force. Not only am I not a "thug cop," I was and continue to be a model police officer. In April of 2015, I filed a $200 million lawsuit against the *New York Post*, the NYPD, and Nassau County for free-speech violations, race discrimination, conspiracy, and defamation. As I write this, the case is still pending.

ACKNOWLEDGMENTS

I always knew that one day I would write my story. I knew that it was compelling and if published would find the right audience. Throughout my police career I kept a journal and even started recording conversations to help keep all the facts straight. My journey from drug dealer to executive in the largest police department in the country was not easy, nor was it easy to tell. But along the way there were so many people who helped me.

First, I would like to thank my creator, Jesus Christ.

I want to thank my mother and father for bringing me into this world. I miss both of you dearly, and I carry you in my heart each day. Willie B (Ma), I could not ask for a better mother-in-law. You are always there to keep the kids and fill my stomach with the best soul food on earth. To my beautiful wife, Brendale: you have been with me through thick and thin, and our bond is unbreakable. That's a true testament to our love. Ever since the third grade I knew you were the one for me. From the day we reconnected my life has changed for the better. I am very thankful to have you in my life and for giving me such beautiful kids. I will always love you. Corey Jr. (Lil Life), Natasha, Kenyetta, Starborn, Cordale (Lil Body), and Cori (Fat-Fat), you are why I continue to live on this earth. I love you so much and wish only the best for you as you go through this journey called Life. Andrew, thank you for being the best son-in-law any man could ask for. Keep taking care of my baby girl. Chelsea (CC), Shaunie (Lil Grand), and Andrew Jr. (Chunky), I hope you grow up and make Grandpa proud. Linda, Debra, Angie, and Tawn, even though Vicky went home to be with Ma, we are still very close. I love you to pieces. To all of my nieces and nephews, I love you unconditionally and will always be here for you. Nakia, Jerel, and Jamal (Mal), God Daddy loves you. To my aunts, uncles, and all my cousins, even though we are spread out, the bond remains strong. I miss those family gatherings so much. Cookie and Chris, you have such a special place in my heart; I can't express in words the love I have for you. Thank you for always being there. Uncle Bro, Coke, and Dwayne, words cannot express how much I miss you guys. I know that if you were still here, you would be my biggest supporters. Until we meet again, I will always love you and miss you so much. Jamal, you are the best brother-in-law on earth. We will be "out" soon. Toni and Val, thank you for being my extended sisters. Virgue and Rosalind, thank you for being great sisters-in-law. Shelia, thank you for not only being a great sister-in-law but also for always being there for me in times of need.

Sean Due, as far back as I can remember, you have been my brother, and we will always have bulletproof love. I will never forget that time you took the jacket off your back and gave it to me. I wouldn't change our journey for anything in this world. Mike (Stoney) and Mike (Barber), you will always be my brothers from another mother, no matter what. Leon Leslie, thank you for always having my back. We had one hell of a career, brother, and you were always the calming voice. June, Will, Ren, Ford (Hakim), Messiah, Conrad, and the rest of the original team with whom I ran the streets back in the day, I will never forget bonding with you guys. I tell our stories every chance I get. Jay Black, thanks for always being there for me, lil brother. Our bond is solidified for life. Mike, Fitch, and Shana, thank you so much for having my back and being my eyes and ears as I climbed the ladder in the NYPD. You will never know how happy you made me feel each day. You deflected a lot of the bullshit that came my way. We will always be friends.

Ed Woods, thank you so much for being there for me when everyone else ran away. You put your name and reputation on the line when you could have gone in a different direction, and for that I am grateful. You secured the book deal—now go get that movie deal! Mike Bellinger, thank you so much for guiding me through one of the roughest times in my life, even though you knew little about me. My family is forever indebted. Alyse Friedman, thank you so much for helping me put out those fires. Hopefully, we will work together again. Judge Greg Mathis, thank you for your guidance when I needed it most, and for just being there for me whenever I needed your advice. Al, thank you for always being there for me whenever I needed someone to talk to or some sound advice. You have never let me down.

Tom Higdon, thank you for being a mentor and father figure early in my career. Douglas Ziegler, Gerald Nelson, Timothy Pearson (TP), and Elton Mohammed, thank you for the guidance and support that you gave me when I became an executive in the NYPD. It really meant a lot to me to have you on my side. Rest in peace, Chief Gianelli; I will never forget what you did for my career. May God rest your soul; you were not only a good man but you were also a good friend. David Barrere, thanks for mentoring me as an executive and showing me how to do things the right way. You definitely left an indelible mark on my career. Police Commissioner Raymond Kelly, thank you for giving me the opportunity of a lifetime, a chance to command two of the most prestigious assignments in the NYPD.

Ruthie Stern, thank you for both believing in me and working with me when I needed help getting my transcript in order. Marc Williams, thank you for helping me with my public speaking; you are truly one of the best speech coaches out there. Peter McGuigan, thank you for believing in my story before it became news and signing me to Foundry Literary + Media. My family and I are truly grateful for the opportunity. Matt Wise, thank you for your guidance early on while I was trying to figure this book thing out. Tanner Colby, I can't thank you enough for helping me bring my story to life. At times when I couldn't find the right words, it felt like you were inside my head articulating all the things I really wanted to say. *Once a Cop* is a masterpiece, and for that I thank you. Todd Hunter, thank you, brother, for coming in in the fourth quarter and sealing the deal. You definitely were the last and key piece to putting this story together. Now let's go out there and sell some books.

Finally, to all my haters—and you know who you are—I salute you for your conviction. But only God can judge me!

To anyone who I forgot to mention by name, thank you. You know my heart.

www.ingramcontent.com/pod-product-compliance
Lightning Source LLC
Chambersburg PA
CBHW011051170125
20462CB00006B/279